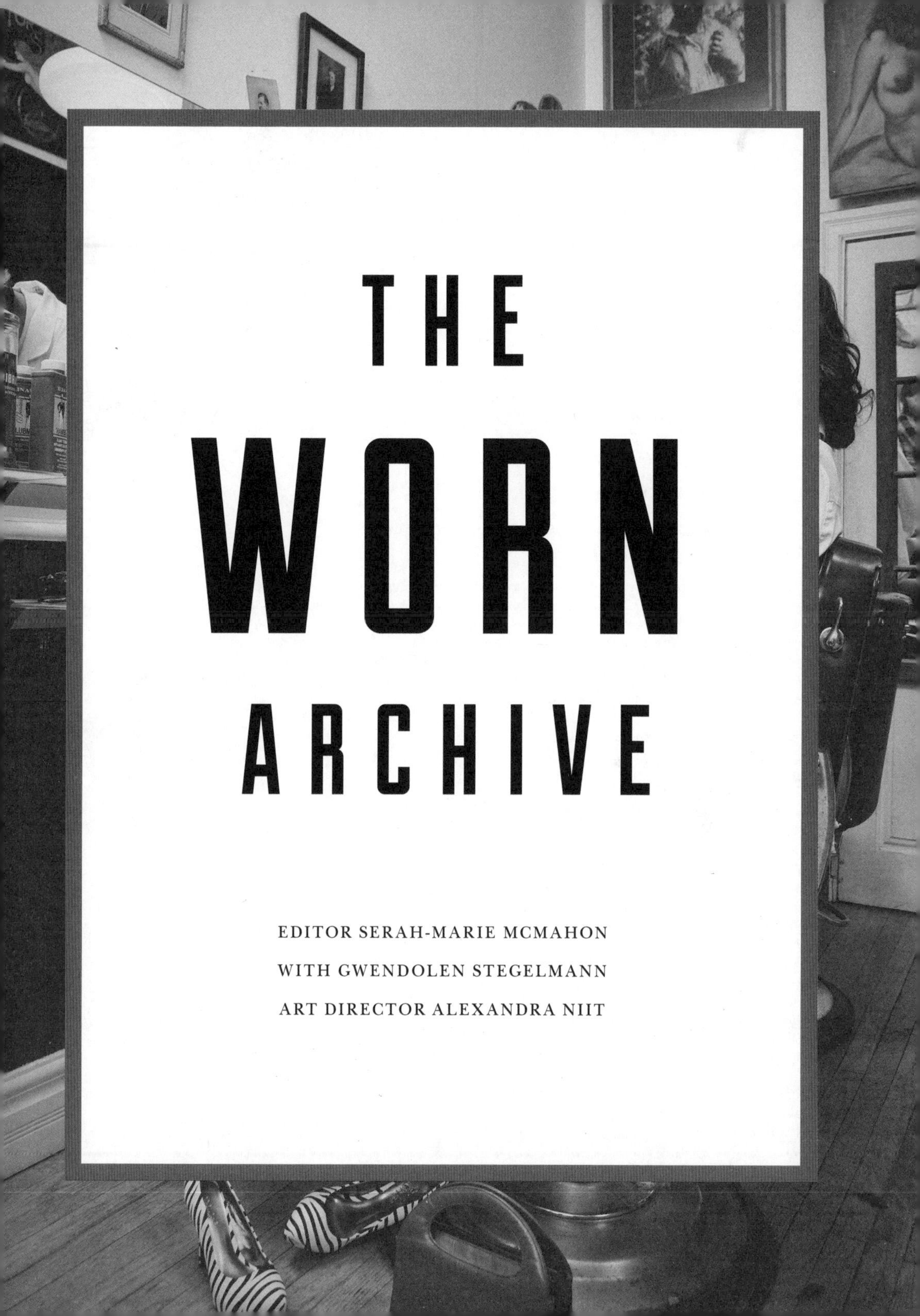

THE
WORN
ARCHIVE

EDITOR SERAH-MARIE MCMAHON
WITH GWENDOLEN STEGELMANN
ART DIRECTOR ALEXANDRA NIIT

Editor-in-Chief // Serah-Marie McMahon
Managing Editor // Gwendolen Stegelmann
Art Director & Designer // Alexandra Niit
Design Assistance // Maegan Fidelino & Peter Ha
WORN Fashion Journal Publisher // Haley Mlotek
Production Manager // Laura Kloepfer
Copy Editor // Kate Schweishelm
Project Editor // Tracy Hurren
Publisher // Chris Oliveros
Associate Publisher // Peggy Burns

Cover design // Alexandra Niit
Cover contributors // Nate Dorr, Alejandro Escamilla, Alyssa K. Faoro,
Isabel Foo, Sara Guindon, Monika Traikov, Arden Wray

Title page photo // Danijela Pruginic

Chapter essays // Gwendolen Stegelmann

To subscribe and purchase back issues of WORN Fashion Journal visit wornjournal.com
For editorial inquiries, email serahmarie@wornjournal.com

For circulation, advertising, and press inquiries, email haley@wornjournal.com

drawnandquarterly.com

First paperback edition: May 2014
Printed in China
10 9 8 7 6 5 4 3 2 1

Library and Archives Canada Cataloguing in Publication
    The WORN Archive: A Fashion Journal about the Art, Ideas, and History of What We Wear /
Serah-Marie McMahon
ISBN 978-1-77046-150-5 (pbk.)
    1. WORN Fashion Journal. 2. Fashion. I. McMahon, Serah-Marie,
editor of compilation
TT500.W674 2014   746.9'2   C2013-906210-6

Drawn & Quarterly acknowledges the financial contribution of the Government of Canada through the Canada
Book Fund and the Canada Council for the Arts for our publishing activities and for support of this edition.

Published in the U.S. by Drawn & Quarterly, a client publisher of
Farrar, Straus and Giroux
Orders: 888.330.8477

Published in Canada by Drawn & Quarterly, a client publisher of
Raincoast Books
Orders: 800.663.5714

Published in the U.K. by Drawn & Quarterly, a client publisher of
Publishers Group U.K.
Orders: info@pguk.co.uk

CONTENTS

CHAPTER 1 »
FASHION IS PERSONAL

Don't look INSIDE unless you love daring Hollywood Fashions!

CHAPTER 4 »
FASHION IS OBJECT

CHAPTER 5 »
FASHION IS DESIGN

image // *myjane*, photo by Jason Madara

FOREWORD

JANE PRATT

DO YOU KNOW WHAT I LOVE ABOUT *WORN?* There's no other fashion magazine that would talk about repairing things instead of telling you to buy something new.

With chapters like "Fashion is Personal" and "Fashion is Fun," *WORN* is reclaiming fashion as something that can be exciting, challenging, different, quirky, and interesting – not just something you have to consume. Here, fashion is open to anyone who wants to participate. It's the most natural thing in the world, but it's not mainstream – maybe that's why it comes off as avant-garde.

People have often described the magazines I've edited as "edgy." But I never did anything in order to be edgy; it's just that I was always really excited about lots of new and different things. That sense of enthusiasm is always present in an issue of *WORN*. The Wornettes are genuinely excited about fashion, and it comes through in the collection of articles they've lovingly assembled here.

So many people feel like they don't fit into the mold traditional fashion magazines want them to fit into. I don't think anyone, including the models working in those magazines, feels like they belong there. *WORN* is the kind of magazine that makes you feel like you belong. A *WORN* editorial isn't aspirational – a *WORN* editorial is inspirational, because it's real. I love that staff members are often the models. When you give readers the freedom to celebrate personal style, especially in a beautiful format like *The WORN Archive*, it feels like a true affirmation.

Since 2005 *WORN* has been offering the parts of fashion that readers don't get in traditional fashion magazines. *WORN* has always been written like two friends talking about what they love about clothes, as opposed to "buy this, buy that" or arbitrary in/out lists. It reminds me of *Sassy* and *Jane* and *xoJane* and all the things that drew me to fashion in the first place.

I want to say thank you, *WORN*, for making a magazine, and for compiling it into this book. When I read *WORN Fashion Journal*, when I read *The WORN Archive*, I am a Wornette. ⬛

FASHION IS
WORN

AROUND THE TIME I DECIDED to start *WORN*, I had a job in a quiet bookstore. My co-worker, an appropriately cynical punk girl, asked me what I was always scribbling in my notebook. I told her I wanted to start a publication about fashion. Her response wasn't exactly rude, but she was far from impressed. She told me fashion had no part in her life, and that it was stupid, vapid, and a waste of time. That made me smile. I pointed out the brands of workwear she preferred. Her Converse predated Nike ownership of the brand, and she knew how to tell. I noted the way she visibly repaired her clothes with dental floss rather than thread to last longer and the silk-screened protest patches and band buttons that covered her knapsack. She used clothing to tell the world her values and establish her place as part of a community and subculture. By the time I was done she had to agree: she actually cared a whole lot about fashion.

People imagine there is this thing called Fashion with a capital F. That it's a subculture guided by its own particular set of rules, behaviours, and aesthetics. Inherent in this is the idea of exclusivity. A binary develops: good, bad; in, out; fresh, so five minutes ago. What is chosen and who can choose it is constantly shifting and never fully established. It's understandable that people are afraid of being told they are doing it wrong, when it's practically impossible to figure out what "it" is. Worse yet, magazines take advantage of that vulnerability, telling readers they need to have the newest bag, cut of jeans, or skin cream to be acceptable (all conveniently provided by advertisers). Not to mention the systematic exclusion of anyone who isn't young, skinny, cis, and white. And then there's makeover TV. And luxury brands. And sweatshops. And and and.

The fashion industry is riddled with problems. It makes me mad! I get all sizzly inside. *WORN* is how I respond to that. Because why not make fashion the way I love it, celebrating the good parts rather than spending my time pointing out the bad ones? Instead of telling people what to do, why not give them a choice and provide an alternative? Because fashion, *oh, fashion*. Fashion is all the other things. It's the how, what, and why of people covering their bodies. We're all born looking one way, but we don't have to stay that way forever.

WE'RE ALL BORN LOOKING ONE WAY, BUT WE DON'T HAVE TO STAY THAT WAY FOREVER. FASHION LETS YOU BECOME WHOEVER YOU WANT TO BE. FASHION MADE ME WHO I WANTED TO BE.

Fashion lets you become whoever you want to be. Fashion made me who I wanted to be.

When I went to art school, I was fascinated by how my fellow students' clothing acted as an extension of their paintings and sculptures. I worked for a few years at a modelling agency and saw the Fashion-with-a-capital-F industry from the inside. I spent some time in vintage, where I met one of the most interesting women I've ever known, who would regularly throw tidbits of utterly fascinating fashion information at me while we unpacked boxes of '70s cycling jerseys and hand-tooled leather purses. I worked at a media retail empire filled with very nerdy music and film fanatics, obsessed with knowing everything about everything they loved.

A lot of people are surprised when I tell them I'd never worked in publishing; they ask me how in the world I came up with the idea of starting a magazine, but it was that all these things came together in my head. I wanted to understand the connection between aesthetic and clothing outside of trend, and reconcile my love of clothes with the problems I saw in the fashion industry. I wanted to know everything about everything I was interested in. I'd been reading my husband's music magazines, and they would have 30-page articles about concerts that happened decades earlier. There was no equivalent in fashion publishing – but as I worked in that quiet bookstore, I realized I could change that.

For issue 5, we asked a
few illustrators to explore
the role of clothing in their
drawings. When reality is
removed, any kind of dress
can exist. Illustration
by Amber Albrecht.

A photo from the very first shoot for *WORN*, featuring one of our earliest and dearest contributors, Liz Byer. From day one we used our clothes as wardrobe, our apartments as sets, and our staff members as models.

I WANTED TO UNDERSTAND THE CONNECTION BETWEEN AESTHETIC AND CLOTHING OUTSIDE OF TREND, AND RECONCILE MY LOVE OF CLOTHES WITH THE PROBLEMS I SAW IN THE FASHION INDUSTRY. I WANTED TO KNOW EVERYTHING ABOUT EVERYTHING I WAS INTERESTED IN.

So I called up that brilliant girl I knew from the vintage store, and she became our managing editor. I posted flyers asking "Do you love fashion, but feel frustrated with fashion magazines?" I added my home address and held a meeting in my living room. A few strangers showed up, and one of them is now our senior editor and an encyclopedia of fashion history. I scoured Montreal for talented friends and strangers. Then we started a magazine.

We made it up as we went along. Some things would have been good to know earlier on, but many of the things that we did our own way became an important part of WORN. Instead of using professional models in photo shoots, we used friends and staff members. Instead of designer clothes, we pulled things from our closets and from local vintage stores. We refused free promotional products, and for the most part, refused to talk about products at all. We didn't report on trends or tell people what to wear. Instead of looking to the runways for inspiration, we encouraged people to look at old pictures, or fictional characters, or '70s pop stars. We wrote articles exploring how fashion related to feminism, performance art, and the washing machine.

As time went on, people began to ask how they could be a part of the publication. That's when we introduced the idea of the Wornette. *Jane* had a big influence on me, and I loved how the writers were like characters in the cast of the magazine. I also loved the Ramones, and how they created a family by giving themselves all the same last name. It was what

WANT TO BE A WORNETTE?
YOU ALREADY ARE.

I wanted WORN to be – a family of people who worked on this little project of love.

Wornettes are not just girls; they can identify as any gender or none at all. Wornettes are not just interns; they are anyone who supports WORN, whether an editor-in-chief or an Australian teenager with a knee sock addiction and a mailbox. In the beginning, it only applied to those who worked for us, but as we grew the definition grew with us. Want to be a Wornette? You already are.

I'm a few years into this and I find myself giving talks to high school and university students. The first thing I usually ask is if anyone has had a fashion magazine make them feel bad about themselves. The answer is sadly, consistently, a sea of raised hands and nodding heads. I started

WORN because I didn't think it had to be that way. That doesn't need to be the dominant relationship we have with fashion. We can do better.

In these pages, we've collected the very best of the first seven years of WORN. We revisited and re-edited our early pieces, applying the lessons we've learned. It was interesting and, frankly, a bit shocking to see how far we've come. The WORN Archive collects articles and photo shoots from our first 14 issues and groups them together to show how WORN talks about style, and how we can examine, and celebrate, and learn from it. Fashion is personal, it's practical, it's history, design, object, art, identity, ideas, and fun. Fashion is WORN.

— Hearts, Serah-Marie Wornette

Over the course of many issues, artist Ariana
created a series of images inspired by makeup –
including sunscreen, lipstick, nail polish,
and, of course, bronzer.

Address & Redress
The story of a brokenhearted dress

I WOKE UP NAKED, nauseous and anxiety-ridden. Next to me on his floor, thousands of optimistic little cylinders glimmered up at my face. I reached out, and they transformed into a sticky sludge of Jägermeister and Sleemans. Outside, it was October, disintegrating leaves littering the lawns. As I lifted the dress from where it had slept, a row of beads broke loose and lost themselves forever under his couch.

That was the last time I wore the dress. And while I would love for my recollection of it to be epically proportioned, this is not where my memory takes me. Instead, when I see it sandwiched between an array of quiet day dresses, I go back to the pounding headache of that Friday morning. I lift the body of black and white beading over my own, silently gathering my belongings; the swirls of its scalloped sleeves weigh like chain mail on my shoulders. As I leave my (now) ex-boyfriend's apartment, it takes everything I have not to chuck the dress in the wood chipper parked not far from his front steps. I imagine running to my bed – skivvies and all – a burst of PVC pearls and pipes showering behind me like fireworks from the metal teeth of the machine.

In the less dramatic version, I hail a cab. I sit in the back seat, the polyester lining of the dress clinging to the sweat of my thighs, until I've travelled the five blocks home. I leave the dress in a mound on the floor. Half a year later it hangs, zipped on a wooden hanger, patiently awaiting resurrection.

Pre-breakup I would have found the dress suitable for any occasion: galas at the Royal Ontario Museum, concerts at Massey Hall, multiple birthday parties, running out for milk. My post-breakup self, however, seems to treat the dress quite differently. Many evenings have come and gone, and many times I have felt the imprint of beads against my palm as I shuffled through a row of hangers. "Don't you think it's too flashy for tonight?" I'd say in the months following the breakup. A more genuine response might have been something to the effect of "I'm not ready to revisit that emotional blunder just yet," or "only if you'd like me to be a slobbering, sobbing mess by the time I put on my shoes." The honesty would have done me some good, but I'm not certain either of those admissions would have made for a fun pre-drink.

Add a few more months, and I have begun to see the humour of getting dumped while wearing such a fanciful frock. How could any guy keep a straight face while his weeping girlfriend sat on the floor in front of him, decked out like Alexis Carrington?

text by Casie Brown
photography by Arden Wray

28

And just like that, its lining comes an inch closer to touching my skin. Other memories come as I pull the slider up the zipper's tape: beads bouncing off the ceramic floor of a bathroom as I held my friend's hair on her twenty-second birthday; being locked out of my second-floor apartment and finally succumbing to sleep midday, on the front porch of our Little Italy duplex. I'm not sure my neighbours had ever seen such a Courtney Love–esque combination of extravagance and wreckage. The zipper snags at the waist as I recall a 6 a.m. walk of shame, sun rising and commuters gawking, my self-stitched hem and self-esteem unravelling down Dundas Street. (Someone had suggested I leave at that hour to avoid walking home in daylight.)

I'm certain there have been more instances of trauma while wearing the dress but, with our combined years together, old memories slip and make way for new ones. In the meantime, there are physical limitations to overcome, as well as emotional.

Patches of beading vanish, and the maze of a pattern is continually altered – if only slightly – with each wear. The dress's residency in the back of my closet becomes an act of preservation for both myself and the dress. The hem that was sewn in a flurry in a hotel room could use a re-stitching; the bare threads that dangle above my kneecaps should be trimmed. The list of repairs makes something that I cannot grasp or measure seem tangible, like learning the ukulele or alphabetizing my bookshelf. I'll get around to it one day. Until then the dress will wait in sartorial limbo. Dust might gather on the neckline, and cobwebs replace the threads that link beads together, but I know it will be there, ready when I am. ⌗

R

BEFORE

THE

BIDDING

STARTS

Stories from a New York auction house intern
text by Pamela Grimaud
illustration by Sara Guindon

I WAS HALFWAY THROUGH A MASTER'S PROGRAM in costume history when I undertook my student internship at a New York City Upper East Side auction house. In my previous internships at museums, I had donned gloves to lay 18th-century silks onto pillows of acid-free tissue and oh-so-carefully removed installation pins from Jacqueline Kennedy's inauguration gown. The frenzied pace of the auction world, however, meant only the most fragile pieces received such treatment. It was an interesting change of pace.

As an intern I reported to Aggie, head of the Couture and Textile Department. Aggie was a diminutive, 50-something woman brimming with energy. As she worked she reminded me of the delicate, determined sparrows flitting crumb to crumb beneath the tables of sidewalk cafés. She wore her hair short in a cut that privileged function over fashion, and her skin was pale from what I would later learn were too many half-eaten office lunches.

Aggie had the enormous responsibility of dealing with hundreds of consignees, all of whom proffered real or imagined treasures for auction. She would proceed to research, document, and measure the selected objects – anything from a '40s-era victory suit (cut narrow in recognition of wartime rationing) to paisley shawls woven large to accommodate the circumference of a Victorian gown.

In the months leading up to the biannual auction previews, I manipulated dozens of objects I had otherwise only read about. The bits of history that passed through my hands were what had brought me to New York in the first place.

Before the bidding started, pieces were publicly displayed for several days, and the nondescript walls of the showroom came alive with art and fabric. A pole drawn through the kimono-like sleeves of a 1910 French opera coat displayed the garment to its best advantage; across the room, there hung a drooping Japanese tapestry. Lime green sandals from Carnaby Street dangled from trees, and beneath rested knee-high boots stitched with the pattern of Old Glory. Vintage illustrations lined the walls; shaky garment racks displayed delicate flapper frocks, belle époque bustles, and the sculpted Dior suits that had ushered in the curves of the hyperfeminine '50s.

In any auction many items are fragile, and I winced as distracted mothers let their toddlers run, arms outstretched, straight for the feathers of a vintage cocktail gown or Lilly Daché hat. At the end of each day iridescent sequins dotted the floor, to be collected in Ziploc bags and reattached to the garments from which they came.

Much of my preview time was spent prying museum-quality pieces from manicured hands and dodging the verbal shrapnel of women unaccustomed to hearing the word "no." I struggled to remain polite as a woman resembling a high-strung poodle who had gnawed through its owner's cosmetic case demanded to try on a delicate Schiaparelli fur and matching cap. "Imagine!" she yelped, levelling her displeasure at my co-worker with a sharp tilt of her head. "This one – who can't even afford a decent haircut – telling me I can't try something on!" Then, shaking her $17,000 Chanel bag an inch from my face, she snarled, "It's not like I can't afford it!"

The hours spent in Aggie's office documenting pieces or prepping frocks to be photographed for the auction catalogue occupied the bulk of my internship and made the extra work I did during the previews easier to bear. As a break from the routine, Aggie let me tag along one day to the home of a potential consignee: a recent widower and practising surgeon whose wife had left behind a cache of pristine outfits. I met Aggie in front of his apartment building on Central Park South.

I had arrived in New York less than a year before, and one of the Manhattan fantasies I'd cultivated had to do with real estate: I imagined having access to the shabby but gracious brownstones of a Woody Allen movie, or the pre-war miracles featured in the Times' style section. This was to be my first peek into this rarefied world. Together we were greeted in the lobby by the doctor, a stooped, elderly man dressed in baggy trousers and a light-coloured cardigan, his hair thin and flat against his skull. His wife had died less than a month earlier, he told us as he led us to the building's basement, and I felt a pang. "She loved to shop," he said wistfully, indicating the enormous wardrobe boxes lined up one against another, "and she looked good in all of it."

Everything smelled of damp and must. Aggie and I sliced open the cartons, slowly removing what we could sell at auction. Each piece was protected by a garment bag – once clear but now opaque and stiff with age – and most still bore price tags. Judging from the labels, the doctor's late wife had favoured the fashions of Norman Norell. Popular from the '50s through the '70s, Norell's designs were once described as social security for the well-heeled American woman, with stiff interlock knits for day and sequinned gowns that provided ready glamour at night.

The boxes were jammed with daywear, and from that we cherry-picked classic jersey dresses and a standout bubble gum pink coat that melted my heart. When Aggie offhandedly mentioned that evening wear often sold for top prices, the man piped up, "I've got more upstairs. Some nice gowns." I had assumed the man's desire to part with his beloved's clothing

was the result of grief, but as he offered up more and more of her belongings (and appeared increasingly disappointed at the suggested gavel prices), he seemed less concerned with staving off memories than with recouping an investment.

Upstairs, whatever view of Central Park the doctor's apartment afforded would have to be taken on faith. The windows overlooking the pond were impenetrable, clouded by age and soot. The path to the living room had been carved through hip-high piles of books and statuary. The folds of Bergdorf bags brought home long ago (and never opened since) were lined with insect eggs. A door had been removed to accommodate the ephemera that burst from a spare room. I had read about hoarders – collectors whose homes and habits have become a kind of prison – but nothing had prepared me for this: the squalor of two lives lived in collusion with one overwhelming compulsion to spend. Any grandiose illusions I'd had about the ranks of Manhattan's privileged were supplanted by a sense of unease.

As we unzipped garment bags revealing one costly suit after another, I realized I was rifling through what was left of a troubled life. This collection was not a celebration of beauty, or even the result of a guilty pleasure. Triplicates of the same outfit, identical but for colour, hung as forlorn reminders of a lifetime spent feverishly dispensing cash, and the things this now-dead woman had spent decades accumulating were being rummaged through by strangers to be sold to the highest bidder.

Aggie gamely went about her work, squeezing between garment bags to push deep inside rooms where hidden treasures beckoned. I grabbed whatever was thrust out to me, her disembodied hand extending

I REALiZED I WAS RIFLING THROUGH WHAT WAS LEFT OF A TROUBLED LIFE

from between layers of plastic. I gingerly foraged through dozens of shopping bags, moving past the dining table where seating for one had been cleared from amid the clutter. In the kitchen, encrusted dishes filled the sink and unpacked Gristedes bags vied for floor space. Canasta-night cocktail mixes sat stacked on narrow shelves, and next to them a set of miniature sherry glasses, stems inverted, supported tiny pyramids of dust. I felt an involuntary heave in my chest and clenched my hand to my stomach. I left the room.

Upon departure, Aggie presented a list of the selected items to the doctor. Her arms filled with all she could carry, Aggie thanked the man and told him that the rest of the clothes would be picked up soon. We bid our goodbyes and headed to the subway to go our respective ways: her back to the office and me home to Hoboken.

Those encounters on the auction house floor, that day at the doctor's – in fact, many of my experiences in New York – were a steady stream of contrasts. Sublime moments and bursts of beauty were rendered even more vivid by the reality of life in that city: cash-strapped master's candidates on 15-minute breaks dashing between the chauffeured town cars of clients they'd just left behind; a vintage Vuitton collar on some oblivious pooch; the solitary guy lying half off the subway platform at 42nd Street. Manhattan felt like a magnet for the best of everything, with those who sought to create it and those who sought to own it always side by side. It was the former who made me want to live there and the latter who, eventually, helped me choose to leave.

Later that year I worked the floor of the auction preview, and there among the pieces was the bubble gum pink coat, its cheerful affect belying its origins. Not surprisingly, it received a lot of attention and went on to fetch a high price. Had I not known where it came from, I would have wanted it too. ⌧

HEAPS ON HEAPS

ARTIST & ECLECTIC COLLECTOR GRANT
HEAPS TALKS WORK, WARDROBE,
HOARDING, AND UNDERPANTS

interview by Serah-Marie McMahon
photography by Lisa Kannakko
styling by Hillary Predko

BY DAY HE MENDS and launders, tending to costumes for the National Ballet of Canada; by night he painstakingly cuts and sews the smallest scraps of colour and texture to form sprawling, quilt-like works. He is a perpetual collector. Grant Heaps's charming home, tucked away on little side street of Toronto, is the perfect showcase for his dozens of bow ties, hundreds of books, and thousands of sailors.

How did you dress in high school?
I kind of hung out with the punk kids. They all wore black, but I didn't wear black at all. I wore a lot of vintage. I'd buy '60s striped pants super cheap because no one wanted them, and take them in so they would be skinny instead of bell-bottom. I wore a lot of those.

Where did you buy them?
Vintage stores, or menswear stores that still had old stock. Toronto used to have a lot of those and they were always cheap – Goodwill, Salvation Army.... I'd wear five shirts at once, each one a little bit shorter than the other so you would see the tails sticking out. I'd add a tie but chop it off so it would be really short. And lots of jewelry – earrings and bracelets and necklaces and rings – mostly cheap '60s ridiculous costume jewelry that you could get for, like, 25 cents at thrift stores.

What do you wear now?
I love stripes, I love plaids and checks, I love combining them. I love blue, I like red, and I think I'm wearing more and more grey as grey becomes more popular. So that's kind of odd, slipping into my wardrobe.... Who thinks grey is odd? Anyways, I didn't actually wear much grey before. And black, obviously, it's just so available. And sometimes greens... but the colour range isn't very wide. When I go into a store, I look for things that are those colours. And in the patterns I like.

Recently someone told me about Thom Browne, a menswear designer who started making these little tiny shrunken suits for men in a kind of Pee-wee Herman look. I have one of his shirts. I spent a fortune, but it was so worth it.

And shoes?
I've worn Converse ever since I was a little kid. Other kids would tease me because no one wore them back in the mid-'70s. I'd get the fake ones for four bucks that said "Made in Czechoslovakia." I just love all the colours and the patterns and I find them really comfortable. And if you do get tired of a pair they eventually wear out. But I always save the tops for my other work, my quilts and stuff. I can pick out the pieces of Converse in my quilts.

Do you often put your clothes into your work?
Yes, other people's clothes too. People give me things sometimes, things that they loved, or that are just a really good colour. It makes me happy when I spot a bit in a quilt.

You use a lot of textile in your work.
I've been obsessed with textiles for as long as I can remember. Even when I was a kid, I loved touching them. My mom always had fabric around, and she made clothes. I remember the sheer things; I just loved to touch them, especially if they had embroidery on top. I found that fascinating. I also loved to wet textiles and see them change. I was a weird little kid. My mom said that once she looked in the laundry room and my wet boots were in among all the clothes, which I'd definitely done. I saved bits of fabric that I probably still have in the boxes of scraps I've had since before I was a teen.

Currently I'm working on a whole series that attaches together like a jigsaw puzzle. They're not shaped like puzzle pieces, just

rectangles and squares, but you can align one beside the next. The picture will tell the story of an audience watching a theatrical event. A person watching sometimes gets mixed up as to whether what they're seeing is about them, or they begin to believe what they're watching on stage is about them and it becomes really personal. I'm interested in the way people perceive things and make things personal, even when they're not.

What do you think of shows like *Hoarders*?
I can definitely relate. I mean I'm not, you know, a "hoarder," but there have been moments in my life when I could tell it was headed in that direction. So I can really understand.

What do you think makes you different?
I haven't become as depressed as most of those people. I think it actually has little to do with how many things there are; it's their state of mind. People get depressed and they literally can't figure out what to do. I mean I do have a fabric collecting problem. I can't say no to fabric. I have more than I can possibly deal with, so I really have to put in some effort to keep it under control. And I know there have been times in my life when there's stuff everywhere and you just have to step over it. If you have stuff and it's organized, that's one thing. But if you have stuff piled on top of itself and you don't even have access to it, that's usually the difference. But maybe it's not organized because they're depressed. I find the whole thing so fascinating.

Tell me about a day in your life.
I usually get up and then I have a shower. And then I choose my shirt. I always start with my shirt. And then from there I choose underwear and a tie that coordinate somehow.

Your underwear always matches your clothes?
Or contrasts. Except today because I'm living in my guest room so all my underwear is in a big basket and it was too hard. So then after the shirt, underwear, and tie comes the pants and then the socks.

If I can, I sit on my front steps to put my socks and shoes on because it's somehow just nicer to do looking out onto the street. Before work I go to a coffee shop, sew for a half hour, or sometimes I'll play solitaire

on my iPod if I really just want to get completely lost.

Then I go to work as the assistant wardrobe coordinator at the National Ballet. I take care of the costumes. People think I make costumes, but I don't. I do fittings, alterations, repairs, laundry, and a lot of organization. I tour with the company and am at almost every show. It's really two jobs. One is the 9-to-5 job, which happens when the company is not performing, and then there's the performing.

I do a million different things at once and sometimes it's just too much. And trying to keep everything tidy, it's sort of impossible. It's a job that's about being able to work in chaos. It's both useful and detrimental. ✂

IMPORTANT STYLE LESSONS
I LEARNED FROM COURTNEY LOVE

TEXT BY SERAH-MARIE MCMAHON
PHOTOGRAPHY BY MONIKA TRAIKOV

THE YEAR IS 1992 AND I'M 12 YEARS OLD. I'm at my best friend Natalie's house, and we're watching MuchMusic on the basement television in the middle of the night. We only get a very fuzzy CBC at my house, and anyway, my mom would never let me stay up this late. I don't listen to the newest songs on the radio (we don't have one) or watch the cool shows on TV. I often miss the point of crucial pop culture conversations that buzz around me at school. I dress in whatever my mother buys, and I end up in a lot of pleated pants and shorts that come with matching t-shirts. I know I want to be something else, but I don't know what.

My eyes are glued to the screen. All these bands I've never heard of are playing: the Pixies, Smashing Pumpkins, PJ Harvey. This intense, wild-looking blonde comes on. It's a clip of a show, and she's not so much singing as yelling. It's angry, emotional, and huge, masculine but feminine as hell. Stranger than the music, though, is the way she looks: crazy, sexy, messed-up hair littered with ribbons and colourful plastic barrettes, pale skin, heavily made-up eyes, and smudged red lips. Her dress is short and dishevelled, black velvet with a white Peter Pan collar and white lacy cuffs. Her nylons are full of runs and holes, and she's wearing chunky black combat boots. She is a porcelain doll come to life and spewing obscenities. She is so girly and yet not in any way behaving how I was told a girl should. It is the coolest thing I have ever seen.

The next weekend I convince my grandmother to buy me a babydoll dress at the Limited. There are racks and racks of them, and I weigh the value of one print over another for what feels like hours. In the end I get one in dove grey with huge pink peonies, fitted long sleeves, and a floppy bow in the back. I like it because I feel grown-up sexy and kid-like at the same time. Much to my mother's distress, I refuse to iron it, though I am not gutsy enough to add the matching ripped tights or makeup. The result is unkempt, but hardly badass.

Once I reach 15 and Hole's *Live Through This* album has been out for a year, I am well into the swing of Courtney style. I pierce my own ears at summer camp (three on one side, two on the other) and layer on long underwear, band t-shirts, workman overalls, and the mandatory plaid flannel shirt, then more layers of necklaces and rings. My friends sport similar looks, and we all think of ourselves as very rebellious, unique, and oh-so-socially-informed. I spend hours listening to grunge music, and I am liberated by the raw, raging noise of it to let out all my teenage frustration.

I am liberated, too, by the freedom of my clothing. It is comfortable, weather-friendly, and non-restrictive. I feel superior to other teens who worry about the cleanliness of their tight, minimalist white dresses and who tromp around in heels too high, trying too hard to exude their newfound sexuality. Courtney helps me get over my feelings of non-supermodel status during what is the Kate-Cindy-Linda heyday. She flaunts her pimples and razor-nicked legs like they are no big deal; this makes it easier to think of my own flaws as no big deal. I can relate to Courtney.

I remember my uncle dropping off a friend of mine at her suburban address and commenting on her trendy outfit. I am outraged! We are not fashionable: we are riot grrrls with attitude, and we don't dress like everybody else. Little did I realize that, back in 1993, Marc Jacobs had put out his now infamous Perry Ellis line of "grunge wear," which was influencing mainstream fashion all around us. There were hundreds — if not thousands — of girls just like us out there, and they all thought they were unique too.

As Courtney gets more and more mainstream, she gets less and less cool with my friends, so I keep my adoration quiet. Even when she goes all Versace on us in 1998, I still love her. It feels as if she's secretly taking Hollywood for a ride. It's an ultraglamorous façade, so beautiful with her tattoos and bleached-out hair. I start to notice designer labels when I hear the names of the dresses she wears: Valentino, Dior, Helmut Lang, and, of course, that stunning white Versace dress.

My style has changed over the years, but many of my Courtney lessons have stuck with me. I still firmly believe dishevelled is sexy. Nothing ever matches properly. I lean toward ultrafeminine, fussy dresses. I don't throw out my tights just because they have a few runs, and my hair is never neat. My style runs closer to cute than to pretty, but I'm never afraid to play dress-up.

TIME SHIFT

WORN Editor Sonya Abrego
models the finest from her closet

Credits

photography // Serah-Marie McMahon

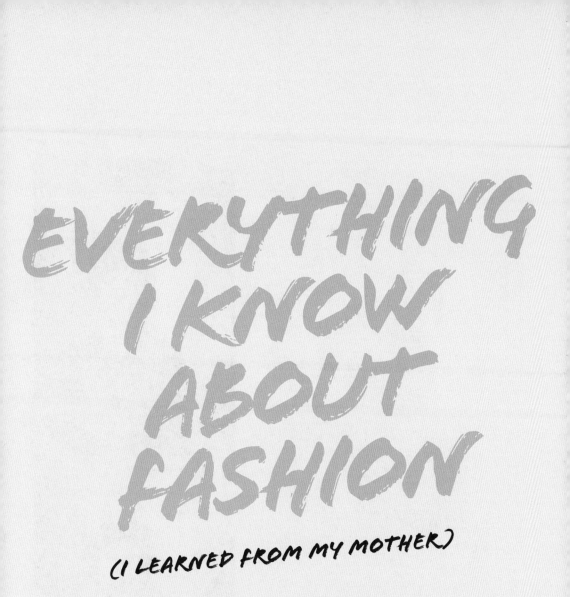

EVERYTHING I KNOW ABOUT FASHION

(I LEARNED FROM MY MOTHER)

text by G. Stegelmann

OUR EARLY PICTURES are those of a Perfect Family. There is one shot in particular I remember: tiny me in my mother's arms, one sister on my brother's shoulders, covering his eyes, and my other sister clinging to their side. My father stands behind us, only his eyes showing. We are all tan and happy, with green garden behind and blue sky above. Our expressions are varied, utterly natural, and if it's obvious we are clustered to fit the lens, we barely acknowledge the camera. You'd never think we didn't want to be there.

We were — and are — a camera-shy family. It was never our first inclination to self-document. A few times a year (at holidays or on some random, sunny summer day) my mother would pull out her old Kodak in its leather case and everyone would scatter, skittish animals catching the scent of a predator. It was useless. She would corral us all together again. "Smile," she commanded, and we did.

When I was very little, it wasn't a big deal. It takes time, learning to be self-conscious. I remember wondering why everyone made such a thing of it, this innocuous lens. My father was the worst, turning his face from the assault of documentation, impatiently waving his hand as though the displacement of air might form a shield. For every picture of all of us looking happy, there is at least one picture of my father (probably taken just before or after) looking annoyed. Ironically, he is extremely photogenic, while the rest of us are... not. As I grew older, more critical – and more able to see myself through the lens of pop aesthetic and expectation – I learned to be that way too.

Going through old pictures of my mom, I was always struck by her beauty. Around the time she married my father, when she was just past 20, she could take your breath away. She was all full hair and pouty lips, her hourglass figure poured perfectly into a cocktail dress or an old-fashioned bathing suit. As we looked through photos she'd tell me where the picture was taken, who she was with, and she would sigh. "I never knew how beautiful I was. I was always worried I was too heavy or that my hair wasn't right," she would say. "I never knew I had such nice legs." She would tell me she wished she had been less self-critical.

I wanted to learn her lesson, but, as the years went by, and as my collection of hideous yearbook pictures and shiny-forehead-big-jaw party snapshots grew, it seemed that I would never learn to love a lens.

When I was 26, I borrowed my boyfriend's Polaroid (a decade later I am, in fact, still borrowing it). I'd never had any kind of camera before and I became obsessed with taking pictures. More specifically, I became obsessed with taking pictures of me. It was the first time I was in control of my image, able to fix it in time, discarding anything I found unflattering and learning to face the lens with an understanding of the reflection it would produce. It was my Great Self-Portrait Experiment. I spent a year or more burning through expensive instant film (I suspect I went through a few thousand dollars of what was mostly student loan money). At the end I had several hundred Polaroids to show – and had thrown away twice as many. I knew how to take a good picture, but I also knew that wasn't good enough.

Flattering pictures were not an accurate reflection of the whole of me. My collection seemed inherently dishonest. I began taking pictures of myself after I'd been crying, or first thing in the morning, my eyes raccooned in makeup. I taught myself not to cringe, and slowly, things changed.

Once I stopped being afraid of my camera – of cameras – I could appreciate my mother's words. Looking at her pictures again, now without her, I realize the photos she would have seen as "unflattering" are beautiful, too. They're somehow intimate, capturing a part of her usually reserved for those who knew her best, with whom she could exist completely and without guard.

Looking at pictures of ourselves is like viewing a work in progress. Whatever we do, make, build, write, or reflect, in the moment we only see where we've gone wrong, what we could "fix." We have no perspective. There's not enough distance for us to appreciate the thing fully; we are filled with angst at how we might fall short. It's said that the camera doesn't lie, but pretty pictures are only half-truths.

And so I have taken up my mother's cause. The last Christmas we were all together, my family bought me a digital camera – and I've made good use of it, chasing them around, clicking madly. Although I only managed to take three pictures of Mom, I think she would be pleased with my ever-increasing digital sketches of the people she loved most (and perhaps even my own absurd collection of self-portraits). I am working to document those I love, too. For my own part, I let the lens find me as it will. Each picture is only a fragment, a little piece of the puzzle of me. The more there are, the more complete the image becomes. Someday I'll be able, and glad, to see it in focus.

"IT TAKES TIME, LEARNING TO BE SELF-CONSCIOUS."

RACHEL DRESSES LIKE A COMMUNIST. More precisely, I would call her style Communist Vampire Bicycle Courier with a dash of Flapper Ninja. For anyone unfamiliar with this aesthetic, it involves a lot of: black; soft, flat boots; army surplus; neglected pedicures; asymmetrical hemlines; and, occasionally, dark lipstick and finger-waved hair. It's not surprising to find her apartment an exotic red jumble of books and stacks of paper, bottles of wine, and strange bits of vintage and sci-fi ephemera. Her most recent purchase, a unicycle, stands in one corner looking not at all out of place.

Michele is an Elegant Minimalist with a touch of Sneaky Chic. Her clothes are always flattering and beautifully made, often in tasteful, understated neutrals (that is until she shows up at your magazine launch in a fantastic, jewel-toned, rustling plaid taffeta minidress and heeled ankle boots). The house she shares with her husband – also an EM, but with Good Man Preppy leanings – is spotless and stylish, practical, and very grown up. You'd almost expect it to be severe, but there is humour in the details – unexpected art and little things too cute to be quite tasteful, comfortable corners to sit in and sunlight streaming through the windows.

Serah-Marie is a member of the Vintage Craft Brigade, with a Militant Joyful streak. Her outfits and apartments have always been impossibly cluttered, strangely cohesive (in the way that no two things alike form a pattern), and optimistically unrelenting.

Oliver is a Clothing-as-Necessity Guy with an unexpectedly keen fashion sense. He cleans up real nice, but only if he has to, and yet he can spot a great jacket/hat/sweater at a hundred paces (a weird aptitude of which I take full advantage). For several years he kept car tires in his kitchen.

It is a rule long established that we should not jump to conclusions. Judging a book by its cover makes an "ass" of "u" and "me." The thing is, that's not how we operate. Every day we make a thousand assumptions based on what we see. They inform our actions and reactions and guide our contact with other people. Not only do we function this way, we're well aware others are doing it too and, often without thinking about it, we construct ourselves accordingly.

Investment bankers wear suits because you can trust the Gravely Conservative with your money. Serah-Marie wears rainbow striped legwarmers because they make her giggle and she thinks we all need to have more fun with our clothes. Aesthetically, the two cannot change places. Individual fashion isn't dictated by what's trendy or tasteful, or even flattering (at least not wholly). Rather, it's a reflection of who we are, what we admire and respect, what we long for, and who it is we want people to see.

My family has a decent collection of photos, but in the '60s and '70s, most of our pictures were developed as slides. When our family was young and all together, we might haul them out for visitors or on a whim, but the projector was unwieldy technology and thus rarely produced. Like 78 records or 8-track tapes, the slides became time capsules locked and buried and, as years passed, the secrets they held all-but-peripherally forgotten. Reels and reels of memory stayed out of mind in a cupboard collecting dust until my brother undertook the daunting task of converting our past to jpeg files.

The pictures have that '70s tone, colour-saturated like old Polaroids. My sisters stand in neatly matching dresses. (Mom dressed them as twins through most of elementary school.) I recognize clothes I would later wear; most were handmade and, whether we liked it or not, incredibly durable. My brother grins in front of the bright red garage. My aunt walks through our summer garden, my father rests against a cheerfully chaotic afghan, and I dance on a picnic table wearing ropes of costume beads. My mother, the driving force behind all this documentation, is nowhere to be seen and everywhere at once. Dresses, beads, gardens, and red paint; before we grew up and made worlds of our own, we lived in hers.

I look at the images and try to remove myself, my knowledge of my mother. I wonder what all the bits and pieces would mean if she were a stranger. There is order: she values her space and sense of control. There is clutter: the world is precious, beloved, and its tokens worth keeping. There is vibrant colour: she is an optimist, ready to see the possibility of joy in everything. It's not hard to apply these patterns to her closet, overly full as it always was of everything and anything – well kept, sometimes shockingly bright, and always deliberately arranged. It had never occurred to me to put all those things together (an oversight that seems quite foolish now), but when I finally did, the connections were overwhelming. I suddenly knew her better.

People have weird reactions to fashion. Just say the word and you'll find everyone has an opinion – and it's not always very nice. There is contempt (fashion is a shallow pursuit, propelled by vanity and ego), scorn (therefore the people who consume it are mindless, trend-driven sheep), and rejection (I don't follow fashion; I'm not the fashion type). Often, there is simply dismissal (it's just not important). But this is a reaction to an industry, not an idea. Whether we are opting out or in, we all participate. Fashion, at its heart, is not propelled by 362 pages of ads in the fall Vogue; it is a choice we make every day to wear this and not that, to consume or discard, to express in some wordless way the things we value.

After taking stock of my apartment (cluttered, but mostly tidy), and my closet (more cluttered and decidedly untidy), I have made some discoveries. First, a whole lot of what I've kept are gifts or hand-me-downs. I acquire things because I associate them with someone or some moment I don't want to forget. Second, though I see myself as both traditional and conservative, I can't keep my hands off a little bit of weirdness here and there. I like things that surprise me – perhaps I like to think I am surprising, too. Also, I keep the things I find most beautiful at eye level. Ultimately, I have come to the conclusion that I am part Detail-Oriented Experimental Classicist and part Sentimental Constructivist. Oh, and I don't mind dust, and I really like shoes.

Who are you?

"FASHION IS A CHOICE WE MAKE EVERY DAY, TO WEAR THIS AND NOT THAT, TO CONSUME OR DISCARD, TO EXPRESS IN SOME WORDLESS WAY THE THINGS WE VALUE."

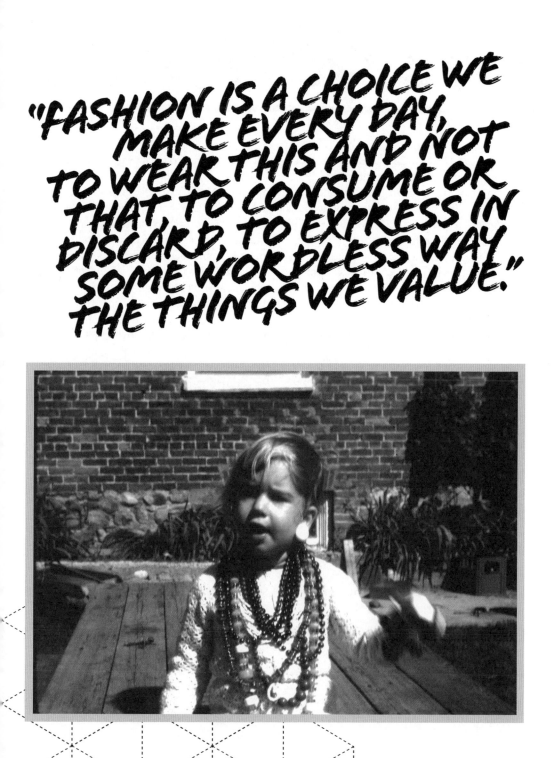

THE GETAWAY

THERE WERE FOUR KIDS in our family. Four kids and one income. We lived in the country, and my parents were models of self-sufficiency. We had three large gardens that produced vegetables all summer, which were carefully pickled, canned, or frozen to last all year. We had chickens for eggs and, eventually, meat. We had fruit trees for jam. My mother baked our bread and sewed or knit a lot of our clothes. "Homemade" was a very big part of our lives. But certain things had to be bought, and shoes were one of them.

Siegel's Shoes was right in the middle of downtown London, a block from Simpsons and Woolworth's and Eaton's. It was a tall, skinny, two-storey house painted robin's egg blue. I remember the smell first, musty and leathery, and the sound of a jangling bell and creaky old wood floors when you walked in the door. The ground floor was filled with new, regular-priced shoes. We might walk around there for a minute or two, but it was only to look, never to buy. Our destination was one floor up, at the top of a dubious flight of rickety stairs.

Siegel's second storey was one enormous room full of bargains. Every wall was covered in pegboard or metal grids that held row upon row of shoes tied together with kitchen string. The floor was filled with standing racks of more shoes and boots and tables piled with mountains of boxes, each stack topped with a sample of the style found below. The tables and racks were so close together there was often only enough space for one customer at a time.

The shoes that covered every available surface were mostly factory seconds or overruns. Many were deadstock: new but never sold and long out of style. Hand-lettered signs were everywhere, boasting prices that started at $0.99! (The exclamation point isn't mine, but punctuation that is inherently part of the notion of Cheap!) I would wander from table to table, wondering what I would buy if I had my own money to spend. I would linger at the one-dollar jelly shoes (my parents would never buy me plastic shoes, no matter how many of my friends had them) and the racks of Sparx runners (running shoes were for running, but would certainly ruin my feet if I wore them all the time) and imagine how cool I could be. I dreamed of sleek nylon-and-velcro trainers, but I'd leave with something much uglier and longer lasting.

One thing I was not, in my most formative years, was cool. I was, in fact, something of a Super Dork. I was too smart – but book-smart, not social-smart. And I was severely afflicted with Knowitallness; it didn't make me popular. I was earnest and literal (a trait I have carried into my adult life), always one step behind the joke, laughing too loud and too late and usually at completely the wrong thing. I was easily cowed by authority, too, and hesitant to indulge in any recklessness that might have impressed my peers. And all this wrapped in homemade sweaters and Mark's Work Wearhouse jeans. I didn't fit in, and worse, I didn't look like I could.

"Fashionable people would rather die than wear a visible label," my mother said.

She didn't like my obsession with trend, though I don't know if it was because she thought it was superficial or futile. Even so, she tried to ease my aesthetic embarrassment, carefully picking tags off castaway clothes and stitching them onto the things she made for me. (Just this past year, as I dug through her old sewing box for a bit of elastic, I found a little bag stuffed with Calvin Kleins and alligators waiting for reassignment.) She would painstakingly mimic popular styles, right down to the piping and buttons. Her creations were beautiful but always a little off, and they never fooled anyone. Pretending not to care was the only social sophistry I ever attempted, but I did care, and it rankled.

One day, in the middle of Siegel's second-floor savings extravaganza, my mother brought me a pair of shoes. "Aren't they so cool?" she asked excitedly in her German accent. They were black suede North Stars. The upper was boxy but sporty – a lace-up walking shoe – with a bright, silver star just below the ankle. The sole was a two-inch silver platform. Nike was King of Shoes that year, and I have no idea what possessed me to agree, but they were cool; they were insane and flash and I loved them immediately. I put them on as soon as I got home, strutting around the house, never once anticipating the firestorm of ridicule about to rain down on my poor, dorky head.

"Peter Pan getaway shoes!" Steve Roes yelled as soon as he saw them. "Are you going to fly away, Peter Pan?" As far as literal association went, it didn't make sense, but he was extremely pleased with his joke all the same. His friend Roger was quick to pick up the cue. The two were relentless, and soon every boy in my class was charging to the banner. "Peter Pan Getaway! Peter Pan Getaway!" I was mortified. These were my new shoes, bought for everyday wear and with room to grow in. They would be my only shoes until snow gave me an excuse to wear boots. I was going to be Peter Pan Getaway for the rest of the fourth grade and possibly my life. I set my nine-year-old face into a stony expression of disdain, but when I stepped off the bus at the end of the day, I crumpled.

I don't know how my mother talked me down. I certainly don't know how she convinced me to embrace my new moniker, only that she did. And then she did something that turned out to be pure genius. She took out one of my favourite shirts, a homemade sweatshirt with tear-away sleeves. Carefully, slowly, she wrote "Peter Pan Getaway" in small script on the front. Carefully, perfectly, she embroidered over the writing. The next day, in a terrifying and unprecedented act of bravery and rebellion, I put on my sweatshirt and my awful, amazing new shoes and went to school.

Those kids didn't know what to do at first. It was a bully's Christmas, and I was gift-wrapped. "Peter Pan Getaway," they'd yell, and I'd cross my arms and laugh and say, "That's me." But it was also Child Psychology 101. The whole fiasco fizzled out within a day or two. Peter Pan Getaway was my nickname for the next couple of years. It quickly dissolved into a meaningless term of endearment. It was my marker of acceptance. I kept wearing my crazy shoes and found myself sorry to outgrow them. In the years that followed, I discovered I could wear any damn thing I pleased. Sometimes it worked, sometimes it didn't, but I never felt like I had to apologize or hide. I don't know if there's any great moral here, but I do know that I have a lot of crazy shoes and I love them, and raising an eyebrow has yet to raise a welt.

And, at the end of eighth grade, Steve Roes kissed me by the baseball diamond fence. I had to bend my knees because he wasn't very tall.

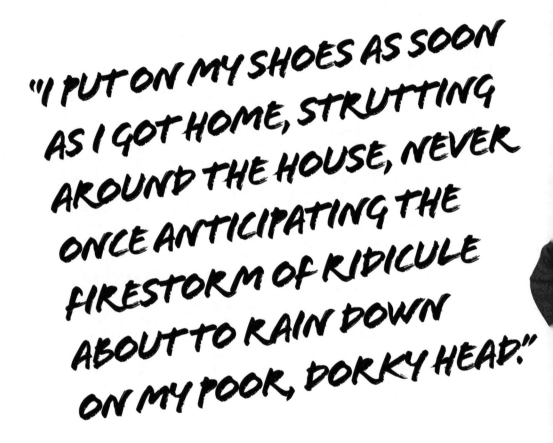

"I PUT ON MY SHOES AS SOON AS I GOT HOME, STRUTTING AROUND THE HOUSE, NEVER ONCE ANTICIPATING THE FIRESTORM OF RIDICULE ABOUT TO RAIN DOWN ON MY POOR, DORKY HEAD."

image // Ann Mann

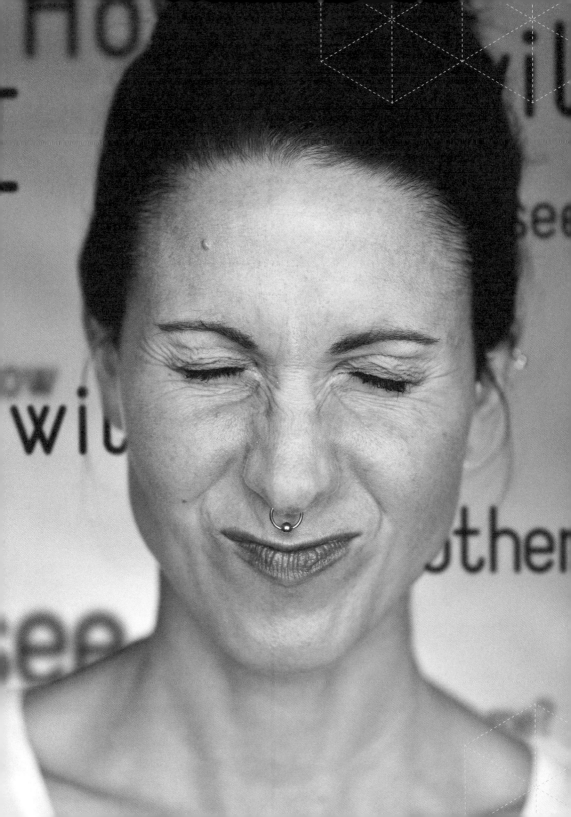

BEAUTY ACTUALLY

TURNING 30 PUT ME IN a remarkable good mood. I had stood in awe of older women all my life. They had beautiful faces and beautiful hands. They were self-assured, as elegant and polished as I was callow and awkward. Now distanced from my emotionally volatile 20s, I was closer to being of their sophisticated tribe. "If this is what 30 feels like," I said to my friend, "I can't wait to be 40." That was 10 years ago.

My mother didn't obsess over her age. She never tried to hide or deny it. She wanted us to know it didn't matter. The year I was born, The Phil Donahue Show went into syndication and I grew up watching daytime "experts" debating Youth Culture, ageing, and plastic surgery. Mom dismissed them all. Getting older was a part of life, she said, and the

more you fought it, the unhappier you'd be. I never saw her fret over crow's feet or age spots, and I was little, so I didn't care either. But I looked in the mirror. A lot.

School years fostered the usual amount of insecurity. My forehead was worrisome, my lips pale, my expression perpetually severe. I was too tall for the new wave '80s, then too short for the supermodel '90s. But I powdered and plucked and permed, undeterrably convinced I could find some cosmetic alchemy to finally make me beautiful.

Magic was not forthcoming. Instead, I made friends with a rebellious and tattooed redhead, a walking lesson in aesthetic independence. I learned to appreciate my strong features, rebuilding my reflection as a whole, rather than a jumble of inadequate parts. At 30, I felt like I had become myself and I was, momentarily, relieved.

My first real grey hair appeared with the adoption of a faux-hawk that same year. The close-clipped sides of my head sparkled with points of silver. One winter, I thought I'd developed a skin condition, only to discover my face suddenly required moisturizer. Daily. Then I needed prescription glasses (the gold-rimmed aviators from the drugstore sale bin were no longer enough). My face held the imprint of my pillow for an hour after I woke one morning and, in a picture, my neck looked strange. None of these things were radical, seismic – some were even amusing – but altogether, they unsettled me. And then....

"You look good for your age," said the intern. She was not yet 20 and it was clearly a compliment. At 37, I might have said those words, but I'd never heard them. I laughed, but there was a sting – this suggestion I might be attractive *despite* my age. And it rankled because I'd already begun to think it might be true and wonder whether it mattered.

What of beauty – where did its value lie? When I was younger I'd wanted it so badly but suddenly I felt ashamed that I cared at all. I was too clever to be consumed with something so shallow. Wasn't I?

We're obsessed with appearance but, it seems, only insofar as it's parceled with youth. Our lexicon is littered with euphemisms: "women of a *certain* age," and "the *mature* woman." Pop media, cultural value, and practical experience encourage girls to pursue beauty relentlessly, to wield it and worship it. That is, until some arbitrary expiration date when they should just forget it; we call that "ageing gracefully." Or we rage and assign words of battle – "the fight against ageing" – and we set ourselves up to fail because, if these are the terms, fail we must.

I had often openly despised women who whined about wrinkles or the Perils of Gravity.

Good lord, I'd think, *suck it up.* I believed, like Mom, that grasping at youth was ridiculous. But we are all beset with messages telling us youth is beauty and beauty, relevance. Superficial complaints disguise deeper fears that our familiar selves are slipping away and, with them, our intrinsic personal value.

"Sometimes I see myself and I get a shock," Mom said one day, glancing in the rearview, as though her hair had turned grey overnight. The truth was, on some level, she had stopped looking in the mirror. Perhaps she'd stopped looking to it. In her mind, she was too old to worry about her looks – and maybe resignation is healthier than agitation – but this approach doesn't sit well with me either. I am older and smarter, but I am always myself and I want to be beautiful.

Isabella Rossellini once said, "If I have to just repeat, 'I am old but I am still beautiful, I am old but I am still attractive,' I don't know.... What I would like is to say something new." I am 40, and flanked by women both younger and older; I want us *all* to say something new – and not just to say it, but to *see* it.

The physical change of years is an aspect of beauty as fascinating – and as wholly unremarkable – as any other. And I'm not talking about "wisdom" and I'm not talking about "experience" (misdirections akin to describing someone as having "really pretty hair" or a "great personality"). We need to recognize the aesthetics of age in a way that isn't stuffed with qualifications or impossible comparisons. Ageing, more than a metaphor, is a physical manifestation of the human condition. It is as lovely as the accident of youth, as awesome as any force of nature.

And beauty is everywhere – not *despite*, not *still*, but simply because it *is*, full stop.

Credits

photography // Lisa Kannakko

"WE NEED TO RECOGNIZE THE AESTHETICS OF AGE IN A WAY THAT ISN'T STUFFED WITH QUALIFICATIONS OR IMPOSSIBLE COMPARISONS."

In 1960 my parents couldn't take their eyes off my brother. Years later, I can't take my eyes off that dress.

ARCHIVE

I PRACTICALLY HOWLED IN DISBELIEF when my mother told me she'd given away those dresses. One was all satiny cocktail drama. The cut of it defined the '50s; with its stiff fabric nipped at the waist and full in the skirt, it was the absolute definition of dreamy. The other, a pale pastel floral, was an ethereal contrast to her jet black hair. "But why," I wailed. "You should have kept them!" I held up the photos of Mom in her lost frocks, evidence of her folly. I couldn't fathom why anyone would discard so much glamour. Her response was an ambivalent-yet-impatient wave of her hand. Maybe I was right, but each of those delectable garments was definitely, irretrievably gone.

I can't seem to get rid of anything. It's no surprise; in my experience, fashion people have a tendency to hoard and collect. Fashion, by its very nature, encourages infinite variety, reinvention, and reproduction. Its dialogue unfolds in reference. When the past is always present (and the fall lines show in spring), it's an invitation to excess. And that's only the half of it. Clothing is an intimate thing, too, kept close to the body and indelibly marked by the wearer. We pilfer our boyfriends' shirts and grandmas' beaded cardigans. Fitting our bodies into

the costumes of their lives brings us closer to them. And that's still not it....

Clothes are inextricably tied to our body image: they are the shape of the body we used to have or the person we could be. I have friends who keep clothes that haven't fit for years or buy new ones in some arbitrary "ideal" size because ownership carries the illusion of control. One acquaintance told me that since she was a heavy kid and all her clothes were awkward and ill-fitting, as an adult she feels compelled to buy anything that looks nice.

My own textile architecture has long sprawled past wardrobe borders, annexing my apartment. For years I've watched my rapid fashion expansion almost helplessly. With every impulse to streamline, I find a reason to delay. I keep things because I might want them again or because they were gifts. I keep them because they remind me of that day the sun was shining in Berlin. I'll just hang on to this for one more year.

I'd venture a guess that this is all pretty common. A whole lot of us have enough clothes to last us two lifetimes each. On the surface (as clothing ought to be) it sounds amazing. It's absurd, storybook-fashion-magazine wealth. Possibility! Reinvention! But it's not dress-up and it's not joyful. It is a wearable levee, shoring up against a flood of fear and desire. (We still can't find a thing to wear.)

For the first time in almost nine years, I am planning to move. Outside of my family home, I've lived in this apartment longer than any other place – and I have the closets to prove it. My walk-in is filled to overflowing; my storage closets are stacked with crates and boxes (some of which have remained packed for a decade or more). My winter stuff has spilled out into the stairwell along with at least 15 pairs of shoes and boots, sometimes ordered but more often in terrible heaps. I used to look into my closet and see an archive of my life. Now I only see the reflection of a self locked in time. (Oh, for the time I could open the door and just see clothes!)

Susan, a member of my mother's church group, told me this story: my mother had come to one of their meetings wearing a lovely new sweater. Susan oohed and ahhed and then forgot all about it. Mom didn't and, at the next meeting, she arrived carrying that same sweater in a bag, carefully washed and folded. "It's for you, because you liked it so much." Susan protested – she shouldn't give away such a pretty thing! I could have told her it was no use to argue.

I can't count the times I told Mom I liked something of hers only to find myself with that thing in my hands. She always had a lot of stuff, no question, but it never owned her. She knew where its value lay.

Now, I'm not suggesting we should all throw everything out, or even give it away. There are things that are beautiful (and beautiful to have). And the past is important – it shapes us – but the form it produces is more than the sum of a drawer. I have clung to things believing they could protect me from loss, somehow, or keep the future at bay. My father's sweater, my sister's purse, that dress I wore the summer I fell in love – it was as though fibres could hold memory fast. Foolishness. Clothes are ephemeral, transient things, prone to stains, prey to moths – and there are always, *always* more.

Even as I write, I have three garbage bags stuffed with t-shirts and jackets and dresses waiting in my office. Filling them was nerve-racking, exhilarating. It was a conscious and physical decision to assign value – and to take it away. It feels good to let things go.

(And don't misunderstand, I have plenty left.) I will let my friends have what they want and give the rest to charity. I will be my archive. My clothes can just be clothes. ⊠

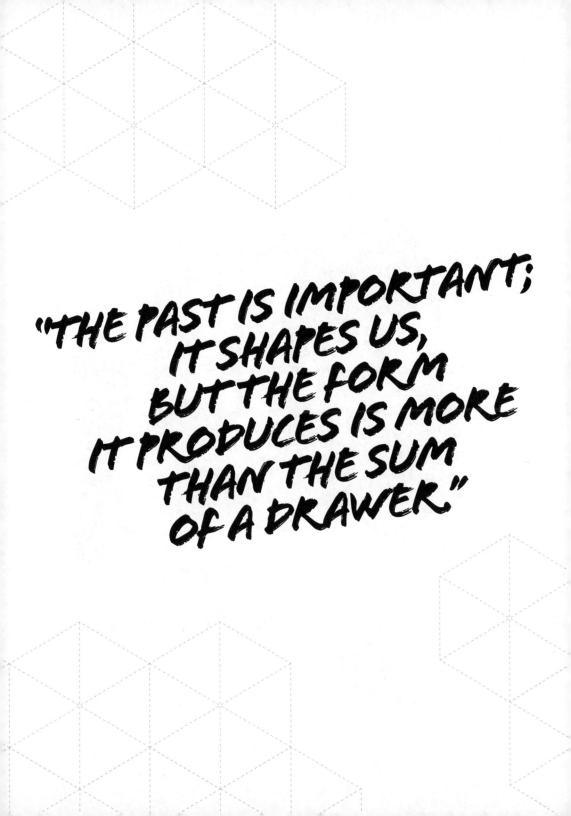

"THE PAST IS IMPORTANT; IT SHAPES US, BUT THE FORM IT PRODUCES IS MORE THAN THE SUM OF A DRAWER."

FASHION IS
PRACTICAL

02

IN A WORLD OF GLOSSY MAGAZINES and lifestyle branding, it's easy to forget that clothing is, at its core, practical. We may want our clothes to reflect our personalities, but we need our buttons to button and our seams to stay sewn. Fashion is ornamentation built on necessity.

Whether we adopt a uniform or dress to kill, all garments require care and maintenance, but the specifics of that care are an issue rarely addressed. The goal of most fashion publications is to convince you to purchase, discard, and purchase again. It is radical to talk about fixing clothes or learning to make them. It means turning away from culturally pervasive notions that newer is better, consumption is a reward (and holding on to what you have is a punishment). It also means we radicals end up with a lot of questions that need answers: what can I put in the washing machine? Is it worth paying a cobbler to stretch tight shoes? How do I tie my stupid tie so the skinny part doesn't hang down past the wide part?

In straying away from the ideological into the practical, we discover a new connection with our clothes – the ability to preserve and alter them and, in making those choices, to define their value. With a more comprehensive knowledge of construction and materials, we find resonant connections with garment history, and create inroads to self-expression, craft, and even art. Fashion is practical – but by embracing its practicality we can find out more about everything else it is, too. ✄

WASHINGis

worn answers your

text by G. Stegelmann
illustration by Tyler Rauman

FOR A CULTURE THAT DEDICATES ITSELF to cleanliness and good personal grooming, we have made our pursuit of it difficult. Nowhere is this more evident than in our laundry habits. This is especially true for anyone who develops an emotional attachment to their clothes, as those less attached will take more risks due to impatience. The latter isn't always a bad thing.

Hand-washing is a nightmare. It's drippy and messy and uses all your floor space. (Lay flat to dry, indeed.) It leaves a ring around the tub. Nothing ever rinses completely or wrings out properly, and if you live in the city and haven't the outdoor space for a clothesline, it leaves great puddles on the floor. That is, unless you're laying things flat to dry, which still leaves you with damp towels, which you still have no place to hang. And yet, looking at the semi-complete wardrobes hanging damply from my friends' shower rods, one would think the washing machine had only just been invented. Why else would we trust it so little?

In the past, I have been known to leave new hand-washables in the bottom of my hamper so long they went straight from the laundry bag to the Goodwill. That is, until my friend Shannon said, "I wash all my wool sweaters in the machine," and turned my world upside down.

Loose your chains – it's time to embrace the future. Here's a bunch of stuff you can jam in the machine with your jeans – and a few things you shouldn't.

Wool sweaters

Shannon was right. Virtually any wool sweater can be washed in the machine, in cold water, using the delicate cycle. (A sturdy sweater in a newer machine can usually handle the normal setting.) It's best to run them together, as there's not much else the delicate cycle is good for, as far as I can tell, except for really (and I mean really) delicate lingerie. Don't wash sweaters with your bras or you'll have a laundry catfight on your hands, and a wool thread will almost always lose to a metal hook. The brilliance of this technique is the spin cycle. Your sweaters will dry in half the time, and unless they're very heavy, the spin will take out enough water to let you hang dry without stretching things out of shape.

Delicate lingerie

You know those lingerie washing bags you can buy? Good, great, use them – that's what they're there for. Or use a pillowcase with a hair elastic around the top because you're cheap, or because you spent your last couple of bucks on lace panties that totally ride up but make your ass look amazing. If you've got this stuff in a bag, you can wash it with your regular clothes (with like colours, obviously) in a regular cycle. Check your bras afterward to make sure they don't dry with dented nipples, as this is never a good look.

Regular lingerie

Just put it in the washing machine and don't be such a baby. Cold water setting, shape the bra cups, hang dry – done. And remember, if you're nervous (and unless you're a coal miner), the delicate cycle still gets regular clothes clean. Use it until you forget to set it someday and realize you were worried for nothing.

Trainers

Virtually any nylon or canvas running shoe can get thrown in the machine. A little leather is okay, too. Shoes are made to withstand some pretty crappy conditions, so a little swishy water isn't gonna hurt. I personally take out the insoles of actually-made-for-fitness runners (I'm not as cavalier as I'd have you believe); the insoles of a running shoe are important in terms of shape and fit. I might also mention many laundromats frown on this. Rightly or wrongly, they believe washing (soft) shoes wrecks the machines. Rightly or wrongly, I believe this is a myth. Nevertheless, be crafty about it and save yourself a world of hassle.

Silk
Delicate, cold. Hang dry. Breathe. You'll be fine and so will your shirt.

Finally, a few handy tips
No more top-loaders ➤ The parts of a wash cycle that do the most damage are agitation and drastic temperature changes. Front-loading machines rely on gravity to agitate your clothes and are less traumatizing to fabrics than top-loaders. They also tend to rinse more thoroughly and fit more stuff; plus, you can use half the detergent for the same result.

Anything you want to hang on to for more than a year, keep out of the dryer ➤ The dryer fades colours and kills elastic and spandex content. It also shrinks and felts wool – which is a cool effect, but only if you do it on purpose.

If you're afraid to wash it, don't ➤ Go to the Goodwill or Salvation Army or whatever, get yourself a $3 garment with the same fabric content, and wash that instead. For a few bucks and a half-hour's work, you can find out if that special fancy blouse/dress/sweater will live or die. But also remember, *stuff is just stuff:* if it's not absolutely irreplaceable, it's definitely replaceable.

Don't put that in the machine for god's sake
Wool pants and blazers, and anything else with a lining ➤ One layer will shrink and shift or twist, and the other won't. It's very sad.

Really great vintage, or anything beaded or sequinned ➤ Who would risk it? But also remember, places that dry-clean often send out their clothes. They have no idea about the process and the damage it can do. (I once picked up a hand-made quilt only to find long slashes all through the top layer.) Check to see if your dry-cleaner has experience with similar items. It's worth finding a few that do, as dry-cleaning uses harsh chemicals, and you don't want to hand one-of-a-kind pieces to just anyone.

Pantyhose ➤ Though mostly you can wash these like delicate lingerie and nine times out of ten it's okay, sometimes they snag. I just don't see the point in risking it. It takes two minutes to rinse them in the sink, and they'll be dry ten minutes later. Stop being so lazy. ⊠

FOR THE LOVE OF THE LINE

POLITICS, PROGRESS, AND WHY LAUNDRY'S SIMPLEST PLEASURE ISN'T ALWAYS CUT AND DRIED

· ·

TEXT BY LISE TREUTLER
PHOTOGRAPHY BY CASIE BROWN

I MEASURE THE SEASONS with my clothesline. From the first buds of spring through autumn's single-digit temperatures, I joyfully hang my freshly washed laundry on a nylon rope strung between my back balcony and a telephone pole. The joy of the clothesline – and how to use it properly – I learned from my grandmother, Babcia.

My childhood summers were spent at my grandparents' cottage, a rustic haven with no indoor plumbing. All our clothes, swimsuits, and towels were washed by hand and hung to dry on three short clotheslines forming a triangle around a small stand of evergreens. Everything I wore smelled like pine and campfire. Now, though my current kitchen has hookups for a washer and dryer, I'd rather walk a block to the laundromat and lug my wet clothes home to hang. Caring for clothes has become my rebellion.

SMELLS LIKE PROTEST, BUT WITH A HINT OF SPRING

It's a cliché to say that the personal is political, but nowhere is this better illustrated than in ongoing clothesline debates across Canada and the United States. Those blissful hours spent hanging clothes on a line are, in fact, hours of activism. In Aurora, Ontario, and many other North American municipalities, the clothesline was banned.

Phyllis Morris, the former mayor of Aurora, led a campaign called Right to Dry. Its supporters worked to persuade the Ontario government to declare the clothesline an energy-saving device. The process began at a municipal meeting during a brainstorming session on energy conservation, when the group discovered local developers' restrictions on outdoor clotheslines. "That was when the penny dropped," Morris says. Although other pro-clothesline campaigns already existed, such as the Project Laundry List campaign in New Hampshire, she believes

Right to Dry's direct connection to energy saving built momentum in Aurora.

In September 2006, the Aurora Town Council voted unanimously to support Morris's motion to the provincial government. World Wildlife Fund Canada and the Conservation Council of Ontario also endorsed the campaign, as did Peter Love, Ontario's former chief energy conservation officer, who recommended that local bylaws prohibiting outdoor clotheslines be overruled in favour of energy conservation. Love and Morris were right: according to StopGlobalWarming.org, line-drying clothes in spring and summer alone prevents approximately 700 pounds of carbon dioxide emissions per household annually. In 2008, clothesline bans across Ontario were lifted, largely thanks to Morris's campaign.

Morris maintains that the right to dry is not just an Aurora issue: she has received hundreds of supportive letters from people across Canada sharing their personal frustrations with similar anti-clothesline by-laws. "In this day and age, knowing we're facing climate change and knowing our energy costs are rising, people want options. There are bigger concerns regarding the environment than underwear hanging outside," says Morris.

BUT THERE'S UNDERWEAR... OUTSIDE

Complaints against clotheslines relate to aesthetics, potential property devaluation, and even money. Irene Rawlings, Denver-based co-author of *The Clothesline*, believes that class associations with clothesline use grew out of the post–World War II euphoria over "labour-saving" devices such as washing machines and clothes dryers. A divide grew between those who could afford such machines and those who couldn't.

Clothesline antagonists argue that undergarments do not belong outdoors on public display. While I'm sure we all have pieces we'd rather not share with the world,

it's strange to think we've been able to reach such an advanced stage of civilization without accepting that most of us wear underwear and that we, at least occasionally, clean it.

How can we accept underwear models plastered on billboards across cities everywhere yet remain skittish about our own hygienic habits? The billboard ads sell underwear with the dubious promise of sex, while a sports bra blowing in the wind tells the story of a woman who exercises and takes care of herself and her clothes – a far more satisfying tale.

THE LINE THAT BINDS

At home in Montreal, I consider myself incredibly lucky to share balcony-community moments with my neighbours as we hang our laundry out to dry. David Fennario's play *Balconville* is about francophone and anglophone working-class neighbours bonding as they hang laundry and discuss politics and factory closures. Instead, my neighbours and I dip into fashion, complimenting each other on our unique styles and occasionally laughing at the prevalence of lingerie. Today's

clotheslines are Luddite-friendly fashion blogs, a preview of street-style. Surely you must be proud of at least some of your wardrobe. Why not display it in all its glory?

Morris, while noting that "most people now are putting the aesthetics aside and the environment first," also recognizes that romantic notions of clothesline use "harken back to simpler times." She believes that a cultural shift regarding past class associations is at work as well. "If it was seen as lower-class once, it's moving up now at least through the middle class." Rawlings holds fast to the clothesline as "one of life's luxuries," an escape from the constant barrage of technology where one can be alone: "There's sort of a spirituality to such an everyday act." This is the universe I enter when putting my laundry on display.

My clothesline tells the story of a vintage-loving, dress-wearing yogi who favours bamboo over cotton. When it comes time to bring my sun-dried clothing inside, I breathe the wind off each piece and once again thank my Babcia for teaching me the lay of the line. ✄

LESSONS FROM MY BABCIA
. . . .

Clotheslines are commonly categorized into three types, each with its own merits.

1) Plastic clotheslines are cheap and easy to clean. They're the most stretch resistant of the three. However, they tend to be the thinnest, leaving obvious clothespin dents and offering the least grip.

2) Nylon clotheslines are also relatively cheap and easy to find. They're incredibly strong and thicker than plastic lines but are often slippery and difficult to tie off.

3) Cotton clotheslines are the least common because they're not as strong as nylon or plastic and often require a full wash instead of a wipe-down. However, cotton lines offer the best grip for clothespins and are the easiest to tie off.

Regardless of whether your clothesline is a loop strung between two wheels or a rope stretched from tree to tree, leave at least some excess at the end after you tie off a strong knot. All clotheslines will eventually stretch from the weight of wet clothes, and leaving extra line makes the re-tying process that much easier.

PANTS: Hang by the bottom of the leg. If you're into creases, fold them where you want the crease to be while they're wet.

T-SHIRTS: Hang by the bottom edge so clothespin dents won't be visible.

SHEETS & TOWELS: Fold them in half and pin the ends to the line together, allowing them to billow in the wind and fluff themselves.

BLACK FABRICS: Don't dry in intense, direct sunlight – unless you wish you'd bought the grey instead.

AND REMEMBER: Put heavy items at the end of the line to reduce sagging in the middle!

LIVE AND LET DRY

THE DIRTY TRUTH ABOUT DRY-CLEANING

text by Risa Dickens

TWO YEARS AGO I inherited a papasan chair, its giant yellow cushion prickly with cat hair. Since I was allergic, but also irrationally in love with the second-hand seat, I dragged it to the dry-cleaner. Sixty dollars and three days later I propped it up in its place of honour, snuggling in with a great book and open

hours ahead of me. I was ejected from the dander-bowl about three minutes later by the laboured breathing, sneezing, and runny eyes I recognized as allergies. What the hell?

I don't know what made me think that there was a miracle cleaning process that would extract millions of thin hairs. "Dry-cleaning," though not "wet," probably doesn't involve magic cat-hair magnets. But it ought to do something. If dry-cleaning didn't get the hair out, what *did* it do?

Perchloroethylene is the short answer. When dry-cleaned, items are checked and treated for stains, then tossed in a machine that's like a super-sized ordinary washer. Liquid chemicals are circulated through the garment fibres; the garments are then heated and spun dry to remove remaining solvent, which is filtered for reuse. Hazardous wastes are produced, in the form of cooked muck and sludge, that need to be disposed of in accordance with safety laws. Mmm, smells fresh.

NOTHING SAYS CLEAN LIKE A CHEMICAL BATH

Paris laid claim to the world's first dry-cleaning service in the mid-18th century. Jean Baptiste Jolly set up shop after an alleged incident in which his housekeeper whitened a tablecloth by spilling kerosene on it. He soon experimented with other chemicals, including benzene, naphtha, and gasoline. By the late 18th century, the first "French Cleaner" had opened in

America in an old dye factory. It closed in 1926 after the highly flammable benzene caused an explosion, killing the owner and the foreman.

Combustibility, however, was not the only concern with these new, unknown chemicals. An investigative article from a 1955 issue of the *Saturday Evening Post* tells stories of acetate dresses dissolving like sugar and buttons disappearing without breaking their thread. Uncovering the truth behind these oddities revealed the complex interactions taking place between chemicals in garments and chemicals in cleaning solutions. The polystyrene plastic used to make buttons was discontinued, ending their vanishing act. Similarly, cleaners ditched the acetone and chloroform they'd used to spot-treat stains, which had inadvertently been melting holes in the gentle acetate.

Just over half a century later, the world's most popular dry-cleaning chemical is perchloroethylene. Perc is used in paint stripper, printing, electronics, and auto part degreasing, but dry-cleaners use it the most. In the United States and Canada, dry-cleaners use an estimated 95,000 tons of perc annually, and Dow Chemical is the most prominent manufacturer. Introduced in the '30s, the chemical was adopted quickly because of wartime petroleum shortages; and because perc is not flammable, it finally let dry-cleaners meet municipal fire standards and move into city centres. In Manhattan, nearly 88,000 New

Yorkers live within 20 metres of a dry-cleaner. In Quebec, there are more dry-cleaners per capita than anywhere else in Canada.

PERCS AND CONSEQUENCES

Of all the toxic contaminants in urban air, perc concentrations are the highest. The food from stores or residences near dry-cleaners contains perc levels up to 800 times higher than normal. Not to mention groundwater supplies contaminated by dry-cleaners are hundreds or thousands of times higher than federal standards.

At the dry-cleaner near my YMCA, the owner stands respectfully when I enter. A woman of the same grey age sits about six feet away, smiling and sewing. Between them is a machine like a front-loading washer, and all around us are Greek flags. For a second I hesitate, not wanting to break the charm of old-world pride and politeness. I ask about the machine, and he tells me it was an investment made when the family arrived from Greece 25 years ago. I ask if he ever had to do anything environmentally conscious to update it. He says he has done what he must to protect himself, his family, and his customers, and that's pretty much when he asks me to leave.

On the way home I think about the smiling couple, their plywood floor, and how close they sit to the Y's underground pool. Possible perc side effects run through my head in the

weird, muggy mist of the climate-changed afternoon: neurological damage, spontaneous abortion, lung disease, headache, nausea, anxiety, cancer, other cancer, more cancer. In bed at night I picture my room filling up with liquid perc. I feel elementally uneasy.

HEADING FOR GREENER PASTURES

Dry-cleaning isn't all evil. It can lengthen the life of garments because stains degrade fibres over time and bugs love food remnants. Fabric is a prevalent landfiller, so a longer garment lifespan sounds good – but there are ways to keep those benefits while lessening the consequences. "Dry-clean only" is frequently misleading. By law, only one acceptable cleaning method needs to be listed, and many manufacturers simply choose "dry-clean only" as a default. Most silks and wools can be hand-washed. Rayon will shrink the first time in water, but after that you can usually continue using water. Polyesters often suggest dry-cleaning, but they tend to be fine in cold water with a gentle cleanser.

And home "dry-cleaning" kits are available, too. These usually include stain removers and a small amount of the chemical cleanser normally used by professionals – one among many "secret recipes." This can be enough for lightly worn garments. Some professional cleaners even recommend Dove dishwashing soap for "dry-clean only"

garments because the solvent is petroleum based and designed to lift oils and grease.

Environmentalists embrace a set of processes called "wet-cleaning," like at the Nettoyeur Vert in Montreal. Wet-cleaners claim to treat 99 percent of "dry-clean only" garments safely with water. Dry-cleaners predictably disagree, but in the case of my chair, I'd have been willing to risk it – especially knowing what I know now about the dry process's cascading effects and non-magical powers.

There are other eco options: SANYO Electric released a new washing-machine/dry-cleaning alternative in 2006 called Aqua, which uses ozone to clean and emphasizes a closed-loop cycle for water usage. These machines are sized to replace household washers, retail at just over $2,000 (USD), and claim to safely wash suits, silks, and other "dry-clean only" regulars. Another option, developed by Micell and the University of North Carolina, reuses CO_2 and actually performed better than alternatives – green or otherwise – in a *Consumer Reports* test. Emissions from compatible factories are captured, compressed to liquid, and used to clean your clothes.

So what keeps this from being the number-one choice of greens? The CO_2 process is proprietary, development speed and marketing are limited, and the machines cost $100,000 or more. This is too much, I'm certain, for the couple with the plywood floors.

And it's important to keep them in mind, these mom-and-pop shops. If you can, try to hand-wash clothes and then bring them in to be professionally pressed. This can be the trickiest part of a cleaning job, so you'll still be valuing the people in front of you and what they can do, benefitting from their skill and supporting the small-business owner without getting tangled up in the ethical and biological complexity of the chemistry.

Skipping the perc step will cost you both less.

DRY-CLEANING VINTAGE

1. CHECK THE PHYSICAL INTEGRITY OF THE TEXTILE.

Remember, just because there's no water doesn't necessarily make dry-cleaning a more gentle process. In an average facility, about 50 pounds of clothes are dry-cleaned at one time. The process weighs down the material with liquid, heats it to 70°C, and spins just like regular laundry. Delicate fabrics like antique lace may not be able to withstand the pressure. On the other hand, if a garment consists of several different types of fabric, dry-cleaning may be the best option to prevent mismatched shrinkage.

Examine your garment for tears or weak spots before taking it to the cleaner, and baste a bit of lightweight white fabric (like cotton) over any area that needs protecting. Do the same thing to keep closed any clasps that might hook the fabric during cleaning.

2. CHECK FABRICS USED IN THE GARMENT, NOTE EMBELLISHMENTS AND CLOSURES.

Protein fibres like silk and wool usually do well when dry-cleaned, but the coating on some notions can be dissolved by chemical solvent, and some fabric dyes cannot be dry-cleaned. If there is any question, ask your cleaner for advice, and if possible, request the fabric be spot-tested in a discreet area before immersion.

3. CHECK THE NATURE OF THE STAIN.

If a stain is greyish, oily, or greasy, the non-aqueous solvent used in dry-cleaning will break it down more easily. If the stain is yellow or brown, or has rings or tide lines, it will be difficult to remove with any system, but wet cleaning stands a better chance.

The key to dry-cleaning old garments is finding a dry-cleaner willing and able to work with you. You may want to request the solvent be fresh, the agitation and solvent extraction cycles be cut short, the heat be kept low, and so on – but finding a cleaner who will take the extra time this requires can be tricky.

Ask stores that deal in high-end vintage, bridal shops, boutiques, and museums which dry-cleaners they recommend. Find a cleaner who does cleaning on site and is used to special handling. It will probably cost you more, but when it comes to your one-of-a-kind treasures, it'll save you some heartache. ⬚

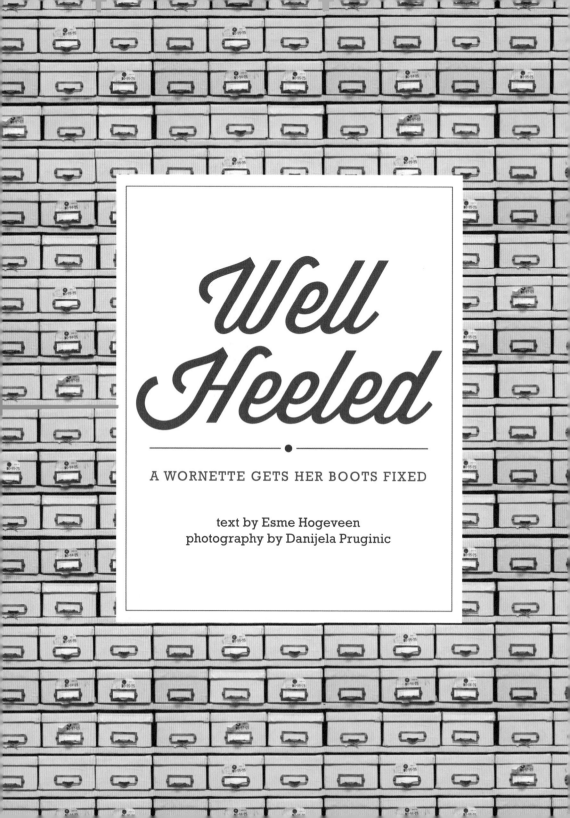

Well Heeled

A WORNETTE GETS HER BOOTS FIXED

text by Esme Hogeveen
photography by Danijela Pruginic

HOW DOES THAT OLD NURSERY RHYME GO? For want of a shoe, the kingdom was lost?

My visit to Toronto's Novelty Shoe Rebuilders Limited begins slightly less dramatically, with a pair of beat-up but much-loved boots. Brown leather, Italian made, and $9, they were a wonderful find my mom brought home one day from a second-hand shop. They fit my feet and my taste perfectly. I had them re-heeled once, wanting my perfect boots to last, but when the sole came away from the uppers and my toes began to peek out, I decided they needed professional help.

Instead of just letting the cobblers work their magic – because let's face it, as with many repair services, most of us understand little about how our clothes are mended – I decided to learn what happens in the days or weeks between when we drop off our broken shoes and when we pick them up, good as new. While I discuss this with Robert, the gregarious manager of Novelty, he abruptly rips off the dangling sole of my right boot. Amused by my shocked expression, he explains that they need to be completely resoled.

Clearly, a shop that is known for fixing Louboutins (they even carry the iconic red sole replacements) will be more than able to handle my no-name boots. As Robert points out a pair of knee-high, bejewelled, red suede boots waiting to be re-stitched to fit a slimmer calf, as well as some coral Manolo slingbacks, I barely notice my boots being whisked away.

The word "cobbler" suggests something old-world and mysterious – think "the shoemaker and the elves" – and the Novelty is no exception. With no view of the bustling Yonge Street I know lies outside, it's like stepping into another time. There are shelves of dusty white shoe boxes of different sizes behind the counter. Rows of various heel styles are on display behind the cash. I especially like the assorted colours of polish – someday I hope to have a need for the bright purple.

When the bustle of customers interrupts my daydreams, I move toward the back room for a basic tour of regular operations. Partly obscured by a glass partition, it buzzes (literally and figuratively) with specialized machinery and four men working briskly in their own particular areas of expertise.

As I watch, Robert explains that Novelty maintains a "bobblehead" policy, meaning they nod "yes" to work that other cobblers turn down.

Soles

A four-in-one cutter is used to fit new soles (as will be done with my boots), which are then adhered with contact cement. Especially worn-out shoes may require repairs to the inside layers of canvas or leather in order to increase durability. One of the cobblers compares shoe rebuilding to fixing a car and the steps involved when replacing parts: stripping, sanding, and refinishing.

Reshaping

Novelty gets a lot of customers who want shoes rebuilt to fit a different size of foot, ankle, or leg. "Lasts" are foot-shaped forms, made from wood and dense plastic, used for support when cutting (like when making a peep-toe out of a closed-toe) or stretching shoes.

Stretching first involves the application of a liquid chemical mixture that loosens the textile (dry shoes would be too brittle to work with). The shoe stays on the last for a couple of days to keep its new shape. There is even a large cylindrical last for stretching the calves of boots.

Patent leather is more challenging to work with because it lacks the porousness of regular leather, giving it less stretch. Making a shoe smaller is a more involved process too, since the seams must be opened and re-sewn.

Stitching

There are two sewing machines, both hulking steel antiques. The "autosole" is for inner stitching, such as attaching leather lining to the sole, and the other machine is for outer stitching around the sole.

Dyes

Colour alterations are dealt with in a room at the very back of the shop. Dozens of small jars filled with different shades of hand-mixed dyes and mysterious gooey substances are jumbled in an organized chaos. Novelty mixes all of their own pigments from top-quality chemical- and water-based dyes imported from the U.S. and Spain. Basic tasks include dyeing new sole sidings to match the uppers.

Certain colour samples can be very hard to obtain, and finding the correct shade becomes a challenge when the customer has something very specific in mind. The bobblehead policy also means accepting the most delicate jobs, like dyeing a pair of the Canadian Stage Company's black leather tap shoes white – a process that involves deglazing with just the right amount of acetone, since it's so hard on the leather.

And ...

When required, the final steps are done with the finishing machine, which "trims, sands, and buffs." Tucked up on a high shelf are brightly coloured leather samples for patching and new insoles. All these materials and the cobblers' meticulous work suggest that shoes really are being rebuilt, and not just fixed.

Before I leave, Robert talks about how shoe repair is a dying art; as is the case with so many services that require specialized and skilled craftsmanship, it is an increasing challenge to find high-quality work. He says shoes used to be better made, and not many people are interested in having their shoes fixed anymore because – like countless other garments – they have become disposable.

As Robert shrugs this off, I can't help but notice his resignation comes with a mild bobblehead motion. Meanwhile, I look forward to getting my boots back. ⚓

GORDIAN NOT

A TIDILY TANGLE-FREE GUIDE TO TYING TIES

▼

text by G. Stegelmann
photography by Darren Curtis
modelling by Elran Oded, Justin Kok, Mercedes La Rosa, & Dessa Harhay

THERE'S JUST SOMETHING ABOUT A TIE. While men's accessories have come and gone, while we have managed to live without top hats and spats and capes and pantaloons, the necktie seems to have woven itself firmly into the foundation of good style. Skinny or fat, long or short, even bow-tied, every one has its place around one neck or another. Not to mention that, between '60s mods and Annie Lennox, it's obvious that what's good for the gander is good for the goose — and every variation thereof.

It's troubling, then, that what used to be common knowledge — how to tie a tie — is becoming less common by the minute. How disappointing to see some almost-dapper dandy sporting a necktie that drifts to one side like it's trying to escape. How sad when a beautiful tie gets ruined because the same knot's been tightened and loosened for years — and why? Because the wearer cannot tie another. No, no — this will not do.

There are four basic necktie knots. (In fact, there may be more, but let's not overwhelm ourselves, shall we?) And with handy instructions for all four, you'll forever feel free to tie one on.

A couple of notes before starting: the following instructions are definitely right-handed. That means the starting position of all knots will find the narrow end of the tie on your left and the wide end on your right. Also, the "noose" referred to in each set of instructions means the part of the tie that encircles your neck.

▲
THE PRATT KNOT
THE WINDSOR
▼

THE PRATT KNOT

This long, narrow knot was the style of choice for my Grade 7 geography teacher, Mr. Gendron. He was a fan of the big knit ties of the late '70s and early '80s. The Pratt knot, with far less wrapping than its cousin, the Windsor, is ideal for thick fabrics. And you have to admit, it looks pretty cool.

STEP 1: Again, with the narrow end of the tie one-third as long as the wide end, this time with the seam facing up all the way around, cross the wide end under the narrow end and bring it up, slipping it through the noose from the front. Pull the wide end down so it's snug but not too tight.

STEP 2: Still holding the wide end of the tie, wrap it over the front from right to left, and pass it through the noose from the back.

STEP 3: Pull the wide end of the tie gently through the little loop you've made at the front and tighten as you did with the Four-in-Hand.

Now, just to be clear, this is still a fairly crappy knot. It will never be perfectly symmetrical. But it makes a nice, trim knot, and it's good for short ties too, since it doesn't eat up a lot of length.

//

THE HALF-WINDSOR

Length of tie is a big factor in choosing a knot. So is the weight of your tie. While the somewhat complicated Windsor is the king of knots, sometimes it just doesn't work. If you're a tall sort (or prefer the short "belly-warmer" ties of the '40s) and want more length in your tie, or if your tie is made from very heavy fabric, the Windsor can get a little unwieldy. If that's the case, and if you're not in the midst of a frantic tie emergency, a half-Windsor is a decent alternative.

THE FOUR-IN-HAND

I hate to be judgemental, but this is four-in-hands-down the laziest knot ever to grace a tie. I recommend it for anyone who, perhaps, just doesn't care. It may also come in handy if you're fleeing a burning building and want to look your best without lingering too long in the toxic smoke, or if you're leaping from a sinking ship.

STEP 1: With the narrow end of the tie about one-third as long as the wide end, seam facing down, cross the wide end over the thin end.

STEP 2: Wrap the wide end under the narrow end and bring it back to the side you started on.

STEP 3: Follow through by crossing the wide end back over the top, then pull it up and out through the noose around your neck.

STEP 4: Pull the wide end of the tie gently through the loop you've made in the front. Pinch the knot lightly at the base as you tighten the tie; keep holding it as you pull it up to your collar, holding the narrow end with your other hand.

Now look in the mirror. See how it's off-centre? Don't bother trying to fix it – it can't be done. That being said, any necktie can be improved by slightly widening the top of the knot: hold the noose on either side just above your knot and tug it apart, just a little.

//

STEP 1: Once again, the narrow end of the tie should be about one-third as long as the wide end, seam facing down. Cross the wide end over the narrow end and bring it all the way around behind.

STEP 2: Bring the wide end of the tie up and over the front, pulling it through the noose, toward the back.

STEP 3: Pass the wide end over the front again, all the way from right to left, and pull it through the noose from the back so that the wide end of the tie is now hanging loose in the front.

STEP 4: Slide the wide end of the tie gently through the loop you've made in front and tighten as with the others. Give a little tug on each side of the noose, as with the Four-in-Hand, to tighten and shape the knot.

As with the Pratt and Four-in-Hand, it won't be perfectly symmetrical, but it will be tidy. Isn't that just what a tie ought to be?

///////////////////////////////////////

THE WINDSOR

My father taught me how to tie this knot for my Catholic school uniform. If you do it right, a Windsor should look perfectly symmetrical – a clean, solid triangle. He showed me the half-Windsor too, but it was understood that this was the "correct" version. I have always been proud of my Windsor knots, and I must confess I still look at this knot, on any gender, as a mark of stylish commitment. Clean nails, clean shoes, and a Windsor – thanks to my dad, I'm a girl who loves the details.

STEP 1: Again, try this one with the thin end of the tie about one-third as long as the wide end, seam down. Remember, though, that this is a whole lotta knot, so the shorter your tie, the shorter the thin end has to be. You might have to re-tie this a couple of times to get your ratios right. Pass the wide end of the tie over the thin end and bring it up behind and through the noose.

STEP 2: Moving to the left, wrap the wide end of the tie around to the back again, all the way around to the right side.

STEP 3: Slip the wide end of the tie through the noose from the front. The wide end of the tie should now be hanging down behind the knot, seam facing out. The front of the tie should look like a V.

STEP 4: Wrap the wide end of the tie around from right to left, covering the front of your knot, and pass the wide end through the noose from the back to the front.

STEP 5: Slide the wide end of the tie down gently through the loop at the front and tighten as before. Give a little tug on each side of the noose (close to the knot) to get that really tidy, triangular shape.

If you've done this right, you'll have a perfectly symmetrical knot, and it will look damn sharp. ⬗

///////////////////////////////////////

DEVIL WITH THE BLUE JEANS ON

TEXT BY SONYA ABREGO • PHOTOGRAPHY BY NATE DORR

THE NAME KILL DEVIL HILL may not offer much by way of description — it might even seem ominous — but for someone like me, whose native province is home to places like Head-Smashed-In Buffalo Jump and Driedmeat Lake, there is something almost familiar, even homey, in the moniker.

Proprietors Mary Beatrice Brockman (wild west) and Mark Christopher Straiton (wild east) conceived the idea for the shop as a way to help an old family friend sell off the contents of a personal collection, an impressive assortment of curiosities that included early Venetian trade beads, at least half a city block's worth of antlers, and an incredible amount of taxidermy. Mark thought filling a shop exclusively with those items would "freak everybody out," so they settled on a concept modelled after the turn-of-the-century Levi Strauss General Dry Goods Store.

Kill Devil Hill offers everything from local, handmade jewelry to pickled asparagus to custom-made frontier pants (solid, handmade trousers with a button fly and other period details), along with vintage and antique curiosities that predate World War II. If the merchandise isn't always practical, it is all functional, and in addition to this mad assortment of wares, Mary and Mark offer denim repair.

Inspiration came, in part, from the fashion industry's obsession with creating new clothes that look old. Mary explains: "There was a pair [of jeans] in here that Mark had repaired and we were selling. They were pretty expensive because they were '40s Levi's, and this dude comes up, takes the jeans off the hanger and instantly walks up to buy them without trying them on.

clothes, they do not make them. "Have you ever heard the adage, 'The cobbler's children have no shoes?' That's kinda like us." The workspace in the back of the store houses an industrial sewing machine and a small portable that Mary's mom bought for her at 14. She has an assortment of denim scraps for patches, and she tries to match them as closely as possible to the original garment. For this work, she says, technique is the key: "I buy a cheap pack of needles and use the larger one, 16 or 14… I don't believe that it's the tool that matters."

The majority of the jeans that come in are valuable to begin with. The shop gets a lot of A.P.C.s (a French label known for their

---

MARK AND MARY OFFER A FEW SUGGESTIONS FOR THOSE ATTEMPTING DENIM REPAIR AT HOME: "THE MOST COMMON MISTAKE PEOPLE MAKE IS PUTTING THE PATCH ON THE OUTSIDE AND STITCHING AROUND IT, BECAUSE IT'S NEVER GOING TO HOLD. YOU SHOULD PUT THE PATCH IN THE BACK AND ONLY STITCH WHERE THE HOLE IS AND GO OVER IT A LOT IN DIFFERENT DIRECTIONS. AND DON'T EVER USE IRON-ON PATCHES! YOU'RE BASICALLY JUST MELTING PLASTIC INTO YOUR PANTS … THEY BREAK AND IT'S A BIG MESS."

He said he worked for a denim company [an unnamed high-end brand] and loved the work on the jeans and was going to try to replicate it."

Mark admits that if he had been present he might have actually cried. But though Mary was annoyed by the customer's flip admission and his "capability to rip us off," she was also flattered their handiwork was good enough to make a fashion-savvy buyer think he was purchasing period repairs. "He didn't realize the effect he was having." The incident spurred them to start offering their own custom services.

Neither Mark nor Mary has formal fashion training, and although they repair their own

use of raw, or "entry level," denim), vintage pieces, Japanese reproductions, and "Big E" Levi's. "I've noticed that generally the jeans that are brought [in] are jeans that people paid good money for." Mary explains that, far from being a mark of poor quality, it's a testament to the desire to keep good-quality jeans alive as long as possible. And while a rapid fashion cycle that advocates replacing old with new is antithetical to the concept of repair, jeans tend to resist this trap better than most garments. According to Mary, "Once people find a pair of jeans they really love, they don't want to give them up." ✠

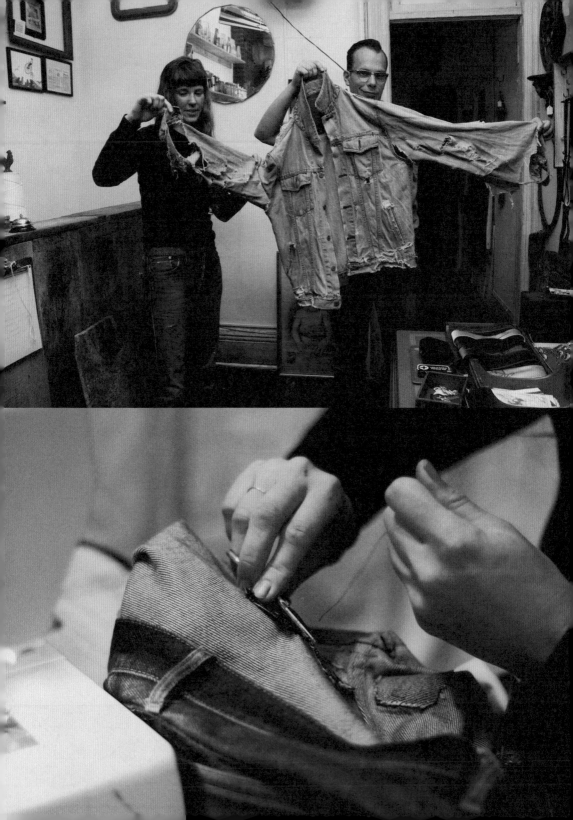

JEANEALOGY

TEXT BY STEPHANIE HEROLD

RAW RAW, SIS BOOM BAH!

Raw denim is denim that is left chemically untreated and unwashed after being woven, producing a stiffer, uniformly coloured "raw" fabric. Jeans made with raw denim whisker and fade depending on wear and usage, resulting in jeans as unique as the wearer's thumbprint. Some die-hards resist washing their rigid raw denim for six months in order to individualize it, leaving their jeans in the freezer to draw out smells. Others are inspired to dip into salt water with their jeans on so that the natural fibres will stretch while wet and eventually dry to their body shape.

PUTTING THE "BIG E" IN LEVI'S

In 1936, Levi Strauss & Co. began to distinguish their jeans in the American denim market by sewing a red tab that read LEVI'S (written in capital letters) on the back pockets of all their jeans and front pockets of denim shirts. In 1971, after corporate rebranding, Levi's began to use lowercase letters on the tabs, and the "Big E" Levi's, now in limited supply, became increasingly collectible. In 2001, Levi's bought a pair of their own Big Es from a seller on eBay for more than $46,000.

SANFORIZING DOES NOT LEND ITSELF TO WORDPLAY

In 1930, Sanford L. Cluett invented the "sanforizing" pre-shrinking process for cotton and cotton-blend fabrics, and in 1936 the Blue Bell Company introduced this new process to denim production. By mechanically stretching the denim before it was processed (through washing and drying), shrinkage after home washing was reduced to only 1 percent.

KIND OF BLUE

Indigo dye is extracted from many different plant species, including the *Indigofera tinctoria* plant in India and Africa, and the *Isatis tinctoria*, or woad plant, in Europe. This deep blue dye has long been prized for its impressive colourfastness (resistance to bleeding or running). Egyptian mummies were wrapped in blue cloth as early as 2500 BCE.

SELVAGE MOTIVES

Originally called "self-edge," selvage (or selvedge) is the small, more firmly woven band of fabric bordering a single piece of unprocessed denim that prevents its edges from unravelling. Textile manufacturer Cone Denim, founded in 1891, produced specially coloured selvages depending on who would fashion the denim. Red selvage was soon synonymous with Levi's.

What we lost when we forgot how to sew

text by Catie Nienaber
illustration by Emily Taylor

FOR GENERATIONS, no girl passed high school without at least a semester's worth of home economics under her belt. She learned the basics of budgeting, baking, and sewing machine mechanics as dutifully as her male counterpart took apart transmissions in shop class. But as the 20th century evolved, so did attitudes toward household skills. What was once a step forward – the recognition of women's traditional duties as skilled labour – became in Gloria Steinem's words, a "cultural ghetto," trapping young women in a life of domestic servitude. With slashed funding and a dearth of teachers, the reputation of home ec soon became as tattered as an old dress.

As this unique skill set has faded, so has our personal connection to clothing. Young women in the '50s took it for granted that socks needed darning, tears mending, and hems adjusting; half a century later, instinct has us reaching for our wallets rather than our needles. In a world more ready to replace than repair, the threadbare practicality of home ec has taken on a brand new significance.

Out of the home, into the classroom

The idea of formalizing home economics began in the mid-19th century. The goal was to make higher education more appealing to women by legitimizing the housework they already performed. In 1841, Catherine Beecher's *A Treatise on Domestic Economy* offered a new systematic way of viewing women's roles and, by the 1860s, classes were taught at women's universities. A group led by chemist Ellen H. Swallow Richards chose the name home economics (rather than "ecology") for the subject that would combine the varied aspects of household management.

In 1854, Boston's school board concluded that "no girl could be considered properly educated who could not sew." In Canada, home economics owed its emergence to activist women like Ontario's Adelaide Hoodless, whose lobbying in the 1890s led to the funding of the Guelph Macdonald Institute, the country's first training facility for home ec teachers.

"From the start this discipline, in which women were the prime movers and most

consistent supporters, focused on issues of knowledge rather than gender," writes Patricia J. Thompson in *Beyond Gender: Equity Issues for Home Economics Education.* "While the early curricula in the schools focused on such then-essential household tasks as cooking and sewing, the tasks were sustained by knowledge of science, human relations, aesthetics, and ethics. Home economics aimed to provide the learning needed for 'right living.'"

Into the '30s, cutting patterns, identifying fabrics, and sewing buttonholes were essential skills for daughters and wives. Small economies were the rule, not the exception, for many struggling families, and even during the Great Depression creativity blossomed under tight budgets, thanks to women who could apply what they had learned in school. Existing garments were reworked to bring them up to date: adding new buttons could freshen up a coat for another year's wear. Rural women, rather than splurge on new fabric, crafted dresses from the large sacks in which seeds, flour, and other dry goods were sold. (Surviving "feedsack dresses" have

become collector's items.) This was an era when "creating your own style" was a literal act. Even a quarter-century later, when home ec had already begun to wane in popularity, it continued to prove useful in practice.

By the time Jeanne Haugh entered her San Francisco high school in 1959, she was confident her future reached far beyond sewing clothes. Still, she took "Sewing" (as that particular class was called) and soon discovered a new set of practical skills.

"We had to make a blouse, an apron, maybe a skirt. I got the basics," she says. "I did learn how to read a pattern, how to use a real sewing machine. I couldn't do a zipper," she admits, "but I could sew!"

And sew she did. Haugh went to the prom in a satin dress of her own design. "Most of the girls for that prom wore long dresses – mine was short. So I was special." She didn't stop there. Entering the business world after graduation, Haugh picked a dress pattern to supplement her store-bought wardrobe and quickly furnished two dresses. "We had to dress for work, *always.* I wore this

one specific dress to work on Fridays. That was my treat for myself." Years later, she made dresses for her daughter and the bridesmaids at her sister's wedding.

Feminism and fast fashion

The year that Haugh made her senior prom dress was pivotal in the world of high school home economics. In 1963, American federal funding that had been specifically earmarked for home ec classes for decades was suddenly removed. Home ec was no longer a protected branch of education. Rather, schools had to find money in their own budgets from the larger pool reserved for "vocational instruction."

As funding disappeared, ideological objections increased. Many in the women's movement felt mandatory home ec classes pushed young women toward the confinement of housewifery. As Thompson explains, "Home economics became a convenient scapegoat for the ills that had befallen women in their traditional roles." Feminism was urging teenage girls to compete in a "man's world"

rather than excel in a woman's. Of course, rejection of one skill set would guarantee no invitation to another, and girls on the cusp of the feminist revolution often found themselves caught between two worlds.

"I never took home ec in high school," columnist Dorothy Storck wrote in the *Philadelphia Inquirer*, explaining she dismissed it as the class for girls who read bridal magazines instead of pre-law textbooks. "But sometimes I'd pass the class and glance in at the sewing machines and nutrition charts and upturned girlish faces, and I'd dash to the hockey field, where, to my mind, freedom from housework lay. It never occurred to me that while I was fleeing the inequality of work in the home, I wasn't running toward much in the way of equal rights anywhere else. Nobody offered me a place on the boys' hockey team."

Linda Duerson taught the sewing component of home economics at various northern California schools in the '70s and '80s. "For years, they either had sewing, or sewing and cooking, and then eventually the sewing kind of disappeared," she explains.

The decline and eventual phasing out of sewing from the curriculum, says Duerson, occurred in the mid-'80s. "That's when girls started wearing jeans and t-shirts; they liked the notion of easier, more disposable clothing. The idea of something that was homemade was not as appealing as looking like everybody else in a pair of blue jeans."

Duerson and her fellow home ec teachers tried to modernize, incorporating newer fabrics (like polyester) into their curriculum so students could create more current garments, but it only went so far. Patterns were always six months to a year behind trends that were seen in stores. The almost-instant gratification of buying inexpensive, trendy clothes right off the rack was chipping away at the appeal of homemade. Besides, in a sea of factory-perfect t-shirts, people might think you couldn't *afford* new clothes.

What goes around comes around

In the John Hughes movie *Pretty in Pink*, working-class teen Andie Walsh creates avant-garde outfits from thrift-store finds. Teased (but not daunted) by her wealthy classmates, she is a beacon of determined individualism, finding enormous joy in her chosen mode of self-expression. Eventually, Andie arrives at the prom: what began as a foamy '60s pink tulle dress is now an angular, modern sheath. Submerged in the power-dressed '80s, Andie was on the cusp of a revival of home-sewing and DIY ingenuity.

Duerson observes that, although North American home ec classes are still woefully underfunded and understaffed, young people are once again interested in making their own clothes. "I know many students who take sewing classes from private people, because they really want to learn." Private tailoring courses and knitting circles are on the rise, too.

Making it yourself doesn't always mean paying less (homemade can be as expensive as high-end, especially when it comes to designer fabrics), but DIY addresses manufacturing practices that deliver savings to the detriment of human lives. "We need to challenge an industry that has done a less-than-stellar job of educating people about the wastefulness and unsustainable practices associated with trying to keep up with the latest fashions," says Dr. June Matthews, an associate professor in food and nutritional sciences at Brescia University College. "How many cotton t-shirts does one really need?"

Some Canadian school boards, in an effort to stylize the homely home ec, now offer sewing instruction in classes called "Fashion," hinting at the possibility of classroom catwalks. But despite the glamorous title the course is serious, teaching students not only to sew but to view the fashion industry, beauty standards, labour practices, and questions of sustainability with a critical eye.

Veronica Tuzi, who teaches a fashion course in Toronto, Ontario, makes a point of describing the sweatshops in which the students' clothes are often made. "This creates an appreciation for their clothing, because they realize that people younger than themselves are working at a feverish pace in order to provide them with the affordable clothing they have," she says. "It tends to be a wake-up call to my students, and they learn to not take their clothes for granted." And this appreciation is, in some ways, exactly where home economics began.

Perhaps the biggest difference between home economics and the DIY revival is that the former was seen as duty and the latter is, for the most part, a choice. But from beginning to end runs a thread of creativity, possibility, and self-expression. We "make" for all kinds of reasons, but the end result is always ours, echoing our ideas and influences and tastes. The resurging popularity of home-made suggests we'd rather be imperfect than identical. That idea is anything but frayed. ✄

FASHION IS

ART

03

COLOUR, FORM, AND LINE are all things we include in our consideration of art. We reflect on an artist's use of materials and question messages and meaning. It is no great revelation to say that art is, in fact, art. But what about fashion?

In our everyday contact with clothing, in the necessity of it, we can fall into the habit of recognizing only its utility; it becomes a collection of tweed hammers and chiffon light bulbs. We neglect its other, more cerebral layers. But even in its usefulness, clothing is more than clothing. On an individual wearer, even unconsciously, it becomes metaphor and memory and a response to the world. So it should be no great revelation to say that in the hands of artists, fashion is art.

Through composition and intent, clothing and craft become powerful media shaped to the human form. Costume exhibitions in museums recognize that fashion is an application of art in life. Artists use clothing to communicate complex ideas about objectification, intimacy, extravagance, and transformation. For someone like the Marchesa Casati, clothing informs a lifelong artistic performance. In editorial photo shoots, clothing is the language of a wordless narrative, creating new realities and questioning our perspectives. Cheap polyester becomes ethereal and sports gear, stripped of its functional use, is reassigned value according to form and colour.

Artist Andrea Vander Kooij suggests that "too often people use medium to make a category." Regardless of the medium, art is art, wherever it appears. To find it in fashion should come as no surprise. ⊠

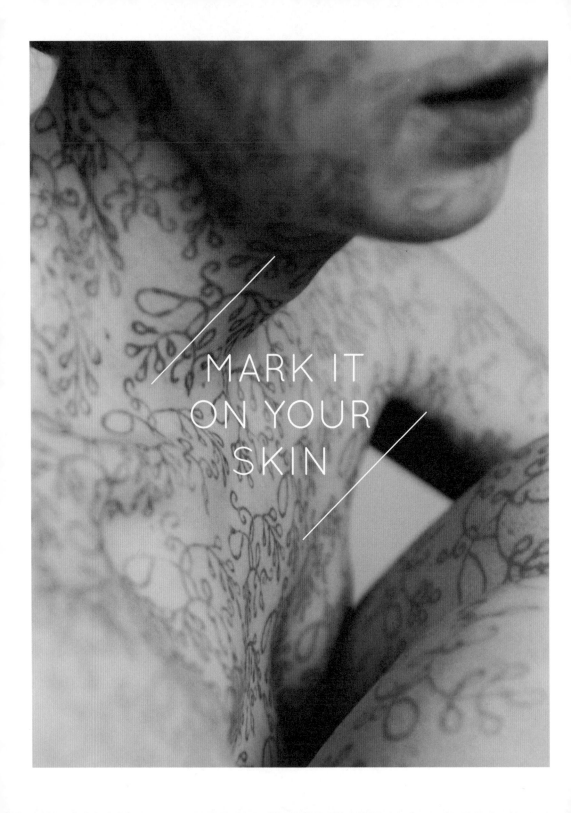

MARK IT
ON YOUR
SKIN

ARTIST ANDREA VANDER KOOIJ TALKS FEMININITY, SEXUALITY, ART, AND FASHION

INTERVIEW BY EMILIE MARZINOTTO
PHOTOGRAPHY BY KATE FELLERATH

ANDREA VANDER KOOIJ LOVES EXCESS. She's motivated by the idea of taking things as far as they'll go, and her studio holds both an enormous red mitten that she knit herself and a still-in-progress portrait of Britney Spears made out of beauty shop acrylic nails.

Vander Kooij's performance piece, *Efflorescence*, was inspired by blackwork: a high-contrast embroidery made most often with black stitching on a white background, sometimes with a flourish of gold, that was popular in England in the Elizabethan and Jacobean eras of the late 16th and early 17th centuries. She originally set out to embroider a man's dress shirt, but her idea exploded into a dress – no, wait – some tights! Ultimately, it seems, clothes were not enough. Vander Kooij set her sights on covering her own body with blackwork using henna.

Vander Kooij sat in various store windows on well-trafficked Montreal streets, her body covered – yes, completely covered – with a traditional blackwork embroidery pattern stained directly onto her skin. As she sat, she embroidered that same pattern onto a pale dress she'd constructed of eight removable panels.

As the pattern gradually faded from her body, it was slowly transferred onto the dress. The designs visually crawled across her body, mimicking how easily and smoothly patterns move through boundaries, through cultures, and through time.

What about blackwork specifically appeals to you?

I'm drawn to the strong graphic feel of blackwork, but also I started thinking about it as viral, as having a life and spreading. Because pattern is really viral.... Pattern moves more easily from one country to another than imagery, because narratives tend to be different in a different country

117

but pattern is mainly visual. What defines an interesting image or a beautiful woman? Those ideas vary. But pattern appeals across borders: a single design can be traced from North Africa to Spain to England.

Some of the photos from your performance remind me of a Vermeer painting: a woman bent over work, warm lighting. The perfect image of subservience, of the ideal domestic demure woman....
I like to think the difference between what I was doing and what Vermeer was depicting is that I display a great deal more than those women did. My work is on me. I engage the viewer. It's not about being a passive object for display.... It's about being an active object. Embroidery is sometimes given a bad rap, is seen as this passive activity, but it's productive, it's interesting. It's not just a prop.

Is your work sexually provocative?
People always bring that up... so I think it must be. I made some deliberate choices about how much I was going to display my body. I could have done this naked. I didn't want the work just to be about that. Susan Sarandon said that your own nipples will always upstage you. And it's kind of true. I didn't want that to be the only level at which people interact with this work.

What do you think the connection is between fashion and art?
I know we need words to describe different things... but it's not the same way I feel about art and craft. It's not the medium that separates it, it's the content. When a person looks at a painting, they always say that's art. Whereas embroidery or a knitted sweater, that may be craft or it may be fashion. They're not sure. I feel the idea or the content

makes it art. There are a lot of paintings
that aren't anywhere near art, or sculptures
that aren't really art. Too often people use
medium to make a category. There is fashion
that is definitely art. And I think there is
art that is definitely fashionable. But at the
same time, that makes "fashion" a pejorative.
And I don't like that fashion is a pejorative.
And I don't like that craft is a pejorative.

I love it when borders can become more
fluid. My favourite fashion is the kind that
people aren't sure whether to call art… and
my favourite art is when you think, "It's
a dress!"… like Comme des Garçons' Rei
Kawakubo's bump dresses. You know, with
the big tumour-y bumps on them? They're
still dresses, but people aren't sure. Hussein
Chalayan had a combination performance,
art show, and runway show in which all
of the models came out wearing skirts
made of glass, and then another model

"WHAT DEFINES AN
INTERESTING IMAGE
OR A BEAUTIFUL
WOMAN? THOSE
IDEAS VARY. BUT
PATTERN APPEALS
ACROSS BORDERS:
A SINGLE DESIGN
CAN BE SEEN
TRACED FROM
NORTH AFRICA TO
SPAIN TO ENGLAND."

came out with a hammer and broke the skirts. Or the models all come out and there's a stage full of furniture and they take the slipcovers off the furniture and make them into dresses, and then the table accordions up and becomes a skirt! I love that kind of shit! But at the same time, I really, really love just wearable Missoni or Marni or Marc Jacobs or Prada. I like it all.

Who influences you?

I always go through fashion magazines and then really want to make art. Often, I'll get the new *Vogue* and feel, "AAAAH! I have so many ideas!" And then you have to let it go for a while... because those are really other people's ideas. I know a lot of the time, for my embroidered work, I source a lot. Most of the time it's from vintage medical manuals, or lifestyle guides, or sex how-to books. In terms of artists, I am very inspired by performance work from people like Hannah Wilke or Janine Antoni. I also love Tracy Emin's work... oh, and Ghada Amer and Annette Messager.

How would you describe your relationship with clothing?

I like to think of clothing as costume....
I think it's one of the clearest ways that we assert our identity in our culture. In terms of my own clothing, I have a very personal relationship with these inanimate objects. I can remember the history of almost everything I own, where I bought it, what was happening in my life when I wore it. The history of the piece of clothing and my own history are very closely entwined.

Obviously a lot of my work manifests itself through or from clothing: I like to use fabrics that came from clothing, and a performance will always involve very clear clothing choices. Using second-hand material in my work is something I love because

there is already a narrative there. Did that person wear that to their school dance, or what was the occasion, how did they feel?

Do you think clothing is like a language?

Everything, including clothing, carries meaning. Comedy writer Cynthia Heimel said once, "If people didn't wear clothes, they would wear sandwich boards that say things like, 'I prefer for you to think of me as athletic,' or 'I'm a Marxist.'" But I definitely think that reading too much into someone's clothing choices can be dangerous. It can be really rotten when people look at you and think that they know what kind of person you are. It's not as literal as all that! Sometimes we dress like the kind of person we would want to be – or sometimes it's the kind of person you'd like for someone to think of you as, but might not be the person you are.

Do you wear embroidered clothing?

I do, but not as much as knitted things. I really like sweaters; it's the thing that I can most easily buy. I have some embroidered pieces, but it's hard to find nice stuff. I don't like the look of shitty machine embroidery. I don't like to see the tracking thread behind, or the sloppy stuff that doesn't have full coverage. I buy a lot of embroidered linens, though. I am obsessed with vintage and have a huge collection of tea party dresses. You know what I do? I take a camera with me when I go shopping, and I get the nice salespeople to take a picture of me wearing the clothes, and then I take that home. I don't have to buy it all the time; it's enough to have a picture of me in it. I try to make good choices: I'll either buy something I'll really get a lot of wear out of, or else things that are just incredible. Everything in between, I'll take a picture. ✉

"IF PEOPLE DIDN'T WEAR CLOTHES, THEY WOULD WEAR SANDWICH BOARDS THAT SAY THINGS LIKE, 'I PREFER FOR YOU TO THINK OF ME AS ATHLETIC,' OR 'I'M A MARXIST.'"

EXHIBITIONIST

FASHION IN THE WORLD OF MUSEUMS

TEXT BY SONYA ABREGO

CLOTHES ARE EVERYWHERE. This means people who love to observe clothing and how individuals fashion themselves are in a privileged position. From recognizing a favourite designer's latest shoes on the subway, to spotting a traditional cultural print on a stranger's backpack, or seeing a jacket from a music video that was a hit three years ago, inspirations abound. If street-style isn't enough, there is no shortage of fashion press – from academic study to runway reports to daily outfit blogs. The ubiquity of fashion retailers means there are racks upon racks of garments for sale, old and new, just waiting to be pawed through. Styles run the gamut (and some are more enticing than others), but they all have secrets to reveal about the culture that produced them: who made these things? Who buys them? This is how it starts – the obsession with drawing

information out of clothing and discovering what style signifies. This rabid curiosity can land you face first in the study of dress history, trying to position taste, materials, and design in a larger cultural context.

The diverse outlets for examining clothing make it accessible, but there is one venue showcasing garments that not everyone (at least outside of major cities) has access to: the display of costume in museums.

In studies of dress history and as part of popular culture, costume exhibitions have enjoyed increasing popularity. But while poring over catalogues from past exhibitions and comparing them with contemporary fashions suggests changes over time, what is really going on at the curatorial level? What does this mean in terms of positioning fashion as art or as a historical document? What are the issues at hand when garments are the focus of museum exhibitions? In looking for answers, I have been lucky enough to confer with four experts, all with experience in costume exhibition. When discussing the challenges they face, they cite issues that extend well beyond the scope of this piece and illustrate some of the common concerns in the study of dress history at large.

Setting the stage

The presentation of dress in a museum context is a relatively recent development. The costume department at the Museum of the City of New York preserves garments and accessories from the mid-18th century to the present in an effort to "engage visitors in exploring the past, present, and future of the five boroughs of New York City." Along similar historical lines is the McCord Museum of Montreal, whose costume and textile collection is the leading collection of Canadian dress and reflects corresponding changes in Canadian history.

The costume department at the Metropolitan Museum of Art in New York became a department in its own right in 1959. Since then, it has become one of the foremost collections of its kind. It was the first experience both Michele Majer and Phyllis Magidson had working in costume exhibition, under the direction of the renowned Diana Vreeland. This former editor of *Vogue* presented her debut exhibition, which was highly theatrical but of dubious accuracy, at the Met in 1980. Despite mixed reviews, it is still credited as one of the first claims for fashion as an aesthetic medium worthy of display in a museum, and it got people talking about dress and its cultural significance.

Although acquisitions by costume collections never marched in lockstep with the development of dress history as a field of study, the two have had significant influence upon each other. The prejudices against fashionable dress are manifold, but for our purposes Elizabeth Wilson best sums up the traditional view: "Fashion is defined by it being not-art, and that because it deals with surfaces and with self-adornment it is a direct manifestation of superficiality and vanity."

However, as Majer points out, costume history is finally getting some hard-earned respect in academia. The divide that had existed for so long between object-based clothing historians (those interested in the material) and non-object-based art, social,

cultural, and economic historians (whose interests are more theoretical) has lessened considerably. Museum collections conserve the materials that provide the evidence for researchers. Whether your investigation is centred on garment construction, or on how a specific shape might reflect an era's concept of sexuality, being able to see the actual garment in three dimensions is invaluable in finding answers to your questions.

While almost everyone has access to at least some historical and contemporary garments displayed in film and print, the museum exhibition offers unique advantages. Shannon Bell Price explains that "museums provide seeing objects firsthand, dressed properly and in the round, in a way that other media cannot purely because of their 2D medium." Magidson also points out how seeing actual garments up close offers perspectives on scale and how people's bodies have changed: "When you look at 18th-century materials and realize how, in the United States, the genetic pool in subsequent centuries has radically changed the body type, it gives a feeling for height, placement of arm holes, and the ways costume affected the way people lived."

Film does have the advantage of giving insight into how garments – particularly historical garments – move on the body, which according to Majer is very important. Magidson has noticed that films in recent years have made an attempt to embrace the structural elements of historical costume, more so than in the past. But despite this, there is a general agreement that costume exhibition offers a unique viewpoint. It affords the opportunity to spend time with a garment in three dimensions

"FASHION IS DEFINED BY IT BEING NOT-ART, AND THAT BECAUSE IT DEALS WITH SURFACES AND WITH SELF-ADORNMENT IT IS A DIRECT MANIFESTATION OF SUPERFICIALITY AND VANITY."

and to see how it compares to related objects from the period, particularly paintings and furniture. Majer cites a 2007 Poiret exhibition at the Met as a highly successful example of what a museum can offer in presenting a fully integrated aesthetic context for a costume display. An institution of that scale, with strong holdings in art, design, and the decorative arts, can create a historical tableau that is informative and yet familiar in its details.

This leads to another aspect that distinguishes the display of costume from other media. Since everyone has to wear clothing, people can relate to it on a more immediate level than, say, an exhibition of sculpture, with which they might not have the same kind of everyday experience. This direct physical connection we have to clothing can be both a blessing and a curse when it comes to exhibitions. On one hand, it can help engage the viewers right away, drawing them closer to the subject and making the balance of the content easier to absorb. However, as Bell Price points out, visitors who look at pieces on a purely subjective level – asking themselves only, "Would I wear that?" – might undermine the larger points the curator is trying to make.

Cynthia Cooper believes that it is difficult for people to see something they feel so familiar with in a historical context rather than as something for consumption. She suggests that "our audiences have largely lost the ability to view objects from the point of view of the producer, and the familiarity with the same objects as consumers leads them to view dress on display in those limited terms."

Yet clothing's role as an "everyday" object can also be used to emphasize the contrasts between the past and present, or high-end

VISITORS WHO LOOK AT PIECES ON A PURELY SUBJECTIVE LEVEL – ASKING THEMSELVES ONLY, "WOULD I WEAR THAT?" – MIGHT UNDERMINE THE LARGER POINTS THE CURATOR IS TRYING TO MAKE.

design and regular off-the-rack items. Majer explains that sometimes the object itself, like an elaborately embroidered 18th-century men's suit or a highly architectural Charles James evening gown, clearly conveys its distance from the everyday. This can help people not only conceptualize changes in style over time, but also what people's lives might have been like to allow for that type of garment to be acceptable. It follows that, as the study of dress progresses and museum exhibitions continue, people will get used to the idea that garments can be appreciated in different ways.

Is it art?

There is a question mark over this subject that needs to be addressed, or perhaps skirted, at this point. Is fashion art? There are museums for art — "fine art," as it is traditionally conceived. There are also institutions that focus on the decorative arts, history museums, and finally, those whose collections are so extensive that they cover it all. Each collection reflects the values of the institution and the stories they are trying to tell. It comes down to specific curatorial choices. Arguments over dress as art, craft, or cultural artifact may never be resolved, but maybe they don't need resolving.

The MCNY and McCord are both history museums and are more interested in garments as social artifacts offering connections to broader historical questions. The McCord's collection documents what was produced and worn in Canada and how that fits into Canadian history as a whole. Similarly, the MCNY focuses on the history of New York City, where the

clothing industry has been very important to the economy from an early date and reflects the multiplicity of the demographics of the city. The MCNY also shows how the local fashion industry compared to the establishment in Paris, as well as preserves specific examples of garments worn by famous historical figures to legendary events and performances. The acknowledgement of items for their fashionable or aesthetic qualities, or as examples of creative genius, is not as significant as their role as missing link in history.

The Metropolitan Museum of Art (where art is right there in the name) is not as tightly bound to a historical approach. The Met's original mission was to "encourage and develop the study of the fine arts and the application of arts to manufacture and practical life." This couldn't be more appropriate to describe the costume department, where they strive to integrate their exhibitions with the larger context of art, design, and the decorative arts. Bell Price explains: "All decorative arts and other art mediums (such as video) have gone through a stage of having to define themselves against more traditional art forms. I am not convinced that costume exhibitions always succeed, or should necessarily strive to succeed, in putting fashion on par with traditional fine arts. But it is important to contextualize fashion in relationship to fine arts and let visitors decide for themselves."

The fashion as art/fashion as cultural history question takes yet another turn when one considers the success of the exhibitions themselves. Those that garner the most attention are monographic presentations that present the oeuvre of a single designer, as

ARGUMENTS OVER DRESS AS ART, CRAFT, OR CULTURAL ARTIFACT MAY NEVER BE RESOLVED, BUT MAYBE THEY DON'T NEED RESOLVING.

opposed to those that focus on larger themes. On the whole, monographic presentations attract larger crowds based on name recognition: Armani, Dior, Chanel. It is easy to be cynical and credit the commercial influence that these names continue to hold, but as Magidson points out, they are historically relevant because although the name may be legend, the actual product can fall into obscurity. It is also easier to follow a single thread in a linear history than to embrace something more conceptual.

The perception that a canon of fashion design exists is comparable to the canon in the history of art. The appeals to visitors (and the criticisms) are also similar: some artists are glorified as geniuses, while those whose work falls outside acceptable standards are maligned or ignored. Cooper believes that history museums play a crucial role in breaking this mold by choosing to highlight the cultural significance of dress as opposed to its merit as a discrete art object. They make space for things that may otherwise have been overlooked.

Whether the focus is historical, aesthetic, or a bit of both, the opportunity to study clothing in the stillness of a museum can help us to understand it in new ways. The small number of institutions with costume collections speaks to how it has been marginalized both as art form and historical document. Although existing departments continue to face challenges, they fulfill a crucial role in the study of dress history for scholars and, perhaps more importantly, as a catalyst in getting the public to reconsider the importance of dress in society past and present. ⊠

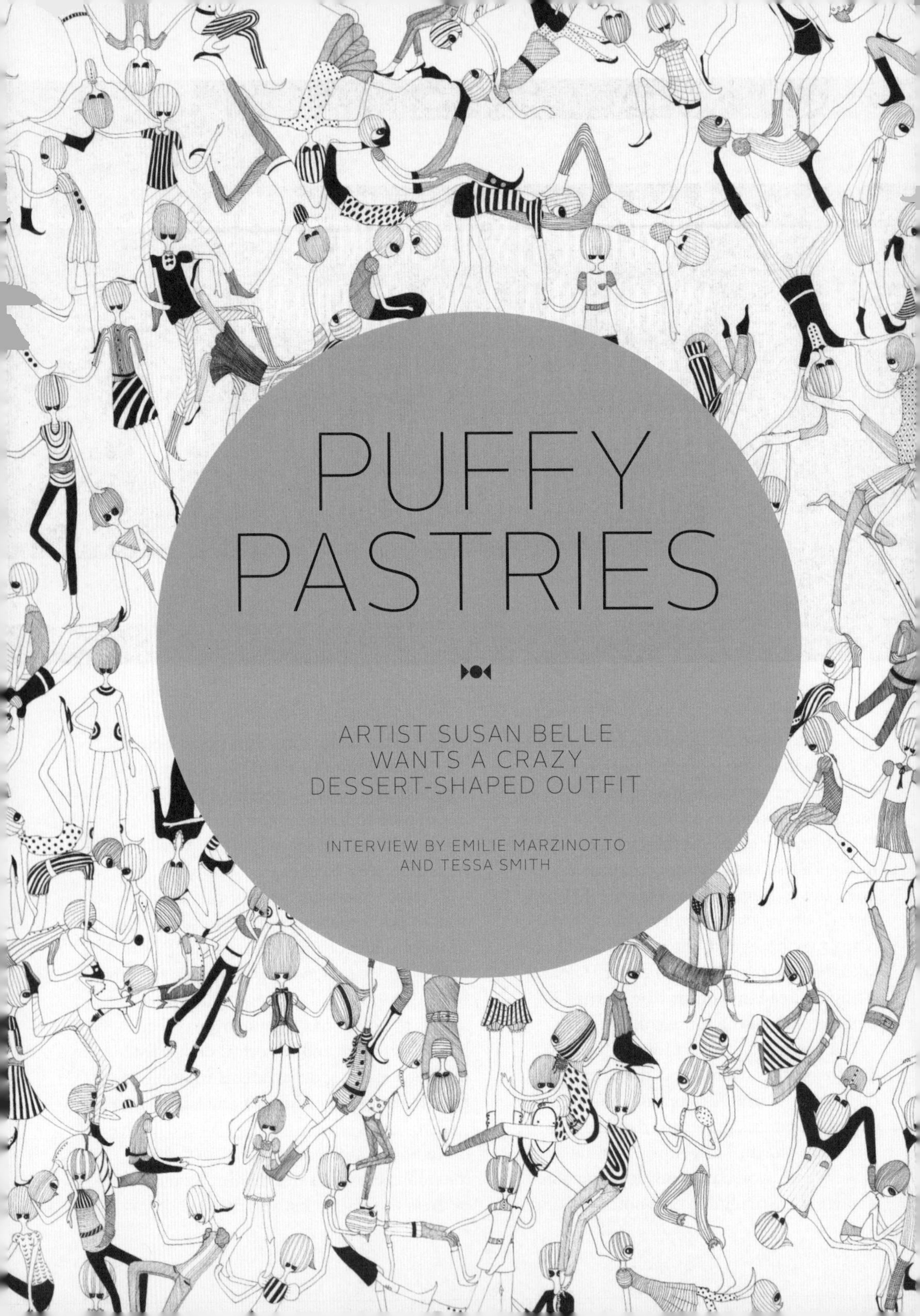

PUFFY PASTRIES

▶◀

ARTIST SUSAN BELLE
WANTS A CRAZY
DESSERT-SHAPED OUTFIT

INTERVIEW BY EMILIE MARZINOTTO
AND TESSA SMITH

GETTING DRESSED IS A LOT LIKE DRAWING A PICTURE: your wardrobe is your palette, and you can mix and match items at your disposal to try to attain an image in your mind. With the right combination – say, by pairing that belt with this frock – you can create a whole new character, an aesthetic sensibility that is truly your own. Of course, this is limited to what's accessible: the affordable, the attainable, and that subscribing to the laws of physics. Enter fashion illustration, in which the boundaries of what is wearable can truly be explored. In our issue 5 cover artist Susan Belle's candy-coated work, her figures don the clothing of her dreams while inhabiting the world of her imagination. If her cupcake-addled art is a window into her mind, here her words exist as a peek into her process.

Are you inspired by the patterns in nature as well as by those in clothing design?

I love the look of manufactured patterns, especially if they have a lot of symmetry. Sometimes I look to nature, but it can get a little too organic for me. I often use the same pattern to depict both hairstyles and hilltops. I feel there should be relationships between people and environments, as if my characters were born out of the land they live on. I do enjoy massive fields of plant life, gems, or underwater creatures like sea anemones. Outer space is also neat.

When I am designing an outfit, it always has to match something, like the hair. I am interested in what I consider an overly "feminine" look, with all the frills and tiny outfits and shoes. The girls that I dress up are really imagined versions of what I want to look like, or somehow be.

The women in your work have bodies similar to those in designers' sketches. Is that intended?

I've been drawing fashionable girls almost my whole life. I think it began when I was a lot younger and I'd try to draw female Disney characters. I had a turning point when I was in my early teens and I discovered this line of graphic t-shirts by Cosmic Debris. That led me to Fawn Gehweiler and Amy Davis, then I got into Japanese anime characters like Sailor Moon, Speed Racer, Urusei Yatsura, and the cute and curvy characters with big hair by Junko Mizuno. Fashion design is very nice and all, but it isn't something I would want to dabble in, unless I was designing some crazy dessert-shaped outfit.

Who or what makes you happy, in regard to clothing?

The film *Qui êtes-vous, Polly Maggoo?* has a lot of fashionable women in it. I also like Lung Leg's style in Richard Kern's short films, Winona Ryder in *Heathers*, Laura Dern in *Wild at Heart*, Laverne and Shirley, and the '80s Belgian singer Lio. People wearing only neon, rainbow, primary, pastel, or monochromatic colours capture my interest. I also like how the women dress in many Czech and French new wave films. A friend and I compiled a list of things we like in clothing: scalloped edges; frilly, high collars; Peter Pan collars; waist belts; high-waisted pants and dresses; yokes; short sleeves cuffed with buttons; bibs with frills or buttons; tiny gatherings; and soft, semi-sheer cotton. I also really like neon splatter paint.

What are you wearing right now?

The outfit I danced in last night! A cream-coloured shirt tucked into black bike shorts, a scarf, and vintage red jelly shoes. My eyeglasses with clear plastic frames are for every day. I wish my outfit were inspired by a pastel rainbow unicorn, though. 🐱

HEAR NOW A CURIOUS DREAM

PHOTOGRAPHY BY HENRY SANSOM

BRUTALLY
INDIVIDUALISTIC

REVISITING THE MARCHESA CASATI, ONE OF EUROPE'S MOST
FAMOUS – AND FORGOTTEN – PERFORMANCE ARTISTS

TEXT BY SARA FORSYTH
ILLUSTRATIONS BY SHEA CHANG

BEFORE THE MARCHESA LUISA CASATI took her seat at the Palais Garnier in Paris, she had her chauffeur slice the throat of a chicken and pour its blood over her right arm. This grisly *maquillage* was further complemented by an entire set of white peacock tail feathers crowning her flaming red hair. As she entered the Palais, this demonic vision reportedly caused several female operagoers to faint.

Lithe and lean, with pupils enlarged by drops of belladonna extract, the marchesa was a scandalous figure of the *belle époque*, known for her wild balls, extravagant costumes, and more than a passing interest in the occult. Today, little remains of her former notoriety, and her biography is pieced together through firsthand accounts of what it was like to be around her, often provided by the many artists who thought of her as a muse. She was more than that, though. The marchesa was a true provocateur, challenging the definitions of fashion and art throughout her entire lifetime.

The wealthiest heiress in Italy

Luisa Amman was born in 1881 into one of Europe's greatest fortunes. Her father, Alberto Amman, was a baron of the Italian cotton industry. He was a self-made man, or a *cotoniero*, as the enterprising nouveau riche of the Milanese cloth trade were known. Luisa had a typical European bourgeois upbringing, full of governesses, croquet, and horses. It was, however, a brief childhood: both of her parents died by the time she was 15, leaving the young Luisa and her sister, Francesca, the wealthiest heiresses in Italy.

Although there is little existing documentation of her life at this time (even the causes of her parents' deaths are conjecture), it's certain that Luisa continued on the trajectory her parents had planned. Casati came out in society in pursuit of a "titled" gentleman – someone to add a touch of nobility to her new money. She found such a man in the Marchese Camillo Casati, and the couple married on June 22, 1900. He significantly deepened his coffers and she became a member of one of the oldest, most distinguished families in Milan.

After her marriage, hints of Casati's future persona begin to emerge, as she traded her hunting horses for pet cheetahs and hosted séances in lieu of garden parties. Scot D. Ryersson and Michael Yaccarino, directors of the Casati archives in River Edge, New Jersey, believe her transformation was an innate progression – though perhaps aided by her poet-lover Gabriele D'Annunzio. Though his name is largely lost on North Americans today, D'Annunzio was one of the most popular – and notorious – writers in Europe. In contemporary-speak, Yaccarino says the marchesa's liaison was "really the equivalent of, say in the late '60s, a totally unknown society wife hooking up with Mick Jagger and conducting an open affair."

The marchesa and Camillo slowly separated. Because of her immense personal fortune, she was able to take up a private residence and lavishly indulge in her aesthetic pursuits. She turned away from the established designers of the belle époque such as Charles Worth and Jacques Doucet, instead favouring the kimono-style gowns and cloaks of Venetian designer Mariano Fortuny, who, like France's Paul Poiret, pioneered an uncorseted silhouette. His gowns were refreshingly simple compared to popular dress of the day – often classically based with soft pleating and draping. It was at this time, around 1910, that the now-popular image of the marchesa as a kohl-eyed, cheetah-walking, masquerade-hosting sorceress emerged.

A radical bubble of her own creation

In Infinite Variety, Ryersson and Yaccarino's biography of the marchesa, they describe the lady on a typical afternoon constitutional: "The mistress of the Palazzo dei Leoni finally made an unforgettable entrance into local lore on the Piazza San Marco. Clad in a Fortuny cloak of antique red brocade, she wore a thick gold necklace and a black fur cap. At her side strolled the contrasting greyhounds, both bedecked with turquoise collars. From behind followed Garbi [her manservant], in turban and waistcoat, carrying a parasol of peacock feathers high above his mistress's head."

The marchesa's burgeoning sartorial escapades also coincided with her patronage of the arts. She opened her homes to artists, such as famed dancer Isadora Duncan, and held exhibitions of the Italian Futurists in the Palazzo dei Leoni (now home to the Peggy Guggenheim Collection). Between 1919 and 1922, a slew of artists portrayed the marchesa in a wild variety of ways. She became the subject of countless portraits by Boldini, Kees Van Dongen, Augustus John, and Man Ray. What's intriguing here is the diversity of artists who were clamouring to capture her image: people associated with everything from Fauvism to Post-Impressionism and Dadaism.

Muses are typically aligned with one particular movement or artist, but not the marchesa. She likely transcended this branding because she was so actively involved in aesthetic experimentation herself. In essence, she was one of the first performance artists, someone who lived her life twenty-four hours a day, seven days a week, in a highly stylized and often radical bubble of her own creation. Her homes, clothes, the hired help, the parties she threw, and the menial stuff of daily life (it is noted that she received guests naked and even slept in a coffin from time to time) were conducted in a calculated, albeit ostentatious, fashion designed to satisfy her artistic impulses.

Even in daylight, the marchesa favoured extremes. When Fortuny's robes and pleated gowns became popular with the fashionable set, she turned to Poiret, whose draped, Asian-influenced designs, harem pants, and hobble skirts confused prevailing ideas of daywear,

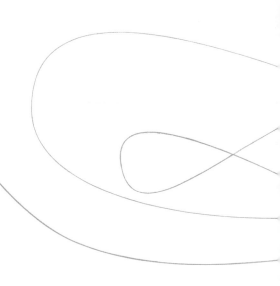

The Marchesa Casati by Adolph de Meyer, Venice, 1912
Image © Ryersson & Yaccarino/The Casati Archives

evening wear, and costumes. It wasn't long before she was commissioning clothes from Léon Bakst, the famed costume designer of the Ballets Russes. Yaccarino argues that the marchesa needed to work with someone whose imagination extended to the same grand, operatic scale as her own. Bakst designed one such costume, complete with a massive star-studded headdress, known as "The Queen of the Night," for the Beaumont Ball in 1922. According to Ryersson and Yaccarino, "It was so elaborate that it required drastic alteration before it was wearable. The costume was made up of a gilt hoopskirt decorated with stars and a train of translucent blue silk. The headdress was an explosion of feathers and silver and gold tendrils adorned with celestial symbols."

The marchesa's creative experiments were not always successful, however. She once wore a costume designed by Picasso made of wire and light bulbs intended to mimic one of his paintings. She had hardly made her entrance before a cable became twisted and Casati was very nearly electrocuted. As she crumpled in a mess of wires and flashing lights, one witness described her as a "smashed zeppelin." Not surprisingly, this wasn't her first experiment – and failure – with electrically operated couture.

Grand in a shabby London flat
Critics of the marchesa are quick to point out that she squandered her fortune (the equivalent of $25 million today) on ostensibly hedonistic pursuits. Due to her own spending, the marchesa was virtually penniless during the last 20-plus years of her life. She lived in London during World War II, remaining there until her death in 1957. This period is poignant because she never lost her interest in the arts and, more importantly, the artistic community. In her own eyes, she was as grand in a shabby London flat as she was in one of her Italian mansions.

Yaccarino believes this period solidifies the marchesa as a true artist. "Some people are hung up on the fact that she wasted [her money]," he says, "but that's not the point. Throughout her life she was passionately interested in making what before was only imagined, real. She had no sense of material value, and it wasn't out of stupidity. The value that she placed on something was its aesthetic appeal to her. So if you were a young artist and you... created this beautiful orange necklace with little worthless baubles attached to it made of twine and plastic – if that appealed to her, she would give you her priceless 17th-century diamond necklace, because in her mind they were equal."

It is undeniable that, given her upbringing and social circle, Casati had an extensive knowledge of art, history, literature, and politics – she was an informed, cultured woman. All of her acquisitions and stylistic choices were based on this education. Londoners probably mistook the marchesa for a bag lady as she strolled through Piccadilly Circus in a threadbare velveteen robe, with scraps of leather and monkey fur attached by safety pins, and a full-length lace veil. It was this severe form of eclecticism, her forward-thinking approach to dress, that made the marchesa such a magnetic figure, particularly for artists. As Yaccarino points out, her post-war London look was Vivienne Westwood circa 1984, a punk aesthetic before punk was punk.

Elsa Schiaparelli once said the marchesa "represented a past age of splendour when a few beautiful and wealthy women adopted an almost brutally individualistic way of living and presenting themselves to the public." Every tantrum, every gilded manservant was a product of her evolving quest to turn her fantasies into reality. It was Casati's brutal approach to life that made her remarkable – brutal because she pushed to the extremities of her vision, but remarkable because she had the courage to do it alone. ⊠

OUT OF BOUNDS

PHOTOGRAPHY BY SAMANTHA WALTON

Credits

creative direction & styling // Eliza Trent-Rennick
additional styling // Rose Flutur & Paulina Kulacz
makeup // Marlena Kaesler
hair // Margot Keith
photography assistance // Jessica da Silva
modelling // Sofie Mikhaylova & Angela Leung

SECOND-HAND STORIES

CONCEPTUAL ARTIST IRIS HÄUSSLER DISCUSSES THE ROLE OF CLOTHING IN HER WORK AND LIFE

INTERVIEW BY SERAH-MARIE MCMAHON

Iris Häussler in a café that occupies a small corner of Honest Ed's discount department store. The size of a city block and adorned with no fewer than 28,000 exterior light bulbs, Honest Ed's looks like a castoff from '70s Vegas. The city landmark was both inspiration and site for Häussler's 2009 work, *Honest Threads*. She displayed dozens of garments gathered from individuals who responded to a newspaper ad. Alongside each item, the owner explained its personal value – the stories their gloves and aprons held. The exhibit was also a kind of library and Häussler encouraged visitors to take home a jacket or a dress, or to literally walk a mile in someone else's shoes. Borrowers were invited to share their own adventures with the clothing on a blog, further adding to the complex history of the item. Häussler is known for contributing to "complex histories" herself. A fair amount of controversy surrounded her previous exhibits that purported to be the estate of an eccentric recluse ("The Legacy of Joseph Wagenbach") and an archaeological dig ("He Named Her Amber"). One national newspaper went as far as to call her a "hoax."

Though the cheeky title of *Honest Threads* seems to address these charges, Häussler speaks as though the garments' histories are real, without clarifying the veracity of the personal stories. In the end, I don't think it's necessary. They are real enough for me.

I saw the *Honest Threads* show; it was refreshing to see artwork that deals with clothing in a thoughtful way.
I have to tell you that the *Honest Threads* show was a surprise for me too. That people opened their closets... they gave away items that meant something to their family, or to themselves, or both, with the potential that it can be lent out and worn by absolute strangers. I find that this is how beautiful Toronto is, that you can do such a piece here. That people participate for real.

You did a sort of similar project before in Europe called *Transition Coat* **– how was that different?**

It took place in two towns across the river from each other, about 100 kilometres east of Berlin. One side was Polish, and the other side German. They were connected through this bridge, and I had a poetic notion of people trading their clothes across the bridge to another country. But basically no one wanted to participate.

As an artist you can develop ideas, you can have concepts, and you can make and do wonderful work, but if you do not have someone who is helping to mediate it, or to advertise it, to bring it out, then you just have no audience. And I would say that was such a case where the curators did this huge troupe show and they were absolutely overwhelmed. They couldn't deal with the practicalities that were required; they were not prepared for interactive work where you need to get your audience before the show even happens. So I can't blame it on the people who didn't participate – it was just not out there. It was hidden.

Why did you decide to deal with clothing?

They are the items that are physically closest to our body, that touch the skin. It's the most intimate thing in a way. And it's also that people care a lot about it. Everybody cares what he or she is wearing. But it's only important often, I think, for the people who do choose and care. The moment those people are gone – let's say they leave because they have a fight with their partner and never return, and all those piles of clothes are left over and brought to Value Village, or the next garage sale – the clothing itself does not really transport the memory. So then it's almost like an orphaned pile of clothes. But it can happen that another person comes by and sees the clothing that she or he responds to and chooses, and again makes it something valuable in their lifetime. That's a fascinating thing.

Do you wear second-hand clothing yourself?

I buy pretty much exclusively second-hand. There's only one exception and that's what I'm wearing. [Stands up to show me her cargo pants.] This is practically my handbag, so I have everything – my keys, my pencil, my sketchbook, my wallet – everything fits in these pants. I more or less accidentally discovered them maybe 15 or 18 years ago. I bought five of the same pants and wore them and sometimes replaced them. Now I have difficulty finding them. I need the big pockets, and with the small, here [indicates the fitted cut at the ankle], these are small down here so you can ride a bike. And then the colour is so forgiving. It's not black so you don't see a white cat's hair – it's really this absolute asphalt colour. They may be a kind of idiosyncrasy that I'm just hanging onto... other than that I'm not too picky with clothes. I'm not looking at fashion.

I'm just looking at second-hand stuff – things speak to me.

Do you see a difference between fashion and clothing?

That's an interesting question. I never asked myself that question. Yeah, I do. I think fashion I can buy. You want to have the visual attraction, you want to be part of your time period, of a style. While clothing is basically just to cover up, to bundle up, to protect your skin, to carry things around in various pockets. Basically a more existential meaning.

How did second-hand shopping play a role in creating *Honest Threads*?

I used to go through thrift stores and reach into the pockets of coats to see if someone accidentally left an old grocery list or something. Mostly there is nothing – that is the job of the people who take care of those things and put them on the hangers, that they remove all the notes. So at some point

"IT CAN HAPPEN THAT ANOTHER PERSON COMES BY AND SEES THE CLOTHING THAT SHE OR HE RESPONDS TO AND CHOOSES. AND AGAIN MAKES IT SOMETHING VALUABLE IN THEIR LIFETIME. THAT'S A FASCINATING THING."

Ageing fabric using tea, coffee, and dirt. These fabrics became part of the immersive installation *He Named Her Amber,* AGO 2008–2010
Image ©Isaac Applebaum

years ago, I started going to thrift stores and slipping notes into clothing, then I just left. It's almost an undisclosed art piece. No one has ever written about it because I never told anyone. I left a little note, like: "Have you looked up to the sky and seen that white cloud that looks like a horse?" and then "3:50 p.m., Friday the 22 of March," or something like that. I still sometimes do such little things spontaneously. I am interested in the stories that are attached to an item. But in a second-hand store you don't get the stories, you only get the clothing. I wanted to develop a project where you get both, and so I thought why not ask people to just part with a piece that they like for a certain period of time, having it insured and everything, but knowing it can be lent out?

Did you borrow anything yourself?

No, I did not. My son did. He borrowed Ed Mirvish's [namesake of Honest Ed's] jacket.

He didn't share his story, but I'm sure he had one. He was out with it and came back in the morning at three o'clock. At the time he was 16, so there's a story, but I will never hear it.

Another common medium that keeps showing up in your work is wax, as in the Amber project, but previous to that you also encased laundry in wax.

I have these clothes that are in plates of wax – sometimes I stacked them up. Each of those plates of wax had a title, and the title was only a family description, like uncle, daughter, grandfather, grandmother. I chose items I got from the flea market, looking at them thinking, "This is children's underwear, this is a daughter," and then I'd decide, "this is a sister." I had a huge show with over 100 of those plates, and I piled them up. All of a sudden there was a grandmother lying on a daughter. It started to build up a relation just by reading.

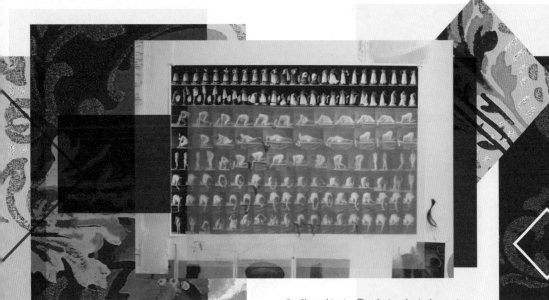

Dr. Chantal Lee's office during the Amber project. The photograph shows a re-enactment of Amber's undressing (she was wearing eight petticoats). It serves as an art historic reference to Eadweard Muybridge. Photo ©Isaac Applebaum

A "grandmother" on top of a "daughter," a "grand-uncle" is under his "nephew."

You clearly love narrative. Even when you're not telling stories, you invoke them in other people's heads. So much of what you're trying to say is related to fiction; it's like a book, only it's not written in words, it's written...
...in your head! I look at you and I can see your head is working. You are doing basically my work; I just give you a little hint. People are so smart and so creative. Some don't know it, but you give them a little bit and they finish the story in their head. It's a beautiful way of communicating.

You feel that clothing is a really good jumping-off point for that?
They are items that are very loaded, very emotionally loaded. I think one thing with your journal that I find fascinating is that you're addressing clothes from a different

perspective. I don't know if sometimes you sit on the subway and look at all the people around you and imagine you would have to wear each person's outfit for a day. Just to check how personality and identity are connected to clothing. Imagine I would make you wear what I wear today. Imagine you would say, "Iris, we are strangers, we just met, but tomorrow you are going to wear this green and white striped t-shirt and you are going to go teaching with that." Imagine that.

It would be crazy. It would be so strange.
And that's what I sometimes do. When I'm on the subway I look at all those people and I think what would I feel if I had to wear those pants and those yellow shoes with the glitter, or those very pink, very tight pants, because my pants are really light. How would that feel on my body? Would I move differently? More careful? Would I feel insecure? Would I love it? Clothes have power. ⊠

FASHION IS
OBJECT

04

FASHION IS MADE UP OF OBJECTS — hats, bags, shoes. These are made up of other objects: materials, like textiles, plastics, and notions; cohesive design details, like collars. Though we might take them for granted as part of a larger whole, these elements can be examined on their own, identified by their characteristics, evaluated and classified by era, materials, form, and use.

By identifying these objects, we discover a whole world of new information about what we wear. Perhaps they are unique to a historical trend or highlight a change in technology, the way the emergence of mass-produced plastics inspired an astounding range of Bakelite jewelry. Sometimes they represent a problem to be solved, as with the dilemma of caring for and preserving historic textiles. The detail of a button offers insight into economics; a safety pin evolves from a symbol of convenience to an expression of rebellion.

Along the path to understanding fashion's history, objects are the clues. They have significance that stands apart from their practical function. There is joy to be had in learning to recognize and read the language of detail, to know what you're looking at and why it exists. You can find all these things when you take a closer look at clothing and, once you do, you can't help but look closer still. ⊠

DOWN THE BUTTON HOLE

CLOSING IN ON COLLECTORS
FASCINATED BY FASTENERS

TEXT // SONYA ABREGO
PHOTOGRAPHY // NATE DORR

THE SPACE IS SMALL and the walls are fully lined; there are vintage clothes scattered throughout. Glass-faced cases filled with cufflinks, jewelry, old spectacles, and cigarette cases make the space a good two feet narrower on either side. With its unassuming window display two steps below street level, Archangel Antiques in Manhattan's East Village is easy to miss – and its specialty even more so. The tiny space holds over two million buttons, tucked away in countless wooden drawers, old apothecary cupboards, and large but shallow wooden cabinets. I open one of these drawers and am confronted with the most visceral invocation of the expression "eye candy" – dozens upon dozens of little, perfectly formed hard circles, each with its own aesthetic flavour, tossed in a colourful mix.

Since the invention of garments, there have been garment fastenings, and the history of buttons closely parallels that of dress. As both practical necessity and stylish accessory, they operate along the permeable boundary between function and fashion. While often simple and serviceable, they acted at one time as markers of status, with some as finely constructed and conspicuously displayed as any valued piece of jewelry. But unlike many vintage textiles, buttons haven't been reduced to shreds over time. Repeated use may result in a little dent or tarnish, but durable materials ensure that more buttons survive to tell their stories than the garments to which they were once attached. They also survive thanks to people who took care to keep them. Countless buttons are stashed away by seamstresses to use and re-use, or collected as keepsakes and artifacts. These buttons, some centuries old, have a human history too – one that values the little differences that make all the difference.

Obsessive collectors and curious crafters

Archangel has been in existence for over 30 years. When Gail and her partner Michael first opened their store, they frequently travelled and worked the antique circuit. Along the way Gail happened to acquire a metal cookie tin full of Victorian black glass buttons, and the reaction was swift – customers went crazy for them. Gail encountered button enthusiasts who belonged to clubs filled with members who compared, traded, and competed with their most prized buttons. Their collections were strategically displayed on cards, mounted like insects in an ento-mology display and organized according to the collectors' own idiosyncrasies. Gail began exploring buttons as a niche market and started buying whole collections when their original owners died or lost interest. Years went by and collections grew, and the little metal tin became a collection of millions.

Collectors sometimes come in with specific goals. Michael tells me about a man who marched in demanding to see all their Victorian red glass platypus buttons and seemed stunned when they were not immediately produced. Victorian red glass exists but is very rare.... The platypuses remain a mystery. Eventually these kinds of encounters became fewer and farther between. The majority of the customers who wander into the store are just people seeking little bits of originality: a crafter who put a lot of effort into a garment and is looking for the perfect finish; a designer or jewelry maker hunting for both inspiration and a source for one-of-a-kind detail; someone looking to take home a little *objet d'art* in button form.

Magic in the details

Michael brings out a tray of delicate 19th-century examples to show me. They date from the late Georgian to early Victorian eras and are called inlay, or pique, buttons. He singles these out as exceptional because "they are evocative of a period when craftsmanship was so important to the individual that was

purchasing. If you look at the pique work, they inlaid the metal [into tortoiseshell] – they cut into the tortoiseshell itself and then sliced the mother-of-pearl and the metal as individual pieces. I would say you needed training in jewelry to do that sort of intricate work. To me it is fascinating when a lot of time and energy was put into something very special."

He skips ahead a few decades to the 1860s and 1870s. One tray is full of perfume buttons in a range of sizes; these buttons, covered in fabric and encircled by fine metalwork, were designed to be daubed with perfume by the wearer to keep clothes and outerwear fragrant. Another tray holds remnants of the Victorian black glass craze, inspired by the mourning Queen Victoria; this period is immediately followed by the "gay '90s," invoked by gaudy jewel buttons, whose shiny brass bases are embellished with big ersatz gemstones. Menswear wasn't neglected during these decades either: the tiny, intricate, gold-set waistcoat buttons that would have studded a wealthy man's jacket

are constructed more carefully than what we are used to seeing in most 21st-century garments. Even more opulent colour is found in cloisonné buttons, where brightly coloured enamel is shaped in intricate patterns on a bronze structure embellished with cut steel details; with each detail individually riveted, they shine like marcasite. I could go on, but the almost overwhelming selection of buttons from just this brief slice of a century shows how much there is from which to draw.

Attaching the past to the present
I'm always curious to know how people who deal with old things (especially those from the ephemeral world of fashion) see the current state of fashion culture, in which the kind of craftsmanship laid before me in these glass cases is practically non-existent. Michael concedes that these sometimes disparate approaches are hard to reconcile: "When you're not aware of something, you don't pay attention to it; more and more you'll find that people aren't

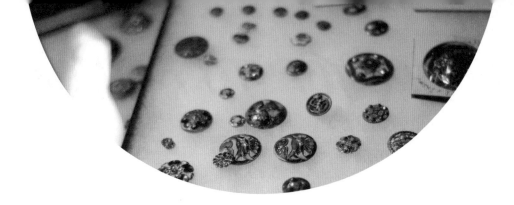

aware that these buttons existed… that something would accommodate a garment so specifically. Along with diminished expectations, people lack understanding, because so little importance is put on these details." Status-marking accessories are hardly extinct, but in the 21st century exclusive items are defined by their price point and logo, not necessarily by their quality of workmanship and attention to detail.

Although I sympathize with the loss of attention to detail, quality, and workmanship that these pieces represent, there is a part of me that feels uneasy bemoaning the loss of a culture in which one's dominant social status needed to be shown off and reinforced right down to the buttons on one's clothes. That's what makes Archangel's buttons so unique – they are separated from their garments, and their original social significance too. The history is writ into the objects, yet these objects can be applied freely and imaginatively by new owners.

Archangel, with all its clutter, represents a part of fashion that has always felt vibrant for me – rather than being a nostalgic mausoleum for past times, the store appeals to the inventive recycling of items and revaluing of materials. Its spirit is not materialistic in a greedy, acquisitive sense, but instead fosters a real appreciation that would spur someone to keep and re-use instead of throw away and replace. It's the same feeling reflected in movements like green design, and one that, according to Michael, is evident both in his evolving clientele and in larger changes in New York City in the new millennium: "We used to have a strong base of Manhattan-based stylists and creative people in the late '90s, and then they all left in one fell swoop – we don't see them anymore. Most of our customers are people who live outside the mainstream. They are not big on Manhattan; they want the energy of these smaller communities …. The people who would come up and say 'show me your Chanel' are not the kind of people who are interested in buttons." ✄

FROM TOP TO BUTTON

PHOTOGRAPHY // CHRIS MEJASKI

No. 1 // He ain't heavy

The paperweight button was popular in the '50s. The hand-blown coloured glass globes look like – who'd have guessed – miniature paperweights.

No. 2 // Neither animal nor mineral

Vegetable ivory (also "palm ivory" or "corozo") comes from the nut of a palm tree that grows in Central and South America. The seed resembles an avocado pit and hardens into an ivory-like solid that is capable of being carved, making it perfect for buttons. Starting in the 1860s, shiploads of the nuts were distributed to button factories in Europe and the U.S., and vegetable ivory became one of the most common materials for buttons.

No. 3 // Compose yourself

If your button resembles the texture of a terrazzo floor, it may be a composite – a composition of ground bone and tortoiseshell mixed with a binder that contains elements of mica (which helps to explain its rough shimmer). Dating from the 1860s–1880s, composition buttons were used a lot for durable work clothing and have an attractive, rustic appeal.

No. 4 // I smell the button of an Englishman

The perfume button, common during the Victorian era, has a textile surface – usually wool – embellished with steel thread ornamentation. The idea was that the wearer would place drops of oil-based perfume directly onto the button.

No. 5 // A fit of pique

The inlay, or pique, button appeared in the late Georgian to early Victorian period (1820s–1850s). Its tortoiseshell base, distinguishable by its lightness and translucence, is inlaid with fine slices of mother-of-pearl and steel wire ornamentation.

No. 6 // Put your lips together & blow

The whistle button has one hole in the front and two at the back. It's attached to the garment through the back, but the hole in the front makes it look like a bead. Sneaky!

ANTIQUE BUTTON COLLECTING is a hobby shared by a small but passionate group of people. "You can't pin down a button collector," says Carolyn Webb, Toronto representative for the Pioneer Button Club. "You'll have 10 collectors in a room and they'll each have a different interest." Some seek out a particular material (like glass, bone, or Bakelite); some are history buffs who might specialize in buttons of a certain era or type (like Victorian or military styles); others simply appreciate the fashion, beauty, and craftsmanship of an antique button. Established in 1960, the Pioneer Button Club is the second-oldest club of its type in Canada. The buttons shown are part of Carolyn's personal collection.

THE REVOLUTION WILL BE PLASTICIZED

BAKELITE AS IT WAS AND IS

TEXT BY SONYA ABREGO
PHOTOGRAPHY BY STACY LUNDEEN

COSTUME CULTURE

COSTUME JEWELRY LEADS A DOUBLE LIFE. One could argue it's better than its "real" counterpart, because unlike jewelry made from precious stones and metals, you know it wasn't mined under dubious political conditions. You also don't have to insure it, and you can buy more of it because it's usually inexpensive. Most importantly, it is distinct because it was made for the fun of dressing up rather than for its mineralogical value. On the other hand, it could also be seen as a cheap, frivolous commodity made to be worn with one season's styles and thrown away the next, another disposable example of fickle consumer culture.

The 20th century was the first to appreciate costume, or "junk," jewelry for its own sake, valuing innovative design that complemented one's costume and celebrated a fun, ephemeral style over the cost of raw materials. Coco Chanel is credited with popularizing costume jewelry when she included strands of glass beads and fake pearls with her '20s designs. She adhered to the principle that jewelry was meant to adorn the person, not to be a marker of class or a sparkling sign of how much money one's husband made. Discussing her famous strands of glass beads, Chanel remarked that

they were "devoid of arrogance in an epoch of too-easy luxe." By freeing jewelry from its connection to status (Chanel herself grew up poor), she made it accessible, democratic, and more reflective of the modern era.

It's no wonder, then, that Bakelite stands out as the quintessential example of modernity in costume jewelry. It's plastic. You can't get any more devoid of arrogance than that.

BETTER LIVING THROUGH FASHION

The first synthetic plastic, Bakelite was created in 1907 by Leo H. Baekeland. Classified as a phenolic resin, it was a product of the combustion reaction of phenol and formaldehyde. Although it was conceived of as an industrial product, Bakelite was firmly enmeshed in the popular sphere of consumer goods – including jewelry – by the end of the '20s.

What most of us would recognize as plastic existed before Bakelite: celluloid was introduced in 1869. But like shellac and the hard rubber compounds that preceded it, celluloid was of natural origin – nitrated cellulose obtained from pulped paper or cotton. In addition to its many filmic functions, celluloid was used for jewelry, most often as an imitation

of ivory or tortoiseshell. Because it was mostly employed in imitation, it never generated the kind of excitement Bakelite did, and it was destined to be considered a mere substitute, inferior to the original.

Bakelite avoided this stigma because it was something entirely new. Most of the colourful Bakelite jewelry we see today is from the '30s. Colourfast cast phenolics were made available in North America in 1928, and by 1934, more than half the costume pieces sold in New York City – including bracelets, necklaces, and dress clips – were made of coloured plastic. The bangle bracelets were created by slicing disks off plastic tubes and hollowing them out, sometimes carving them for ornamentation. They were lightweight and easy to wear, and since they were inexpensive, people could buy stacks to mix and match according to outfit or mood. Surfaces could be clear or opaque, and the hue was always brilliant and didn't fade. These Bakelite pieces were bold and clearly artificially pigmented, lending themselves nicely to the streamlined designs popular at the time.

Another reason for Bakelite's popularity was that it was lauded as the product of innovation, of man's (yes, I mean man's – specifically one man's) dominance over nature through chemistry.

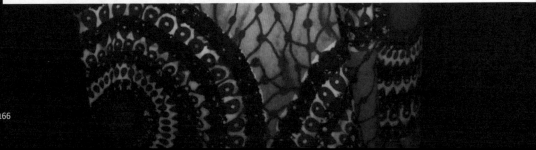

THE MYTH OF THE CREATOR

Baekeland was a Belgian émigré trained as a chemist, working in the United States. He had already achieved success by selling the rights to Velox (a photographic printing paper he had developed) to Eastman Kodak when he decided to start looking for an artificial substitute for shellac to use as an electrical insulator. The end product was in fact better than the original because it did not melt at high temperatures or shrink and contract with age. Baekeland's process was patented in 1907, and Bakelite was formally announced in 1909. Dubbed "the father of plastics," Baekeland graced the cover of *Time* magazine in 1924 accompanied by the cryptic caption, "It will not burn – it will not melt."

Bakelite is not technically a brand name. Different companies used Baekeland's process, but Bakelite has become something of a blanket term for labelling all phenolics. The General Bakelite Company controlled the rights to use the process of fabrication. They promoted it to different molders and fabricators in the chemical industry, so the material suppliers were separate from the producers of the finished products. The majority of the jewelry was produced by the Catalin Company, mainly because

they were the first to introduce colour. The early industrial uses for which Bakelite was created – varnish for electrical coils, insulators, and gearshift knobs – were quickly surpassed. Once it became a part of the marketplace, manufacturers and consumers played a crucial role in defining the new material. Rotary telephones, ashtrays, cutlery, and streamlined radios all made use of Bakelite.

We take plastic so much for granted today that it's hard to imagine a time when people were just beginning to think up uses for the stuff, but that's exactly what was happening with Bakelite's inception. Jeffrey Meikle describes it best in *American Plastic: A Cultural History*: "Bakelite's emergence marked a triumph of the frankly artificial celebrated for its own sake, a perfect machine-age material evocative of precision, rational control, and unearthly beauty."

In the years between its announcement and its eventual replacement by other materials, Bakelite came to be a cultural product that stood for the properties and promise of all plastics.

BRAVE NEW MATERIAL

The kind of optimism expressed by Bakelite's promoters touches on the utopian. This

material was a human creation that improved on nature, and it could do anything. Meikle evokes the historical context perfectly by describing how plastic was seen as "a child of the depression," arriving at a time when public faith in technological progress served as a counterforce to economic and social stagnation. It also coincided with an era in modern art when artists and designers were articulating the meaning of industrial modernity – think Futurism's glorification of the machine or Art Deco's sleek industrial look.

In other words, plastic was no cheap substitute. It was a better option; it would literally bend to our will. It was an exciting, tangible example of progress, and progress was good. In addition to commercial accolades, plastics were subject to philosophical enquiry by Roland Barthes. In "Le Plastique," an essay from his 1957 book *Mythologies*, Barthes describes how the freedom to manipulate plastic into anything would reduce differences between things, leading to "the hierarchy of substances [being] abolished – a single one replaces them all: the whole world can be plasticized."

The General Bakelite Company sold Bakelite as "the material of a thousand uses," with the infinity symbol as their logo, no doubt referencing its many functions and also its indestructibility. The sense of excitement surrounding Bakelite is nowhere more obvious than in *The Story of Bakelite*, written by John Mumford in 1923. Written as a promotional book to help endear the product to the general public, Mumford's work combines accurate historical information with an almost romantic acclaim for industry that resonates as incredibly naive today. Phrases like "our modern magician – the chemist," who would continue to improve the world by concocting "marvels which the earth had never known," or descriptions of Bakelite as "a wonder stuff, the elements of which were prepared in the morning of the world, then laid away until civilization set them to work" sound strange to contemporary readers. The text feels alien because it's rooted in another time. Its blind faith in science and technology is lost in a world let down by modernism's belief in the inherent good of progress.

Bakelite was no longer produced after World War II, having been replaced by new plastics that were cheaper and easier to fabricate. It makes sense that the importance and promise associated with it became irrelevant around the same time humanity became aware of the full destructive impact that resulted from scientific innovation and technological might. In "Le Plastique" Barthes writes that plastic as a material embodied the

concept of infinite transformation; we can now look back and see that the perception of plastic has transformed over the decades.

Plastic has surpassed the thousand uses described by the early promoters of Bakelite; it is an unavoidable and ubiquitous part of our lives. Instead of celebrating its versatility, today we think of how it is filling our landfill sites and taking millions of years to decompose, or how toxic pollution is infusing the air as a result of its production.

TWIST OF FATE

So the cheap Bakelite bracelet is a relic from another time. Barely distinguishable from any plastic bangle made today, it represents a moment in history not too far from our own but unquestionably distinct. I would argue this is one of the reasons for its popularity. Andy Warhol was probably one of the most famous collectors of Bakelite, and a fan of abolishing hierarchies in his own right. He even named his ground-breaking multimedia performance events "The Exploding Plastic Inevitable." And it was inevitable that Bakelite would end up as one of the hottest collectibles on the vintage jewelry market.

"I have seen Bakelite sell for more than its weight in 18-karat gold," a New York antiques dealer once told me. He wasn't exaggerating.

Pieces of uniquely carved, multicoloured items fetch very high prices, with some bracelets approaching $1,000. This not only makes finding a special piece for cheap more thrilling, but also brings us back to the paradoxical nature of value in the realm of costume jewelry. Items that were never scarce in their own time are now considered rare and valuable. Over 70 years later, those Bakelite bangles that reflected an ephemeral popular style are now falling into an elitist camp that had previously been the exclusive territory of "real" or fine jewelry.

It is almost as if Bakelite's relevance has come full circle, from being a wondrous material with transformative power, to representing an era that valued such beliefs. It is the context surrounding plastics that has really transformed, and Bakelite once again stands out as something unique and exciting. The look of Bakelite will keep it from ever becoming a symbol of wealth and status like, say, diamonds, but it is hard to deny the certain smugness in knowing that my armful of bright plastic bracelets is worth more than someone's precious heirloom cameo.

But the educated (or maybe just the nerdy) can see the difference. The moment of recognition conjures images of the past. It's not romantic nostalgia, but more of a fascination with how time changes values, both monetary and otherwise. ⊠

RECOGNIZING BAKELITE

The best way to identify Bakelite is by having experience with it. Looking at jewelry books and visiting antique stores will help you get a sense of characteristic colours and shapes, as well as pricing guidelines.

Many "fakelite" copies are made nowadays, so if you see a whole row of identical bracelets you can assume they are not old. Your best bet is always to compare it to an old piece.

▶ Bakelite is heavier than most plastics, and it is very hard. Two pieces of Bakelite make a characteristic "clunk" sound when knocked together. Since it's not rubbery, it can also shatter when it hits a hard surface, but it's probably best not to test for that.

▶ It will not have any "seams" on the surface. Thin mold lines are evident in newer plastics that were pressed into a form, whereas Bakelite was cast from liquid in tubes or sheets and then carved out.

▶ Bakelite has a characteristic smell of carbolic acid or formaldehyde when heated. You can check for it by rubbing it between your fingers to make it warm from friction or by running it under hot water.

▶ It will not melt when heated. You can test this by touching it with a hot pin – but I wouldn't recommend it. If it's not Bakelite, it might be ruined, and if it's celluloid, it might burst into flames. That said, just because it won't melt with a hot pin doesn't mean you can put Bakelite tableware in the microwave. If it was made before the time of microwaves, it shouldn't go in there. End of story.

▶ If you have a brooch, pendant, or clip that has a pin or backing on it, look for screws. Bakelite is hard and not glued or molded around a base, so it was always drilled into and the backing attached with little screws.

▶ Simichrome polish is a product used to polish chrome and found at some mechanics' shops. If you put a small amount on a bit of cotton and rub it onto Bakelite, the cotton should turn yellow. This is also supposed to work with other cleaning products like Scrubbing Bubbles and OxyClean, although I've never tried those. It won't hurt the Bakelite and actually polishes it up nicely.

low vamps and peep toes

WHY THE '40S PUMP IS PERFECTLY PROPORTIONED
AND PIN-UP PREFERRED

TEXT BY SONYA ABREGO // ART BY BREE APPERLEY

I LOVED SHOES FROM THE '40s before I even knew what they
were. To me, they were just those shoes with the perfect shape,
the ones pin-up girls wore, the ones with the killer heels,
the perfect arches, the sexy straps. The look has been often
imitated, particularly in the '70s and again in the late 2000s,
but nothing compares to the quality and style of the real thing.

Like most vintage items, the best way to identify '40s heels
and get a sense of how they look is essentially a gestalt thing:
the more you see, the easier they will be to recognize. Here are
a few pointers for those of you looking to find the perfect pair.

the material

To identify anything vintage, a working knowledge of history can help a lot. During World War II most materials and imports were limited, which affected the look of clothes and accessories; it's the reason why shoes from the early '40s are different from later designs. War rationing in North America and Europe led to designers using innovative materials like cork for heels, and rougher fabrics were often substituted for leather. Post-war, the end of the decade saw more intricate details added to more luxurious materials. The embellishments echoed an earlier Art Deco style in their streamlined look and included the use of multiple straps, leather bows, and lots of metal or rhinestone studs.

A typical '40s high-heeled shoe is made of leather, inside and out, including the soles — although there may be fabric lining on the sides. The heels are wooden and the shanks metal. A handwritten size might be visible on the inside, but don't rely on this too much, as it could have worn away. A wide range of fabric can be found in addition to leather, including brocade, cord, canvas, and satins and velvets for formal evening wear. Shoes were often originally sold with matching bags, though it's rare to find such sets intact.

the colour

Shoe shades vary from standard black, brown, and navy to gorgeous reds, greens, and yellows. If you're familiar with the decade, some colours stand out as distinctive, but it helps to remember that colour palettes were generally more conservative, unlike the pastels and atomic looks that followed in the '50s. However, the pigments themselves are intense, and contrasting colours are often combined for a dramatic look.

the toe

A smooth, rounded toe is common, whether in heels or flats. This, combined with a low vamp, makes the foot look smaller – they were often referred to as "baby-doll shoes." The term "peep-toe" originated in the '40s and is used to describe that little cut-out section at the tip of the toe box through which one or two toes can be seen.

the heel

It's hard to pin down exactly what makes the '40s heel unique. It starts directly beneath where your natural heel rests in the shoe and is just as wide at its base. It tapers down gradually (but not to a point like a stiletto) and has a subtle curve that is more visible in higher heels and less so in lower ones. Along the inside (heel breast) you will always find what looks like a seam, where the fabric or leather is folded under and joined to the wooden heel. I've often heard the terms "stacked heel" or "Cuban heel" used in reference to '40s shoes, but they're not always accurate. Stacked heels usually look chunkier, like '70s platforms; Cuban heels tend to have a more '30s shape – like ballroom dancing shoes.

The allure of the '40s heel is in the illusion it creates. Because the width at the top is the same as your natural heel, and thus in proportion with your ankle, it makes a long, column-like line down the back of the leg. This is a *very* good thing. Also, these heels are sturdy, so most women could (and can) walk in them with confidence. This is always more attractive, not to mention comfortable.

the strap

This is tricky, since there are so many variations, but proportion and placement are key. The ankle strap with the buckle in the middle is very distinctive of the '40s and is thin (usually just less than one centimetre), made of leather, and lined.

There is often a little concealed bit of elastic right next to the buckle. High ankle straps were called "Yankee-catchers," two high ankle straps "double Yankee-catchers," and so on. Apparently, boys from the northern states fancied the high straps. Slingbacks were hot, particularly on platforms, with straps that start off wider and taper at the back of the heel. Straps that criss-cross in an X shape at the back of the heel in an open shoe were also popular, and it's no surprise why: they look amazing.

the platform

Platforms didn't originate in the '40s. The style goes back centuries, beginning in Europe with the chopine in 16th-century Venice and even earlier in Japan during the Heian period with the geta sandal. Despite its rich past, the platform usually triggers images of freaky disco shoes or Elton John's Frankenstein moon boots. Put those out of your head. Platforms from the '40s can go from a slight rise under the toe to a full two-inch lift. Regardless of the height, the '40s platform always follows the shape of the shoe; again, think Deco streamlining.

the wedge

Salvatore Ferragamo claimed to have invented the wedge heel in 1936 for the house of Schiaparelli. Wedges from the '40s are graceful. They follow the contour of the shoe and often curve slightly inward to create an elegant, fluid line. The heel itself can be leather or cork, or combine twisted fibres to create a rope-like effect. Wedge heels were popular and practical, especially in daywear. During World War II, women were more likely to work outside the home at jobs that required they be on their feet – in nice shoes – all day. Find yourself a pair of these, and you'll soon see those dames knew what they were doing. ✄

SAFETY DANCE

HOW THE SAFETY PIN BECAME A REVOLUTIONARY FASHION ACCESSORY

TEXT BY TED KULCZYCKY

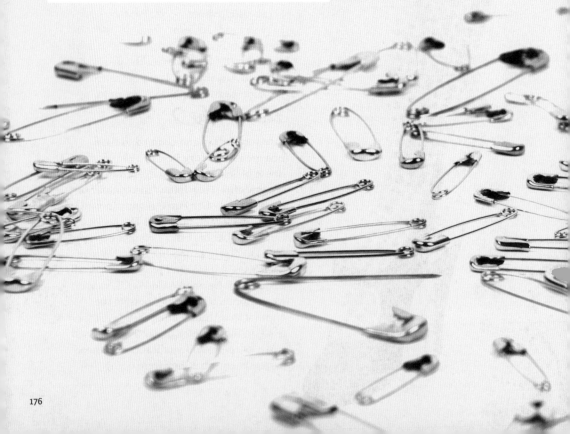

IN THE SPRING OF **1849,** inventor and mechanic Walter Hunt nervously fidgeted with a small piece of wire while trying to figure out a way to pay off his debts. Among this New Yorker's inventions had been a streetcar bell, street-sweeping machines, an ice plough, a semi-automatic rifle, and an early sewing machine (which his seamstress sister wouldn't let him patent because she believed it would put too many people out of work). Despite his immense productivity, Hunt was frequently cash-poor, due to his equally immense gambling habit. But his anxiety managed to convert a small wire into a prototype safety pin, which won him $400 when he sold the patent.

Hunt probably should have held out for more. The recent invention of the microscope had revealed microorganisms as the cause of much disease, and hygiene was beginning to be seen as more of a health concern than a social problem. The washable cloth diaper rapidly replaced the hide-skins that had previously been the norm, and Hunt's safety pin replaced the clumsy ties that held them. Cloth diapers were being mass-produced by the 1880s. By the '40s, diaper-washing services were used in middle-class cities across North America, and Hunt's invention was attached to each and every "present" Junior gave Mommy.

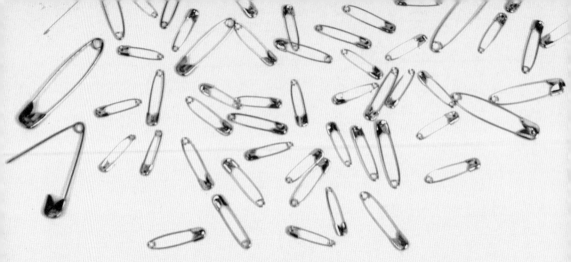

But the introduction of the feminine sanitary napkin gave parents ideas, and by the early '60s, a number of disposable diapers were on the market. By the mid-'70s, Pampers basically eradicated their cloth counterparts, and the safety pin was replaced by sticky tape. At around the same time, however, a young poet-musician-addict accidentally discovered some new uses for Hunt's safety pin: political statement and fashion object.

Richard Meyers moved to New York City in the late '60s with his prep-school chum, Tom Miller. After several years of working in bookstores and operating a small press, Meyers and Miller changed their names to Richard Hell and Tom Verlaine and formed the band Television. Unlike most bands of the era, Television wore their everyday clothes when they performed. Hell's filthy unkempt hair and generally dishevelled appearance had already made an impression before he arrived at punk mecca CBGB, his shredded t-shirt held together by safety pins.

Hell has long maintained that this wasn't meant to be any kind of statement, but was simply a way of holding his clothes together. This explanation has never really made much sense: why not just wear another shirt? Photographer and friend Bob Gruen filled in the missing details. What Hell

neglected to mention was that, after a very recent fight with his live-in girlfriend, she took a razor blade to all his clothes.

As it happened, Malcolm McLaren (husband of fashion designer Vivienne Westwood and aspiring music impresario) was spending a good deal of time in New York, looking to find musicians to steal and to steal from. His plan was to package his Dadaist politics with his wife's confrontational fashion sense and graft them on to a prepackaged '70s boy band (think of The Osmonds or the Bay City Rollers). Although he was unable to mold any New York musicians to exactly his ideal, he returned to his native England full of fashion notes and musical concepts from the New York scene, including Richard Hell's unique garb.

By mid-1975, McLaren had formed the Sex Pistols, drawing from the disenfranchised youth who hung out at his wife's boutique, Sex (later called Seditionaries). Littered among the S/M garb, spray-painted t-shirts, and dog collars that the band wore were clothes held together by safety pins.

One of the employees at the McLaren-Westwood shop was Jordan (born Pamela Crooke). By common consent, Jordan was not only the first "punk" in the United Kingdom, she was also its most consistent

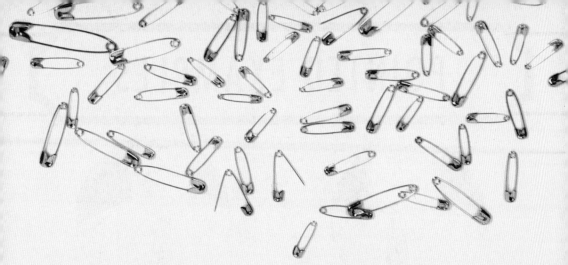

media image. Virtually every British television report and newspaper story that appeared on punk in the late '70s featured an image of Jordan in her suggestive outfits with cropped and sculpted dayglo hair.

Much credit is due her for defining punk's image, but she often claims to have also invented the safety pin as fashion statement. "Johnny [Rotten, lead singer of the Sex Pistols] always tells the story of how he went into Sex one day – I had on this t-shirt with a big rip right across the front, so I'd put in a safety pin to cover it up. Johnny thought it was great, and the safety pin thing started there and then."

Since both McLaren and Rotten dispute this account (and give proper credit to Richard Hell), Jordan's memory seems faulty. However, she may have been the first to use a safety pin as jewelry. There are pictures of her in the early punk era with safety pins piercing various parts of her body, whereas the other punks from that era seem relatively unscathed. By the late '70s, this was standard practice among aspiring punks. There were (unsubstantiated) rumours that certain clubs had "dress codes" requiring piercings. If you showed up without the appropriate gear, the doorman conveniently had a safety pin and pencil eraser (but no antiseptic ointment) ready to improve your image.

By the early '90s, punk had morphed into grunge and "alternative," and the days of mohawks and safety pins seemed as quaint as ducktails and zoot suits. The late-night drunken bathroom piercings of yesteryear gave way to midday drunken visits to "body artist" boutiques. The stainless steel barbell became the standard starter piece.

Of course, the safety pin continues to be used as an ad hoc clothing mender and fastener for badges and buttons. But as a symbol, the safety pin is no longer dangerous. It is worn like a support ribbon to promote patient safety measures in the medical industry, and every September 10, many American schools celebrate Safety Pin Day.

But in the spring of 2005, Vivienne Westwood launched her "Hardcore Diamonds" jewelry line. For the low starting price of $400, any street punk could use a gold safety pin (with a .05-karat diamond setting) to hold their ratty t-shirt together. Perhaps, if he were alive today, Walter Hunt would use the $400 he received for inventing the safety pin to purchase one of these must-have fashion items. ✄

Credits

photography // Monika Traikov

POINTED EXAMPLES

the TAB COLLAR

- An often high shirt collar with a small tab that attaches the two sides of the collar with a button underneath the necktie to keep it neatly in place
- It is rumoured that in 1923 the Prince of Wales (whom Fred Astaire called "unquestionably the best dressed young man in the world") debuted this collar as part of his casual look
- Seen crisply represented on Donald Rumsfeld, Secretary of Defense under Presidents Gerald Ford and George W. Bush (some credit Rumsfeld for the collar's current unpopularity)

the DETACHABLE COLLAR

- Separate collar attached to the back of the dress shirt, often with a metal stud
- Invented in 1820, associated with stiff, middle-class morality
- Cluett, Peabody & Company ran the Arrow Collar Man advertising campaign from 1905 to 1931, featuring this collar on more than a million billboards and car cards
- Desperate to look dapper, poorer men would buy cheap detachable collars made of, or reinforced with, paper (the jig was up if a launderer accidentally washed the collar…)

the CARNABY COLLAR

- Typically a white, small collar with rounded ends, paired with a printed shirt
- Named after the birthplace of mod fashion: Carnaby Street, London
- Young men of the Carnaby mod tribe engaged in fashion wars with their rocker nemeses on Britain's beaches in 1964, fighting against archaism and championing everything "new and consumable"
- Post-dandy and pre-metrosexual, Carnaby Street fostered "The Peacock Revolution"

Some Advances in Men's Shirt Collars in the Last Hundred Years or So

◄ ►

TEXT BY STEPHANIE HEROLD, ILLUSTRATION BY KAROLIN SCHNOOR

the SOFT TURN-DOWN COLLAR

► Any collar that folds onto itself, or the shirt, in contrast to a single, stand-up collar
► Soft collars were typically not stiffened using starch, but by inserting tabs into their collar points, or by "trubenizing" – fusing the outer surface of the collar to its inner lining
► Worn with giant ties before and during World War I by figures like Oscar Wilde and Rupert Brooke, who reacted against stiff garments symbolically attached to the "Establishment"
► In Britain, the Men's Dress Reform Party rallied for soft collars, while in France the "Anti-Iron Collar League" "called for social disobedience"

the RUFFLED COLLAR

► Standing on the neck in a single band, often made of gauzy material, edged with lace or gathered material
► Popularized on "Party Shirts" from the '60s made by Michael Fish, owner of British boutique Mr. Fish
► References small lace-edged "ruffs" from the beginning of the 16th century (think Shakespeare)
► Mr. Fish, in his book *Doing Your Own Thing*, advocates dressing according to the revolutionary idea of "self-expression" – later to become the dominant philosophy of '70s fashion

• COLLAR ANATOMY 101 •

COLLAR BAND: the material of the collar that wraps around the wearer's neck
COLLAR HEIGHT: how high the collar sits on the neck
COLLAR POINTS: the ends of a collar
COLLAR STAY: a narrow piece of plastic or metal slipped into the collar points to ensure stiffness and jauntiness

RUFF: supplanted by the collar at the beginning of the 17th century; a pleated, stiff collar radiating from the neck and protruding outward to varying degrees
SPREAD: the space between the collar points
STUD: ornamental button originating in the 18th century; fit through a metal ring or eyelet, to attach a detachable collar, neckband, or shirt front

the NEHRU COLLAR

- Stand-up collar worn in the '60s, occasionally made with rounded front collar points
- Named after Jawaharlal Nehru, Prime Minister of India, 1947–1964
- It was claimed to have been "invented" by Gilbert Feruch in 1962 on a tuxedo for French mime Marcel Marceau; however, earlier incarnations were seen on political figures such as Vladimir Lenin, hence its alternative moniker, the Lenin collar
- Also called the Mao, Mandarin, or Oriental collar
- This collar's popularity was due in part to the Parisian infatuation with Mao, who also sported this collar, often coupled with Mao suits
- In 1967, a faux pro-Maoist parade was launched by French television program *Dim Dam Dom* to celebrate the marriage of fashion and Mao

the STAND *or* STAND-UP COLLAR

- A stiff piece of material permanently attached to the shirt, standing straight up and tight to the neck, usually white
- Began to be worn primarily for formal occasions – often with bow ties and cravats – at the beginning of the 20th century when men's fashion became more casual
- By 1896, the stand-up collar stood upwards of three inches high
- Very tight and very white, the stand-up was a chore to keep clean, encouraging avoidance of perspiration and necessitating a constant flow of fresh shirts and/or collars
- The stand-up was utterly impractical for manual labourers, who often sported blue turn-down collars (hence the term "blue-collar")

the BUTTON-DOWN COLLAR

- A classic two-piece, turn-down collar, with its collar points buttoned down to the front of the shirt
- Invented in 1896 by American menswear pioneer John Brooks, of Brooks Brothers, after noticing that polo players' collar points were commonly fastened down at the ends with buttons
- Adopted by French teenagers in the 1960s yearning to sport the "Kennedy look" thereby developing the "Frenglish style"

the LONG-POINTED COLLAR

- Long, larger-scale collar with pointed ends, worn in the '70s
- Seen famously on John Travolta in *Saturday Night Fever*
- The Dog's Ear collar was a common variation of this collar: the collar points were rounded like a dog's ear and often drooped down to the chest, making for one of the most bizarre and exaggerated collars of the 20th century

the ASCOT COLLAR

- A narrow scarf, also called a stock, approximately four to eight inches long, attached to the back of a shirt, and then looped in front
- Named after the race course at Ascot Heath, England, this style was popular in the '20s and the late '60s
- This collar is often confused with the wide ascot necktie, introduced in 1876, also worn to the races at Ascot
- The name "Ascot" appeared in 1711, when someone misheard Queen Anne choose "East Cote" as the ideal place to race her horses

the TENNIS SHIRT COLLAR

- René Lacoste debuted the soft, flat tennis collar in 1936
- Made of jersey petit piqué, which allowed it to be easily turned up to protect a tennis player's neck from the sun, and easily unbuttoned to help cool one down during a match
- In 1935, a reporter in the south of France commented that polo shirts created "the oneness of the sexes and the equality of the classes," and said, "[p]ersonality, extinct … the Riviera has produced a communism that would be the envy of the U.S.S.R." ⊠

· NOW GO POP YOUR COLLAR ·

FROU FROU SHOE

· · · · · · · · · · ·

VINTAGE STORE OWNER
MATTHEW MORAD HAS A LOT OF SHOES

INTERVIEW & STYLING BY SERAH-MARIE MCMAHON
PHOTOGRAPHY BY ALYSSA K FAORO

SOMETIMES HE REPEATS HIMSELF. Maybe it's nervousness at being put on the spot, or excitement over the subject at hand, but there are not enough words. Hands gesture, cheeks flush, and a slow-moving smile creeps over his face. Matthew Morad is the most charming mix of knowledge, intensity, and unbridled enthusiasm. The French accent doesn't hurt either.

His tiny Toronto vintage store, Frou Frou, houses shoes from the '20s to the '80s – some on display, a few tucked into cabinets, still more nestled under racks. Matthew delights in the history and craftsmanship of everything in his shop. However, as with many vintage dealers, the things he loves best never get there – indeed, they never leave his home, and they are definitely not for sale. And among those favourite things are many, many shoes....

How did you get involved in the vintage industry?

I grew up around my uncle who was into antiques, and he would drag me to auction rooms. I would be looking at Victorian this, Edwardian that, and I noticed that the clothing – hats, whatever – was being over-looked. I started buying, as if I knew that this was going to be popular one day. I had a stash from the good old days, when you could buy shoes by the pound, or by the boxful. I rented some storage space and bought some more.

Was it relatively cheap to buy things back then?

It wasn't bad. There was the odd dealer, but if you were not looking for a specific label you were okay, you were doing well. I had no intention of selling anything, you know? I was buying for the sake of buying.

Is your shoe collection art?

Oh, definitely. They're so architectural.

They're *objets* to me. You'll find there are a lot of "one ofs" – there is only one shoe, they are not always a pair. But I still love it on the shelf.

How did you start collecting shoes specifically?

The auction rooms helped, but there was also Queen Street. Queen and Dundas were littered with "Momma-Poppa" shops, and as I was growing up they were at the end of their rainbow, their life cycle, because that generation was dying. So I would walk in there and be like, "Oh my god, those shoes!" to the ones no one really wants because they're old. I would buy them. I would buy them by the shelf full just because they are collectible to me. I have bought whole collections of shoes from one or two stores, some that have never been worn. Those shoes were just sitting there coated with dust, and I would go and the guy would say, "Are you sure you want this?" and I'm like, "I'll take it all!"

How do you take care of them? Are you nervous about handling them?

I'm not nervous to touch them. Right now they are in boxes, and I try to keep the shoe paper in them to keep them from collapsing. In my bedroom I have a couple of galoshes, like neat old slippers. People are begging me to sell them, but no, no, I can't. For one thing, that is very early rubber, and they are very '30s and '40s. They are not for sale.

Do you have a favourite era? A favourite style?

Well, there are lacy ones that movie stars would wear in the '30s and '40s, with delicate lace – I don't know how to describe it, but it coated the foot. Those are so, *oh my god*, for a movie star! I have a couple like that; they are my favourites. Then skip all the way to the '60s square toe if they have

nice buckles. I like a sturdier shoe, one with a thicker heel. They are like dancing/walking shoes, more practical. I like a bit of a heel, but none of those big stilettos. Some of those are trashy; they are styled with certain people in mind. You need a shoe that you can walk for miles in. Although I do love Roger Vivier, the right arm of Dior. He didn't just make stilettos – he made good stilettos.

Do you think you could be a shoemaker?
Oh god, no! I'm not very dexterous. I have an eye for things, but I'm not very practical.

What do you think of new shoes made to look like vintage? Modern interpretations?
The '40s-style shoe was just on the runways and in stores in the fall. Of course they don't get it right. The lines are not as nice, there is always a flaw in the design, and the material is always – excuse my language – shitty. It's not as perfect as it should be. They are just farming the work out to Timbuktu. I'm sure back in the day the designer and the shoemaker would work together in the same workshop, so you have the dialogue. But that isn't happening now. Appreciation and standards for shoes are much lower. They cut corners.

Can you name one of your ultimate style icons? What would she wear?
Wallis Simpson. She is dead now, but she was hot in her day – she is a goddess. She is that American divorced woman who married the king of England. She was very, very well dressed, and the '40s shoe would be her favourite for cocktail parties.

Do you ever wear your shoes?
Oh gosh, no! I wish they would fit, but they are all too small, sizes five and six. They're dainty and cute. ⌗

TO CONSERVE AND PROTECT

UNPACKING THE MULTI-LAYERED WORLD OF TEXTILE CONSERVATION

TEXT BY SARAH SCATURRO

"THIS BABY'S SKIN IS LEATHER!" I exclaimed as I summoned everyone over to look at the dried skin peeping out of the wrappings of the small mummy I held. Though I knew leather was just another word for desiccated skin, it took me a moment to register the gravity, awe, and unease I felt handling this mummified baby. It was January 2005, and I was in the middle of vacuuming a small pre-Columbian mummy bundle as a member of a group of volunteer amateur textile conservators visiting Peru. I could see carbonized dust, bones, and leathery skin peeping out of the hole at the bottom of the cotton-wrapped package – a hole caused by body fluids draining out of the body as it sat in its grave for centuries.

How had I become someone who was trusted with the preservation of this mummified child, discarded in a coastal Peruvian desert by grave robbers? I was just one semester into a conservation graduate program at New York's Fashion Institute of Technology. My classmates and I had survived crash courses in fibre science and identification, museum theory, and the history of fashion and textiles. Before

entering the program, I really had no idea what I was getting into – I just knew that I liked old clothes and textiles, history, museums, sewing, and, oddly enough, science. Even more, I knew I wanted to do something meaningful – and conservation melded everything together.

Objects "live" much longer than people; they are tangible proofs of past human experiences. Conservators are a link between past and future, and by preserving the objects under our care, we keep history alive. But what exactly is conservation?

This ain't the Restoration

Let's begin with what conservation is not – and that's restoration. When people ask if I restore things, I cringe. To "restore" something implies a desire to make an artifact appear as close to new as possible. That means doing whatever is necessary to get it to its previous state, including taking it apart, removing old materials, adding new ones, and even falsifying details. Restoration irreversibly changes the object in some way.

In contrast, conservation seeks to preserve an object by protecting it from harm. Though conservators often make objects better, it is our adherence to a strict code of "do no harm" that distinguishes us from restorers. Reversibility (meaning our actions can be undone) is a crucial tenet that guides everything we do. According to the American Institute for Conservation of Historic and Artistic Works, conservators are ethically bound to preserve cultural heritage. Essentially, we try to leave the objects we handle better off than we found them. It sounds simple, but the subjective nature of conservation means there are no absolute answers. Every situation is different, and the outcome of a conservation treatment depends on a conservator's goals, experience, training, and resources.

Let us use an early 19th-century cotton gown as an example. Sometimes wet-cleaning (conservation-speak for laundering) ensures the longevity of a garment by removing acids and dirt. But if the gown has an original glaze on its surface, although that glaze might be the very thing causing the degradation, it might also be adding body, stiffness, and sheen. Washing the garment destroys the glaze, and as a result, the gown will never again drape, handle, or look the same. What to do? For me, using conservation ethics as a guide, the answer is clear: I will not do what cannot be undone – so, I do nothing.

Well, not exactly *nothing*. I might not be able to wet-clean the dress, but at least I can make sure to store the dress in a way that will slow its deterioration. This is where "preventive conservation" comes in. This type of conservation attempts to prevent further damage from occurring to an object by keeping it in a sort of holding pattern. The hope is to preserve it as long as possible for future generations of conservators and scholars.

An ounce of prevention…
The principles behind preventive conservation involve maintaining a stable environment during storage, transport, and exhibition. (For fashion, this usually entails keeping the environment at around 45–55 percent relative humidity and a temperature of 20–22°C.) It also means creating sturdy mounts, containers, and padded hangers to protect objects being handled, stored, or displayed. Preventive conservation also keeps objects safe from dirt, damaging materials, pests – and light. Have you ever wondered why fashion exhibits are so dim? It's because ultraviolet light damages fibres by causing polymer breakdown, while non-UV light causes colours to fade.

In our search for safe, inert materials and tools, we have turned to many interesting fields, including medicine (for surgical tools), aerospace and building industries (for things like vapour barriers and hi-tech non-wovens and laminates), pool and air-conditioning industries, and even entomology (insect pins are perfect for pinning delicate fabric).

So, what have you done for me lately?
Conservators work on pretty much anything related to fashion and textiles. Gowns might spring to mind, but we also care for flags, quilts, and samplers. We work with mummies because they are wrapped in ancient textiles. We mount and prepare objects for exhibitions, rehouse objects for storage, and perform wet-cleaning, stabilization, humidifying, and flattening treatments. We do a lot of documentation. One of my most glamorous responsibilities is to ensure that insects are not eating our collection.

According to the museum, I help manage the "integrated pest management program." I am the go-to girl when bugs are found in the building. It's not at all unusual for me

CONSERVATORS ARE A LINK BETWEEN PAST AND FUTURE AND, BY PRESERVING THE OBJECTS UNDER OUR CARE, WE KEEP HISTORY ALIVE.

to reach into my mailbox and find a spider in a jar left by a concerned coworker. (As an aside, spiders are not known for being "heritage eaters," so it's safe to let them go.) But it's not all paperwork and pupae.

One of my favourite tasks is dressing mannequins for exhibition. As conservators, we learn what type of padding, rigging system, or support is needed to get garments looking the same on mannequins as they would on people (carefully, of course). Nicole Bloomfield, a newly minted conservator with an MA degree from FIT's conservation program, recalls taking a course in mannequin dressing with celebrated dresser June Bové (a talented professor who developed many of the standard dressing techniques museums use today). "My partner and I were having a hard time getting the chest and butt area

right. At one point we were on either side of the mannequin shoving batting on and pretty much feeling the mannequin up in an effort to get the proportions right. At the same time we both looked up and sort of realized what this would look like to anyone walking by. We fell on the floor in hysterics."

There are, of course, more serious challenges to being a textile conservator. Just as sitting in front of a computer all day strains eyes and hurts wrists, intensive treatments stress the body. Imagine repetitively sewing one small stitch after another using floss so fine it's actually called hair silk, or painstakingly vacuuming something so delicate that you can only use a tiny brush while looking through a microscope. Apart from mold, soot, fibres, dust, and frass (insect excretion), a major hazard for textile conservators is the possibility that the object

UNLIKE OTHER CONSERVATION FIELDS, WE HAVE A TANGLED RELATIONSHIP WITH OUR OBJECTS BECAUSE WE WEAR AND EXPERIENCE CLOTHING FIRSTHAND, EVERY DAY.

we are working on has been treated with hazardous chemicals like arsenic or mercury. In the 19th and early 20th centuries, these were often applied to deter pests.

She works hard for the money

Despite conservators' fine and highly skilled work, one of the greatest challenges they face is the ability to eke out a living. As Maria Fusco, a textile conservator at a museum in New York City, confides, "There are some serious drawbacks to this profession, mostly financial and in terms of self-determination in work location. It can be very challenging for those without support from their family or spouse.

Salaries are very low in comparison to the skill set and level of education required." A graduate degree, internships, and volunteer work are all mandatory.

Annual salaries start at $25,000 to $35,000 (USD) – that is, if the newly graduated conservator can find a permanent, full-time job (rather than contract work or fellowships). Even experienced conservators with decades of experience rarely reach six figures. There's the option of private practice, but like anything freelance, the workflow is erratic and clients often balk at the high rate a trained textile conservator rightfully commands ($75 to $200 an hour). This all leads to one inevitable question: why is our field so poorly paid?

"I think the culturally ingrained assumption of textiles and sewing as 'women's work' plays a part," says Bloomfield. "The idea that it isn't 'manly' to sew or weave is ingrained in American culture, even though historically men have done a significant amount of sewing, weaving, and embroidery …. If you combine the already established propensity for low salaries with a field deemed to be 'women's work,' then you end up with a highly skilled labour force with very low wages."

She's right – women dominate the textile conservation field. Although we work on a variety of objects, the relationship between traditional female consumption patterns and fashion ensures that many of the garments we conserve were made for the female consumer. Thus, we end up in a non-lucrative system in which women are the primary caretakers of other women's things. It's a sobering thought, but there are always reasons to be optimistic.

It's getting better all the time
The increasing reliance on technology is opening new doors for the next generation of conservators. Isa Rodrigues, an independent textile conservator, suggests that "the 'younger' generation is more acquainted with scientific tools and equipment used for conservation and research." Bloomfield expands on this idea: "The use of photography, video, and the internet to share conservation treatments and museum collections is relevant not only to people in the field, but also to educate the public on the importance of conservation."

And the "younger" generation isn't necessarily young. Fusco points out that "many conservators seem to come to the career late after having an odd mix of previous careers. It is one of the few places they can combine technical/hand skills, focus, and knowledge of art history and design." Textile conservation is an opportunity to combine diverse (and often lifelong) interests into one profession. It is, for its practitioners, uniquely rewarding.

Even with all of the pitfalls of this profession, Fusco acknowledges, "I look forward to going into work every day, and I'm proud of what I do. I like being able to use my hands, slowly improving the stability or aesthetic of an object in a way that is conservative and scientifically informed, and seeing tangible results of my workday." And Rodrigues agrees, citing her ability to preserve objects for future generations as a great motivator.

Mary Lou Murillo (a freelance textile conservator and scientific assistant for textiles at the American Museum of Natural History) values the idea of bringing artifacts back to life: "Sometimes I talk to the artifacts, too, which I've been told is an occupational hazard." Though she's half-kidding, Murillo's admission isn't surprising. The physical manifestation of long-lost owners is especially poignant and pervasive in garments – we wonder what caused some rip that was haphazardly mended; we marvel at how well-loved this sweat-stained, and still smelly, dress must have been. Unlike conservators in other fields, we have a tangled relationship with our objects because we wear and experience clothing firsthand, every day.

Ultimately, textile conservators know that everything is ephemeral. No matter what we do, we cannot stop the inevitable decay. Yet despite endless challenges, odd (and sometimes dangerous) conditions, and dismal compensation, we never stop trying to delay that absolute truth. To some it might seem a strange and futile drive – but it is also a sort of cockeyed optimism. After all, we just want to slow the ageing process down, just a little, just *enough*. Then perhaps, somehow, somewhere, sometime in the future, humanity will develop the means to let the evidence and weight of history last forever. ⧖

no.1   no.2   no.3   no.4   no.5

Loden Coat

BEFORE ALPINE SPORTSMEN could rely on space-age synthetic fabrics, there was loden: a brushed, milled, and waterproofed wool used to craft the loden coat or loden jacket. Originating in Loderers, Austria, in the 16th century and popular throughout mountainous Central Europe, loden coats are still worn as *Tracht* (folk costume) at festivals like Oktoberfest. A surge of American interest in the '30s and a revival in the '80s made these jackets more readily available in North America. The slim silhouette and fitted shoulders of this meticulously detailed piece by Julius Lang of Bavaria suggest it dates from the late 20th or early 21st century. No need to dry-clean: unwashed loden develops a sheen over time; all the better to resemble a von Trapp family singer or a *Jägermeister* (master hunter).

Credits

text // Stephanie Herold
photography // Lisa Kannakko

196

no.2

no.1

Typical of *Tracht*, the embroidery displays a naturalistic pattern inspired by pastoral Alpine scenery; this can include native flowers such as the edelweiss. This particular design is popular in the Niederdorf province in Northern Italy (once Austria) where similar stitches would decorate the front of men's lederhosen.

After a stag was hunted and killed its antlers were used to make these prized buttons. Shapes vary based on their usage – long buttons fasten and flatter lapels, round buttons decorate. Colour variances and a slightly grainy surface help determine whether buttons are made from authentic antler.

no.3

no.4

This green loden appliqué is reminiscent of oak leaves found along the Inn River, where farmers' pigs would feed on acorns. Similar shapes can be seen on 19th-century women's jackets from Tolz, Germany. Decorations indicate provenance; for example, the outline of a goat represents the popular skiing town Kitzbühel.

The use of grey accentuated by forest green mimics Alpine landscapes of rockface and forest. Red lining typically serves as an accent, giving a visceral peep into a mountain dweller's second skin. These days, the fabric once supposedly praised by Emperor Charlemagne for its durability is often outshone by its modern techno-rival, Gore-Tex, in hiking circles, anyway.

no.5

Handcrafted buttons of solid silver or brass are stamped with regional or designer symbols; MCMLXXVIII reads 1978, presumably the year Julius Lang founded his label in Germany. Decorative bodices on dirndl dresses can be displayed easily if, as in this example, a metal chain acts as the sole functional fastener.

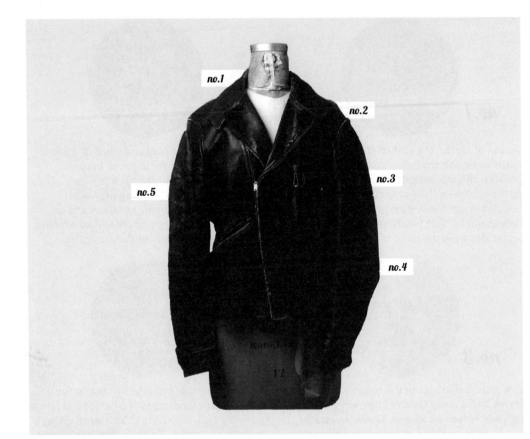

no.1
no.2
no.3
no.4
no.5

Motorcycle Jacket

ONE LUCKY BUYER FOUND THIS '30 s motorcycle jacket at the famed Los Angeles Rose Bowl flea market, spending $50 on what turned out to be worth between $500 and $1000. Thanks to Marlon Brando's iconic portrayal of gang leader Johnny Strabler in *The Wild One* (1953), black leather biker jackets achieved legendary style status in the '50s, but their mass production for U.S. military pilots, and popularity among civilians, predates World War II. Their durability made them an instant favourite as sportswear, especially among motorcyclists, and they were manufactured all over the U.S. and Canada.

Credits

text // Sonya Abrego
photography // Nate Dorr

no.1

no.2

This label reads *made in San Francisco*, but comparable examples came out of both East and West Coast leatherworks. Different regions favoured different details, adding local charm to an iconic look.

The leather is black steerhide, although many were made of horsehide as well. Horsehide will have a slightly more pebbled texture.

no.3

no.4

This is called a "D" pocket (for the shape) but it's also known as a pistol pocket. Both it and the little steel ball-chain zipper pull are distinctive markers of '30s and early '40s styles.

Another period detail is the horizontal band at the back of the jacket – a sort of belt – set in for a slight narrowing at the waist. Steel buckles sit low at the side for adjusting the perfect fit.

no.5

The heavy-duty front metal zip is stamped with the *Talon* name and embellished with Art Deco–style radiating lines – very '30s. The typeface, unique to its age of manufacture, helps identify the approximate age of the garment. I'm still unconvinced that a zipper pull works faster, but it sure looks nice, doesn't it?

no.1

no.2

no.3

no.5

no.4

Sun Suit

POPULAR IN THE '50S AND '60S due to the increase in private pools and seaside travel, "sun suits" were play-clothes that could follow you into the water, if you were so inclined. In American vintage parlance, a one-piece sun suit is called a *maillot*, borrowing from the French word for swimsuit, *maillot de bain*. This Jantzen example from 1960 sat on the cusp of the shift in swimwear from childrenswear-inspired one-pieces to revealing bikinis. Early '60s Hollywood good girls like Doris Day and Sandra Dee sported maillots in their beachside films; two-pieces were reserved for bad gals like Brigitte Bardot. With a matching skirt to accompany you to the burger shack, a girl could, as the ad suggested, "Just wear a Smile and Jantzen."

Credits

text // Stephanie Herold
photography // Lisa Kannakko

no.1

Tiny metal spirals inserted into the suit's bra seams helped the bustline stay in place. The result was the distinctive '50s/early '60s semi-pointed shape, strong enough to last through any kind of play date. Jantzen advertised that their spiral apex stays created "figure control" and "bra bewitchery."

no.2

The fold over or "cuffed" bra was part of this friendly design, named *"Jeune fille."* During the early '50s, this popular neckline could also be found on the play-clothes worn with these maillots. The "little boy leg" of this suit, cut across the top of the thighs, typically finished the look.

no.3

Jantzen once sized suits based on body weight, using an in-store scale for fitting assistance. The more regularized fit system was introduced in the '50s and ranged from size 10 to 18. Salespeople were instructed to use positive language in the changeroom, suggesting what did fit rather than focusing on what didn't.

no.4

Introduced in 1920, Jantzen's red "Diving Girl" was reported to have been the seventh most recognizable trademark in the world by 1932. In 1948, her pompomed swim cap and unisuit morphed into a pompomless low-back maillot ensemble, which remains basically unchanged today. Cole of California was another popular American swimwear brand of this era.

no.5

"Quick care Oxford" cotton was part of a wave of quick-dry and wrinkle-resistant fabrics used in swimwear of the '50s. By the '60s, cotton was blended with even quicker drying synthetics like Spandex or elastane. Bright and bold stripes were especially swingin' during this period, as were Persian prints.

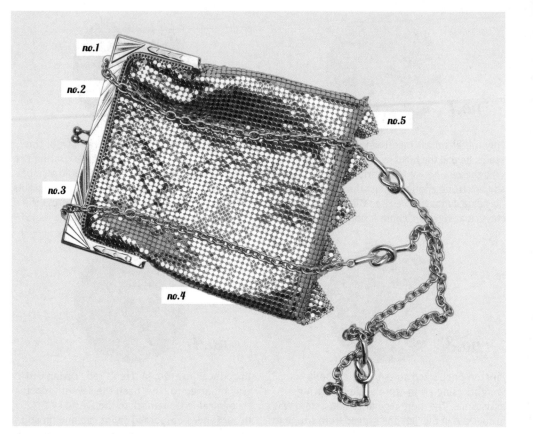

no.1
no.2
no.3
no.4
no.5

Gunmetal Mesh Purse

GUNMETAL MESH PURSES FIRST APPEARED at the end of the 18th century, paving the way for this modern example from the famous metal mesh purveyor Whiting & Davis, and its competitors Mandalian, Evans, and Deauville. Purchased in 1948 to brighten a Toronto woman's wedding ensemble, this golden beauty was typical after World War II when women stopped seeking more elaborate Art Deco designs in coloured enamel mesh and started opting for gold and silver materials in designs that retained Art Deco's geometric motifs. Metal mesh bags have won over fans from Shirley Temple to Shirley Manson, creating a coveted collectible.

Credits

text // Stephanie Herold
photography // Lisa Kannakko

no.1

Beginning with their first purses in the late 19th century, each "spider" in the W&D mesh was attached by hand to its ring base, often by poor families. Despite Pratt's invention of the mesh-making machine back in 1909, W&D silk purse linings continue to be sewn by hand onto interior metal spirals.

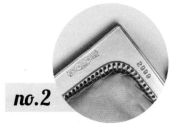

no.2

In 1921, W&D started attaching a shield-shaped tag to its purses – blue tags for soldered mesh, white for unsoldered. The removable paper tags were then joined by interior metal tags, and then incised W&D logos before the end of the '20s. Fabric tags were later sewn into the lining.

no.3

The postbellum clean lines of this frame differentiate it from some of W&D's 1,200 other purse frames, which feature enamel, Bakelite, openwork patterns, delicate filigrees, and even jewels. Mandalian, W&D's rival, also often garnished its purse frames elaborately, creating Mandalian's strong reputation for the ornate.

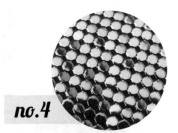

no.4

Composed of octagonal "spiders," each four-armed piece of gold-plated brass is attached to four golden rings, creating armour or flat mesh. Mandalian's armour is typically set diagonally, while W&D's is usually set horizontally and vertically. Party-proof, this mesh can collapse in both directions, resist cuts and perforations, and ultimately withstand fire.

no.5

Mesh as a medium inherently comes with design limitations, often restricting these bags to somewhat pixelated, geometric shapes. The Vandyke skirt, named after the short, triangular beard it resembles, was predominantly used as a decorative feature for purses in the '20s and '30s. ⌗

FASHION IS

DESIGN

05

IF IT IS TRUE THAT FASHION IS DESIGN, how better to view it than through the eyes of designers? While clothing is influenced by art, history, and experience, designers are like translators deciphering cultural messages. And each designer filters those messages differently, shaping them according to their own unique perspectives. The processes (and the results) are fascinating.

Nothing crystallized this transformation for us quite like our *Art and Sole* project. We gave identical pairs of shoes to a diverse group of designers as a basic design to build on. As each pair was returned, some in pickle jars, some lifted onto platforms like chopines, some crocheted or winged, they were a lovely (and often amusing) testament to creativity and the possibility of style.

So much of our clothing is mass-produced. We walk into a shop or a mall, and we see racks of items: thirty pieces in three sizes and two colours. It's as though the garments have no origins at all – they simply exist – but that couldn't be farther from the truth. Sometimes we're lucky enough to see designs at their inception, sometimes not until long after they've lost context, but the things we wear all came from somewhere. They came from someone who made decisions about how to balance reference, materials, and structure. Every garment is deliberate. There is no fashion without design.

Tangled Up in Shoes

John Fluevog's quirky soles have adorned the feet of heiresses, shock-rockers, movie stars, and even regular folk

text by Sara Forsyth • illustration by Adriana Komura

IN A PILE OF SHOES, his designs are always unmistakable – and deeply personal. Fluevog has bypassed the scenes and trends to make, arguably, footwear that is timeless. He's associated with everything from rockabilly to steam punk, Gen X to new wave.

Fluevog characterizes himself as the quintessential baby boomer – an "old school trendoid." He's been hip to every mania of every decade, and it all began in the '50s, at his father's business. Well, perhaps "family business" is more appropriate, since the whole Fluevog brood lived under its roof.

The lap of Luxury Freeze

Father Sigurd Fluevog owned the Luxury Freeze – an ice cream parlour located on Kingsway, one of the busiest streets in Vancouver and, at that time, the only route in and out of town. Add a high school next door, and you've got one overrun living room. "My house was full of people all the time," Fluevog says. "It was just Grand Central Station. I was inundated with high school culture, kid culture, car culture – it was rockabilly, greaser – all of the things that were going on in the '50s."

Little Fluevog had a room in the basement. Most mornings he would sneak up to the kitchen before his parents were awake, open the door to the Freeze, and have Swamp Water (that's a gourmet term for a blend of fountain pop – usually Coke, 7Up, and Orange Crush) and maybe a scoop or two of chocolate chip ice cream for breakfast. And while he did not develop diabetes, he did acquire a passion for cars and car culture. There wasn't a particular model that fascinated him; he was more interested in the seemingly endless modifications people made to their rides. "One season people would be jacking the fronts of cars up, or painting the rims white with black walls, or taking the grills off," says Fluevog. "There was a time when, if you borrowed your family car to go out on a Friday night, you'd take the hubcaps off, so that it could possibly look like your car."

Fluevog noticed the connection between customization and individuality. Those who wanted to stand out used their bodies, their clothing, and their cars to make a statement about who they were as people. To disassociate yourself from the more polished and conventional world of your parents, you took the hubcaps off their car, thereby making it a little more tough, a little more rock-and-roll, a little more like you.

Falling into it

When he was 19, Fluevog drove a dilapidated Citroën down the west coast of the U.S. It was the late '60s, and he wanted to catch a glimpse of the social revolution firsthand. Though he never considered himself a hippy – "I was far too slick for that" – Fluevog ended up in an adobe house in a commune outside San Francisco. But California was not the epicentre of peace and love he was expecting: "It was crazy times. The cat was on acid in the backyard, people were running around naked … I remember I went to Haight-Ashbury and it was all over. All the love turned into hate, and there was a disillusion you could feel."

At some point, Fluevog made friends with a group of guys, including a senator's son, who were anxious to leave California and return to their cushy lives in Florida. He could have gone with them, but he decided to go back to Vancouver. He describes it as a pivotal moment in his life. "I remember laying my hands on [my] car and praying that it would get me home," says Fluevog. "It had no windshield wipers, and it was winter on the coast, so it was pouring rain the whole time … I drove all the way home with no windshield wipers and parked it in the alleyway of my parents' house. The car never moved after that."

That's when Fluevog met Peter Fox, a shoe retailer 15 years his senior looking for a "hip, trendy kid" to work the cash register. Meeting Fox determined the course of Fluevog's adult life, though he's quick to dismiss the notion that anything was a conscious decision on his part. "People ask me how it started, you know, 'Did you go to school?' But I was just there," he says. "I had no idea. I was just there to look good – I had embroidered, flowered, velvet bell-bottoms on.'"

Six months later, Fox approached Fluevog's dad for a loan of $13,500 to open up his own shoe store. "My dad said, 'Sure, if you make my son 50 percent partner,'" Fluevog remembers. "And I'm going, 'Oh cool! You mean, instead of making $45 a week I could be making $60 or $70?'" And thus, Fox & Fluevog was born.

Fox & Fluevog

The pair ran a smooth operation. Fox was designing the shoes, and Fluevog was managing the retail store and "looking good." At the beginning of the '70s there was a stylistic turn toward all things old-world, including turn-of-the-century footwear. Their store, located in Gastown, Vancouver, attracted, as Fluevog says, "anybody doing anything illegal in town." They sold shoes to high-end hookers, hip rich kids, and celebrities and musicians who would fly up from Hollywood for a pair of Fox & Fluevogs. And at $350 a pop, they were fairly expensive shoes.

"We probably had the hippest, coolest shoe store in the entire universe at that time, and we didn't even know," says Fluevog. "We had these patent leather, knee-high boots for men, lace-up or pull-on, in six colours. We were selling high-heeled 'D'Artagnan' over-the-knee boots for men that we had made at a women's factory because no one else would do it." Shortly after opening their store, Fluevog met a supermodel. They married three months later. He maintains he was still passive about the direction his life was taking: "I thought, 'Wow, I got this cool store. I got this hip chick. Things are rollin'….. She entered me into a different world. The first house we bought, we bought with the engagement ring Peter Sellers had given her."

Fluevog's love affair with the rich and famous was fleeting, however. Drug-addled celebrities quickly lost their sheen, and any allure that lifestyle offered disappeared. The marriage only lasted five years. Looking back, Fluevog thinks of it as a great lesson in disguise: "It sort of robbed me of my youth, I think. But [it made me realize] that there isn't something way cooler out there that I should be doing. I realized that all of that stuff is pretty shallow."

Ten years passed, and Fox moved to New York to start his own line. Fluevog bought him out and soon found himself in ambiguous territory. At that time there were Fox & Fluevog stores in Edmonton and Victoria, and a few in Vancouver. Shortly after he bought the company, a recession hit, and Fluevog was nearly bankrupt. "I ended up shutting all the stores

down, except two in Vancouver," he says. "One was making money and one was losing money."

Eventually, Fluevog closed the weaker location and put everything into a truck. He snuck out of town in the middle of the night and headed for Seattle.

The birth of the Vog

It was the late '80s when he opened his shop in Seattle, and Fluevog was getting into the youth alternative scene – the beginnings of grunge. He began importing Dr. Martens from the U.K. (the first retailer in North America to do so), and soon the phone was ringing off the hook. In addition to the original, plain Dr. Martens, Fluevog produced "Dr. Marten Vogs," which he would decorate with pink pony hair and stencils.

"At that point people thought I was a designer," he says. "I wasn't really. I didn't totally design things from scratch. When Dr. Martens became mainstream, they [the shoes he was doing with pony hair uppers] weren't what the mainstream wanted... so I quit selling them altogether."

The Fluevog stores in Seattle and Vancouver were doing well initially, but after a few months he ran out of capital. Sales went down, and Fluevog contemplated getting out of the business for good. He now had a young family to provide for. "I remember saying to my wife one morning, 'I've got to find another source of income, because this is killing me.' And on that day I had an epiphany. I had a dream of the name and the line and what it could be. That event affected me to this day. [It made] my whole career." Fluevog characterizes his epiphany as a "God-ordained event." He now felt he had the affirmation to act on a feeling in the pit of his stomach – he had the courage to design his own shoes.

With little experience in design, Fluevog developed a technique of "seeing" that he still uses 20 years later. "I'll see a shape or I'll see

> "I don't want to give my customers a rehashed version of someone else's design. I want the stuff that I do to make people feel original, like they're actually made by a person who thought about them."

somebody wearing something, and then I'll imagine what it could look like," he explains. "The very first shoe I did I was influenced by a girl wearing pointy-toe cowboy boots. They were too big for her, and they were all cut up on the toe. So I designed a little flat with a turned-up toe and a big, huge buckle on the front of it. They were called pilgrims … and I actually sold them. They did quite well."

Vogism

Today, Fluevog has 10 stores in North America. His shoes – the exaggerated points, bright and contrasting colours, and hourglass heels – are instantly recognizable. He may be Canada's most famous shoe designer. That's a pretty big deal for someone who claims to have fallen into the business. He attributes the brand's longevity to the fact that he has always tried to stay true to himself – always easier said than done, of course.

"To love truth and beauty… those are the things that are going to make you happy," Fluevog says. "I don't want to give my customers a rehashed version of someone else's design. I want the stuff that I do to make people feel original, like they're actually made by a person who thought about them."

Cars are still a source of inspiration for Fluevog – particularly the car culture from his childhood. That modification aesthetic is something he's carried into his professional life. Cars, like shoes, are bound by set parameters – there are certain components you need in order for them to function. "For me, it's not about doing a pretty sketch on a piece of paper," he says. "It's about putting it all together and actually making it work. Which is why I like looking at cars – it has to work. Footwear, you know, they haven't changed how it's made in 150 years. So I'm bound within certain conventions, yet within that, there's room to manoeuvre." ⊠

TYPOGLYCEMIA

Norwegian Wood designer Angie Johnson in her label's prize-winning collection

Credits

photography // Alyssa K. Faoro
art direction // Serah-Marie McMahon
& G. Stegelmann
styling // Serah-Marie McMahon
styling assistance // Chelsea McBroom
& Avyn Omel
makeup // Bella B.
hair // Jamie Furie
modeling // Angie Johnson

NO. 01

NO. 02

NO. 03

NO. 04

ART AND SOLE

WHEN IT COMES TO WHAT WE WEAR, it is often difficult to navigate the push and pull between function and fashion; shoes walk a fine line between both. Though often lumped into the ephemeral category of accessories, they are also utterly utilitarian, cutting across nations and cultures, aesthetics and ideologies. Sneakers hold a special place in the history of dress: they slip between fashion/function boundaries in ways most garments never will.

KEDS AND THE HISTORY OF THE SNEAKER

When sneakers appeared in the history of international exploration, technological innovation, and industrial evolution, they helped punctuate a shift in North American lifestyle and culture.

The first rubber-soled shoes were invented in the late 19th century – but it wasn't as simple as all that. Natural rubber was unstable. Although Europeans were impressed with the novel properties of this mysterious substance from Central and South America, they had a hard time harnessing its powers. Charles Goodyear was the first to vulcanize rubber, a process that kept the benefits of flexibility, waterproofing, and durability without the melting and cracking that occurred in extreme temperatures. Rubber-soled footwear preceded rubber tires, and the term "sneaker" – referring to the stealthy movement afforded by silent rubber soles – was coined sometime in the 1870s (although like so much popular culture etymology, the specifics remain a mystery).

In 1916 Keds introduced the first standard white canvas rubber-soled shoe that we still recognize as a sneaker today. Combining the word "peds" (from the Latin for "feet") with "kids," the company, originally known as U.S. Keds, created the ideal lightweight, supportive, casual shoe for sports and, along with it, one of the few shoes with a claim to truly iconic status.

Modern sneakers have expanded from strictly athletic gear to everyday wear, and from aesthetic statement to status symbol. Yet despite these twists and turns, the little white Keds have stayed true to form. Their look has a tenacity most artists and designers can only hope to achieve.

THE ART OF THE SHOE

Issue 8, *WORN's* "Shoe Issue," was the first themed issue we'd ever produced. Naturally, we wanted it to be a big deal – more than just talking about or looking at shoes. We thought, what if we could *make* them?

Thus the *Art and Sole* project began with an idea and a template: a basic pair of clean, white Keds. We sent our templates out to 23 artists from Montreal and Toronto and asked them to do, well, whatever they wanted and send them back. And when it was done we would put all their contributions together in an exhibit and an auction.

What resulted was, on some level, a perfect illustration of what we all do with fashion every day. Though most of us start with variations on the same basic items – a shirt, a skirt, a pair of pants – we interpret and wear them differently, slowly transforming them into a communication of who we are.

So it was no surprise that when we gave artists Keds, they made art. ⊠

NO.05

NO. 07

NO.06

NO. 01 // WHO: Clayton Evans, designer, complexgeometries. **WHERE:** Montreal. **THIS DESIGN:** "I like working with comfortable, hardwearing fabrics like cotton jersey, canvas, and fleece. I tried to make a shoe I'd like to wear. I like the simplicity of Keds and didn't want to change too much."

NO. 02 // WHO: Elif Saydam, craftswoman. **WHERE:** Montreal. **IN THE WORKS:** A recipient of the 2008 Prix du Centre des arts et des fibres du Québec, Elif is planning to ride her bike to Arizona. **THIS DESIGN:** Inspired by quilts, *Saved by the Bell*, Turkish janissary boots, and the Sonoran desert.

NO. 03 // WHO: Hilly Yeung, sculptor, crafter. **WHERE:** Toronto. **PREFERRED MEDIUM:** Anything. **INSPIRATION:** "Some of my favourite shoe designers like Roger Vivier put a lot of drama in their design, and I wanted to channel that into a pair of sneakers."

NO. 04 // WHO: Dana De Kuyper, artist, Damned Dollies. **WHERE:** Toronto. **KNOWN FOR:** Dana's dolls have been featured in British *Vogue*, and one was purchased by one rock star to give to another rock star. **THE SHOES:** Something beautiful and delicate that her studio-mate called "lace puke."

NO. 08

NO. 09

NO. 10

NO. 05 // WHO: Patrick Lundeen, painter. **WHERE:** Montreal. **WHERE ELSE:** Shows in Calgary, Montreal, Stockholm, Quebec City, Gothenburg, Chicago, Saskatoon, and Dundee. **TAKE HEED:** "Please don't put laces in my shoes. They might be a little toxic so don't let kids, dogs, or boyfriends suck on them!"

NO. 06 // WHO: Samantha Purdy, crafter, Pin Pals. **WHERE:** Montreal. **MATERIALS:** 16-count aida cloth, DMC embroidery floss, gems, and shoelaces. **INSPIRATION:** "My submission is based on traditional embroidery and cross-stitch designs from eastern Europe. The pattern possibilities are endless."

NO. 07 // WHO: Tim Mitchell, artist, Team Macho. **INSPIRATION:** "Once, on the internet, I saw this horse that fit inside of a shoe; I thought it was pretty funny. On further thought, I found it quite sad. I mean don't get me wrong, I am all for miniature large animals… but that horse is in for a life of loneliness and misery."

NO. 08 // WHO: Tyson Bodnarchuk, artist. **WHERE:** Montreal. **EDUCATION:** A steady diet of Muppets, horror and sci-fi movies, and my mother reading Maurice Sendak. **INSPIRATION:** "The birds are taken from other works I do… but usually they are being eaten by some sort of giant worm or monster."

NO. 11

NO. 13

NO. 12

NO. 9 // WHO: Dane Richards, designer, Danegerus. **WHERE:** Montreal. **BOOK LEARNIN':** Winner of the Puces Pop Emerging Designer award, Dane studied art in his parents' basement, the Salvation Army, and various alleyways. **THIS DESIGN:** Geishas, Galliano, Grass, and the High Class.

NO. 10 // WHO: Danielle Meder, illustrator, fashion blogger. **WHERE:** Toronto. **PREFERRED MEDIUM:** A 4B pencil and my Mac G5 + Wacom tablet. **THE PROCESS:** Danielle found inspiration in a 1926 Singer patching machine, traditionally used for shoe repair – "it was quite the workout."

NO. 11 // WHO: Hollie Dzama, artist. **WHERE:** Montreal. **ON HER PLATE:** Diverse projects include cartoon voiceovers, painting, and music. **THIS DESIGN:** "I wanted to re-create the shoes as something I could wear to a KISS concert."

NO. 12 // WHO: Tyler K Rauman, artist. **WHERE:** Montreal. **THE FINISHING TOUCH:** "And then finally, to completely remove any sense of the shoes being wearable or inviting, the insides, which are normally a pleasant, towel-like fabric, were filled with cement, sparkles, and gloss (which I only slightly regretted when I had to ship them in the mail from Montreal to Toronto)."

NO. 14

NO. 15

NO. 16

NO. 13 // WHO: Renata Morales, fashion designer. **WHERE:** Montreal. **SHOUT-OUT:** "The embroideries on the shoes were made in Haiti by the Jeremie Les Abricots co-op, a project in the works with my beloved friend Regine Chassagne."

NO. 14 // WHO: Sonja Ahlers, author, artist. **WHERE:** Toronto. **RECENT PROJECTS:** "I've spent the past two months trying to track down a pair of Kork-Ease sandals. Super epic verging on total embarrassment." **THIS DESIGN:** Angora abstract-expressionist Keds.

NO. 15 // WHO: Angie Johnson, designer, Norwegian Wood. **WHERE:** Montreal. **INSPIRATION:** Reptilian armour in metallics and pearls. **SHE GIVES AND SHE GIVES:** "I discovered after making them that I really wanted to keep them...."

NO. 16 // WHO: Allyson Mitchell, fibre artist. **WHERE:** Toronto. **THE TROY MCCLURE FACTOR:** You might know her from such acclaimed installations as *Lady Sasquatch* and *Brainchild*, which toured across Canada.

BROKEN
frames

art direction & styling // Pascale Georgiev
photography // Arden Wray
set design & graphic design // Vanda Daftari
assistant styling // Gabrielle Gagné
hair & makeup // Liz Furlong
modelling // Sadaf & Ming
featuring pieces by 2010 Fashion Pop winner
Natasha Thomas from her line By Thomas

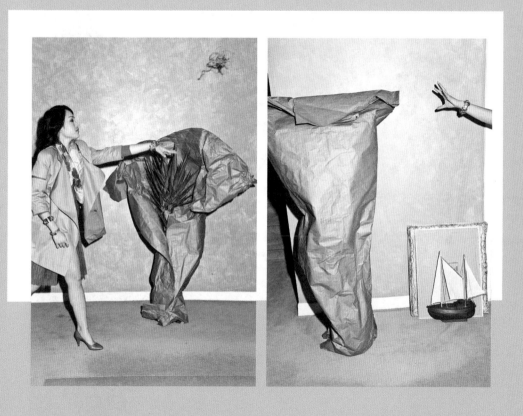

The Elusive Mr. Frederick:

Searching for the story behind Hollywood's naughtiest lingerie label

text by Sonya Abrego   art by Alexandra Barton

I believe you MUST look
truly feminine to enjoy life.
Our aids to nature assure
that look INSTANTLY!
Order yours now.
Mr. Frederick

Don't look INSIDE
unless you love
daring Hollywood
Fashions!

OF COURSE I'D HEARD OF FREDERICK'S. I knew they were one of the first popular producers of risqué lingerie in the United States. I knew they'd been around for ages, and that they were still operating. I would even see the odd item fetch a high price on the vintage market, but that had been the extent of my knowledge and, for a long time, it never occurred to me to look for more. That is until I found *Frederick's of Hollywood 1947–1973: 26 Years of Mail Order Seduction.*

Published in 1973, the coffee table book reproduces selections from the original illustrated catalogues with little editorializing. Expertly rendered figure drawings of girls, flawless and curvy to the point of ridiculousness, wear garments with names like "Treasure Chest," "Air Borne," or "Double Dipper." Alongside their half-dressed sisters were ladies fully-but-no-less-provocatively clad in complete outfits with equally enticing names like "Danger Ahead" and "Temptress."

The lack of photography, though unusual today, was quite common up to the middle of the 20th century. According to Jane Farrell-Beck, former professor of textiles and clothing at Iowa State University

and co-author of *Uplift: The Bra in America,* photographic lingerie ads began to appear as early as the '30s, but line drawings were still used well into the '60s. She suspects that, in the case of Frederick's, models may have been apprehensive to be photographed in something so blatantly sexy.

With up to four typefaces *per page,* text angling in every direction, and myriad figures floating in empty space, the layout was a modernist's nightmare. There were text boxes, exclamation points!!!!, and haphazardly sprinkled disembodied busts. It made me want to re-evaluate everything I learned about pop art, Dada, and constructivist collage. Laura Gottwald, the designer responsible for the 1973 graphic compilation, was drawn in for similar reasons: "I had never bought it or worn it," she explains. "I was fascinated with these tacky graphics, the way the type was set, the ridiculous copy, the style of illustration – they're so funky and goofy."

And then there was Mr. Frederick himself. Debonair in portrait form, he floated over the pages with tips like, "The Hollywood look is the look he'll love," or "Keep the love in your life and the life in your love!"

Building a Better Bustline

Little is known about Mellinger's original design team, and it has been suggested that it included an industrial designer from the army corps of engineers. These lingerie novelties are considered Frederick's of Hollywood firsts:

Mr. Frederick says:
"YOU'LL NEVER SUE ME FOR NON-SUPPORT!"

FUNDERWEAR!

"Heaven's Helper"
The Padded Bra (1947)
Though padded bras inspire mixed emotions about deception, they were undeniably encouraged by Frederick's. Why settle for the bustline you're born with? According to Mr. Frederick, "The right bra spells the difference between sag and surge."

The Thong Panty (1981)
Interestingly, this design was released just before Frederick's began to tone down their image in 1985. Previously only for strippers, the thong was marketed to a wider audience and, to the horror of parents of teens everywhere, became insanely popular.

SCENE 4
DON'T have a droopy aging bust!
AFTER
BEFORE
To give a higher bustline, plus glamorous cleavage to the small to average bosom . . . these wonder-workers feature stitched-in push-up pads.

PADDED HIPS AND SEAT!

"Rising Star"
The Push-Up Bra (1948)
Hailed as a technological masterpiece, the idea is to push breasts in and up. Frederick's illustrated schematics show little has changed in the principle of this design.

"Living End"
The Padded Girdle (1951)
Also known as "fanny pads," girdles were pretty common mid-century to smooth lines and slim silhouettes. But not *too* slim; thinner girls could fill out their girdles with "miracle" foam rubber pads that slipped into pockets over the hips and "derrière."

"Blow-Ups"
The Inflatable Bra
It's not more ridiculous than anything else, but seeing a model (in a rare photograph) with her chin tilted down and lips around a straw in her bra is just too funny. The straw was included for free.

The man behind the women

Frederick Mellinger was born in New York in 1914. He worked in the lingerie retail business as a teenager, but it was a stint in the U.S. Army that honed his focus. Mellinger's fellow troops told him they wished their girlfriends would wear the same alluring underpinnings as the popular pin-up girls of the time. He took their directions and, upon returning to the U.S. in 1946, started his business as a lingerie retailer in New York, specializing in provocative styles. A short year later, he moved westward and named his company Frederick's of Hollywood.

Along with his ability to crystallize a good idea, Mellinger also understood the effectiveness of advertising. His company's saucy ads were featured in romance and movie magazines, as well as more mainstream publications like *Seventeen*, *Harper's Bazaar*, and *Ladies' Home Journal*. He marketed to men, suggesting sexy lingerie was a great gift, while offering mail order discretion for the more bashful. By the mid-'50s, the company was manufacturing and business was booming.

Mellinger appeared as "Mr. Frederick" in the catalogues, his portraits resembling actors' headshots. Other times he was captured in action: lending a creative hand, taking pictures of models, or measuring them in what look like re-enactments of dress fittings – "Frederick measures whistle-waist of French model in his own glamour design." His authoritative expertise didn't end with fashion. Fatherly recommendations and witty quips often strayed into the territory of romantic advice that could be summed up like this: Frederick's of Hollywood makes women look better; if they look better they will feel better, they will have more success in life and love, and they will be more pleasing to men.

Advertising juggernaut and post-feminist minefield – this was definitely part of the Frederick's puzzle.

Location, location, location

What did it mean to be "of Hollywood" in 1947? This was the oft-cited "Golden Era" when a few major film studios (concentrated in Los Angeles) created most of the public's cinematic entertainment. Although the West Coast didn't have the same historical connection to the garment trade and fashion industries as the East, it was not only catching up – it was innovating. Desirable styles capitalized on the novelty of modern casual dress and leisured lifestyles connected to West Coast living. This was true for clothing as well as lingerie.

"Frederick's was by no means the only one to put Hollywood in their name or who thrived in California," Farrell-Beck explains. "It was a magnet for jobs in munitions factories in World War II, there were lots of women going out there again, swelling the potential audience for bras ... and [California] did have a particular style, the outdoorsy style, sporty style that adapted quite well to American women, who wanted clothing that was comfortable." Along with the established glamour of the film industry, this presented a highly profitable marketing opportunity.

Living the fantasy of a stylish, carefree lifestyle meant fitting into a particular physical mold. Farrell-Beck found that more

think there is a thing I welcome like my Frederick's catalog.... What would we do without you?" Such affirmations work to convince the reader that, in buying this product, she really could reap the same rewards as the Hollywood inside track. The proof? They also include comparable

women in California were wearing bras than in other parts of the U.S. New clothing designs were more modern and flexible, and undergarment design followed suit: "Bras made it possible for different kinds of shaping to be achieved. In the era of the corsets there were limited shapes ... you could squash the breasts or you could cradle from below. Whereas there's rounding, pointing, exposing the nipple, push-up, all of those things are possible with bras." Frederick's designs did all of this and more – squeezing, padding, or pushing to make sure wearers could fit into all the latest styles.

But more than geography or design, Hollywood was about fame and fortune. Frederick's catalogues featured testimonials from actresses and models, some famous (like Jayne Mansfield), but most not. All are full of rousing praise: "It was a Frederick's dress that helped me get my very first role in the movies," and, "I don't

testimonials from "regular" American women. Mrs. Kathleen Morgan from Clear Fork, West Virginia, exclaims, "I was wearing a Frederick's of Hollywood creation when I met my future husband. That stunning date dress caught his eye, and his love."

It's a clever tactic, comparing a homemaker from Iowa to a beautiful actress; it encourages the fantasy of Hollywood and offers vicarious participation through consumption. Looking back, Gottwald likes "the socialist concept that even women that lived in trailer parks could improve their love life and make their man love them by wearing these clothes and turning him on. It was kind of sweet... [Mellinger] really felt he had a mission."

Using language incongruously borrowed from the women's liberation movement of the '60s and '70s, he asserts, "I knew there *had* to be ways to reproportion women and give every lovable one of them EQUAL OPPORTUNITY in the eyes of men!"

Fake it till you make it

The gender dynamic played out in these pages is disconcerting. Readers are repeatedly told that the fashions will make them appealing to men, which is what they should want. It's brazenly sexist. Not to mention the specious implication that having a "balanced" figure means having a big bust, tiny waist, full hips, and long legs. But the sense of humour is palpable, too, and the celebration of sexuality-without-prudery is refreshing. Gottwald didn't feel at all conflicted about immortalizing Frederick's brand of publicity in the early '70s: "I thought it was fun. I didn't really have terribly strong ideas about it from a feminist point of view. I mean, I was already a feminist... and I never felt that displaying my body or dressing seductively was un-liberated. Ever."

The drawings are provocative, yet much of the copy is written in a conspiratorial tone as if "us girls" (and Mr. Frederick, of course) are all in on a joke. The padding and lifting are treated matter-of-factly as though the reader should know perfectly well that this kind of beauty is a construction. Fakery is more than just okay, it's encouraged and it's what women do to look good. In a world of photo-manipulated deception it's nice to see something unapologetically, gloriously fake. There's honesty in the artifice.

Mr. Frederick retired in 1984 and passed away in 1990. The company still exists, but with waning success. Farrell-Beck thinks it might have to do with the nature of the product itself: "I don't really think the very sharply contoured bras at Frederick's are as suited to present-day styling. They had a very aggressive torpedo shape and in the '60s the rounding of cups started and persisted." Gottwald thinks that Frederick's trailblazing populist sex appeal has become mainstream: "I guess everybody took it away from them, it's sort of like Franklin D. Roosevelt taking the socialist party platform and then there was no need for the socialist party... there's no need for Mellinger anymore. Sexy attire is so acceptable and mainstream in 2011 — it exists from couture to inexpensive junior shops."

So where does that leave us?

I was hooked and went looking for more information, but it turned out there wasn't much more to find. The appeal of vintage and vintage-inspired style is only getting stronger, yet as more and more companies profit from heritage branding, for whatever reason Frederick's has not joined in. When I contacted the company they claimed that they didn't have much older material left. They confirmed what Gottwald noted in 1973: "All the original artwork had been lost or destroyed." While I'm not saying that we need to bring back the bullet bra, it seems a shame not to value this material as a historical and design archive. The fact is, lingerie tends to remain subordinate in fashion history. Not that it wasn't essential in creating the silhouettes, but according to Farrell-Beck, "the outerwear takes new shapes and then the lingerie responds to it." If lingerie is already given short shrift in fashion history and Frederick's was actively targeting a lower-middle-class customer, perhaps there wasn't enough cultural cachet to make it serious fodder for design historians.

Not long ago I was rummaging through a vintage shop bin full of lingerie and came across a Frederick's bra. It wasn't especially wild, no conical padding or exposed nipples. It was black lace and pretty with that bright pink label — but I didn't really need the bra, I wanted more of the story. I guess that despite my pushing and squeezing, I would never fill it out. ⊠

more of you
SHOWS
NOW!

FASHION IS
HISTORY

06

THE THING ABOUT FLIGHT ATTENDANT UNIFORMS is that they have changed so radically, so often, in such a short time. But the thing about men's suits is that their origins go all the way back to medieval knights. Winston Churchill wanted to see the home front in lipstick. Wondering how to navigate the complicated path of human history? Just look at what we wore.

Whether through object analysis or anthropology, we can focus our understanding of the past through the lens of fashion. Materials change according to availability and need. Styles reflect the evolution of gender equality and highlight entrenched ideas about masculinity; they cling to an age or a monarch or a culture; they reflect our values in times of war and become

the anchor for political protest. When we view fashions in the context of the conditions from which they emerged (and with the perspective time allows), trend transforms into collective cultural commentary.

Fashion doesn't exist in a vacuum. Created by people influenced by a particular set of circumstances, ideas, and experiences, clothes are necessarily informed by their age. Documenting fashion history preserves an accumulation of those ideas – we can borrow from the past to make meaningful, layered statements about our own time, and to form our ideas of the future. Plus, it's got bullet bras, bubble helmets, and two battleships' worth of corset stays. How did we never learn this in high school? ✗

DRESS BLUES

The military's covert operation in men's closets

TEXT BY ROBERT EVERETT-GREEN

ILLUSTRATED BY CHRISTOPHER MORRIS

THERE ARE GOOD AND LESS GOOD WAYS to wear a hat, and I think I know a few of the better ones. But when I tried on a snappy fedora in a Toronto men's store, the sales clerk took the hat from my hands and told me that my way of putting it on was "ridiculous." I had put it on from the brow end, the way Fred MacMurray does in *Double Indemnity*. The clerk showed me the "right" way, by slipping it on his own head from the back. "That's basic British Army stuff!" he said. I should have told the sergeant major that I hadn't enlisted yet. But he was only giving me the kind of instruction meted out even more freely to any man who shops for the central signifier of dressy menswear, the business suit.

Shop at all seriously for a suit, and you enter a realm of things you must always or never do. Never button a bottom button or show less than half an inch of shirt-sleeve. Always wear pants that break once on the way down, and that cover roughly two-thirds of the shoe. Ignore the rules, and accept the punishment: being ridiculous.

The rules are laid down in virtually every guide to menswear, including designer Alan Flusser's lavish 2002 book, *Dressing the Man: Mastering the Art of Permanent Fashion*. Note the astounding certainty of the subtitle: *permanent fashion*. Flusser's rules aren't just for this season or this year, but for all time. And yet the suit isn't eternal: it has a definite history. Its immediate ancestor was a casual tweedy outfit worn by British toffs when shooting things for sport. That gradually moved into town, got spruced up with finer fabrics, and went into business.

The suit's military lineage isn't as obvious. You have to look back to the medieval suit of armour, or the military doublet that was part of the standard "suite" of clothes for 17th-century gentlemen. You have to examine the effects of three centuries of military uniforms on our ideas of what a "real man" should look like.

One suit to rule them all

"Without uniform, there is no discipline," said Frederick the Great, the 18th-century warrior king of Prussia. He was one of the first to put armies in uniform, and not just because it looked tidier. Frederick realized that clothes could reshape the minds of those obliged to wear them. Having to keep an elaborate outfit looking exactly the same as everyone else's forced a relentless attention to detail. Uniforms had to be cleaned, were expensive to replace, and displayed hierarchy at a glance. According to fashion historian Elisabeth Hackspiel-Mikosch, uniforms helped promote a new masculine identity based on "obedience, frugality, and discipline."

It helped that most uniforms were designed to cut a dashing figure on the field and in the ballroom. *The Whole Art of Dress!*, an anonymous guide published in 1830, devotes an entire chapter to a style analysis of European uniforms. Many sacrificed comfort and ease of motion for a sleek design. In William M. Thackeray's novel *The Luck of Barry Lyndon*, the young hero is fiercely envious of men from his town who wear the king's uniform. "A red jacket would mightily become me!" he moans. Many felt the same way.

Brooks Brothers started as a ready-to-wear civilian clothier in 1818, and began making uniforms 17 years later. It has since kept a foot in both camps, designing civilian suits for the likes of Richard Nixon and Stephen Colbert and launching a new line of U.S. Navy dress uniforms in 2004.

The measure of a man

A masculine uniform for civilians really took hold after the invention of the tape measure in the early 19th century. As Norah Waugh notes in her 1964 book, *The Cut of Men's Clothes*, standardized measure led to cutting systems based on proportions of the body. These systems emulated the standardized cut of military uniforms. They also became the basis for the mass production of men's suits. Their "geometric logic," as Flusser puts it, is the basis for many common rules, such as the axiom that the length of a jacket should be half the distance from the back of the collar to the floor.

Shop at all seriously for a suit, and you enter a realm of things you must always or never do.

By the second half of the 18th century, says Hackspiel-Mikosch, the masculine ideal displayed in military dress had seeped into civilian culture: "Men began to adopt the aesthetics of soldiers' uniforms." In many cases, they used the same tailors. Hawkes, a leading English clothier, "was established as a military tailor and dictator of regimental uniform regulations in 1888," says the website of the successor company, Gieves & Hawkes. "Officers were told to get their uniform from Hawkes," the site explains – "otherwise they would be 'out of line.'" Gieves & Hawkes remains a fixture on Savile Row (the centre of British menswear), and still dictates to stock traders and executives.

By the time the tape measure came along, epaulets and bright colours had vanished from most uniforms, and menswear had become sober and dark. The rising business class associated a drab look with discipline, frugality, and reliability. The cut and colours of their clothes had changed since Frederick the Great's time, but the mentality had not.

The cut of personality

Complete uniformity, however, can't always withstand the desire to stand out. An issue of the English magazine *Punch* from May 1942 includes a satiric account of two officer cadets spending double their official allotment for

uniforms from a private tailor, reasoning that "extra smartness may mean earlier promotion, with a consequent increase in pay." The designer Hardy Amies, who served in British intelligence during World War II, used loden fabric imported from Austria to lend his uniform panache, and even designed brass buttons embossed with "a pansy resting on its laurels."

Similarly, a businessman shopping for a suit can bend the rules. Nadia Serraf, an image consultant who advises business types at Brooks Brothers in Toronto, says her clients shop to match their position in the office hierarchy, or a spot just above. Top executives go for high-class

The mentality of the uniform, with three centuries of social history behind it, remains embedded in the culture of the business suit.

conservative cuts, she says, but sometimes flaunt their power through flashy ties and collars. Middle managers "don't want to attract attention," and "starters" want a slim, tailored fit to show off their gym-tooled physiques. Like *Punch's* officer cadets, they figure that extra smartness may mean earlier promotion.

Of course, one suit can look very different, and serve different occasions, with changes of shirt, tie, and pocket-square. Variety is possible, within the general colour tyranny of grey and dark blue suitings. But the mentality of the uniform, with three centuries of social history behind it, remains embedded in the culture of

the business suit. It's held in place by corporate hierarchy and the need to express a sober, disciplined work ethic. This is the reigning dress culture of the 1 percent: those rich enough to do anything they want — except in this sphere.

Surveying the standardization of men's dress over two centuries, Waugh asks whether the fitting of a suit need be "just another engineering problem," in which cloth is fitted to body, as body is fitted to corporation. "Hasn't something been lost, the old creative spirit stifled, all endearing extravagances ruled out?" she asks. Yes, and that was the point. Without uniform, there is no discipline. ✠

TINKER, TAILOR, SOLDIER, STYLE

THE GORGE VS. BUTTON STANCE

Menswear terminology is often more historical than intuitive and can even change according to your geographical location. Ask for a "vest" in New York and you'll get a sleeveless, buttoned garment to wear between your shirt and jacket. Ask for the same thing in London and you'll get an undershirt – because the British term for what you want is "waistcoat" (pronounced "weskit"). Here are a few terms that, produced at the right moment, will make more than your outfit look smart.

The "gorge" is the point on a jacket where the collar meets the lapel, usually marked by a notch (or a "peak" if the notch tilts upward). The "button stance" is the position of the top front fastening button, relative to the natural waist. Many men say "gorge" – as in, "that jacket's low gorge is so '80s" – when they really mean "button stance." No, okay, they don't actually say that, but they're thinking it – and even if they're not, you will, now.

THE DINNER JACKET

SIX-ON-FOUR

Americans call it "formal" and the English call it "dress." Americans (who first named the tuxedo for the New York club where the English style was introduced) like their dinner jackets white and their tuxedos black. Brits prefer the opposite. But the French (why not?), who call the black version *un smoking* (after the English term from the mid-19th century), decide whether your jacket is *un smoking* Deauville or Capri depending on the collar style. Well, unless you're on the French Riviera, where it's called a Monte Carlo. Got it?

Double-breasted jackets have two columns of paired buttons, with the top row flaring out toward the shoulders. Six-on-four means there are six buttons in total, with four in rows that may be involved in keeping the jacket closed. But only two of those buttons actually have a hole, and most menswear gurus insist that only the upper one should be fastened. Four-on-two means there are four buttons in total, with two in the buttoning row, and again only one gets buttoned. But all double-breasteds have a secret weapon: a hidden inside button, to keep the coat's overlapping front from slipping out of line.

THE
TICKET
POCKET

Along with the pockets found on either side of a sport or suit jacket, there is occasionally a third, smaller one above the right-hand pocket, known as the "ticket pocket." This was introduced in the 19th century in tandem with the rising popularity of rail travel, allowing gentlemen travelers to keep their tickets handy and separate from items in other pockets. Unless, of course, they were taking the train to the theatre....

SURGEON'S
CUFFS

The buttons on the sleeve cuff of a sport or suit jacket are purely decorative, and most are sewn straight onto the fabric. Surgeon's cuffs, however, are functional buttons – a souvenir of the pre-Pasteur days when it was common for a doctor to remove an appendix without changing out of street clothes. These days, surgeon's cuffs are more likely a sign of bespoke tailoring than a willingness to roll up those pricey sleeves and do a messy job.

THE
HACKING
JACKET

In the 19th century, the English hacking jacket was developed for casual horseback riding (or "hacking"). Usually made of a sturdy fabric such as tweed, it had a high button closure for warmth and rear vent(s) for ease of movement. Slanted pockets (with flaps to keep stuff in and rain out) offered better access while riding. Most single-lapelled jackets without matching pants are still called sport coats, and a slanted pocket is always called a "hacking pocket." Saddle up, old chap.

THE
TROUSER
BREAK

The "break" is the beginning of a fold in the front of the trouser near the ankle. It's caused by cutting the pant slightly too long, so that the top of the shoe forces the fabric above it to buckle slightly. The idea is to eliminate any gap between shoe and trouser when standing or walking. For the most common length (a "medium" break), the back of your pant hem should stop about an inch from the floor.

BEAUTY AS DUTY

PATRIOTISM, PATRIARCHY, AND PERSONAL STYLE DURING WARTIME

TEXT BY HAILEY SIRACKY // PHOTOGRAPHY BY CARL W. HEINDL

STYLING BY G. STEGELMANN // HAIR AND MAKEUP BY BELLA B. // MODELLING BY HILLARY PREDKO

JULIA ROGERS'S FIRST-EVER GROWN-UP BALL wasn't quite what she'd hoped for. In 1942, her soldier father took 16-year-old Julia and her mother to the Annual Regimental Ball. Just one year after Britain's Utility Clothing Scheme was implemented, there was nary a ball gown in sight. "All the women in short dresses," says Julia of the occasion. "It was disappointing."

Her own dress was all practicality. Her mother, a dressmaker by trade, had fashioned the frock for Julia as she did all of her family's clothing. Cherry red, lightweight, and easily washable, with a sweetheart neckline and a flowing skirt that came just past the knees, the dress was undeniably pretty – but hardly the elaborate gown one would expect to see (or wear) at such a fancy occasion.

Julia, who grew up in a family in which money was scarce, was used to having homemade clothing intended to last for years. "When the war broke out I had all the clothes I needed," she says. "My mother made my dresses with enough seam allowances and hem lengths to make alterations as I grew." When the British government introduced a system of clothes rationing during World War II, Julia hardly felt the blow. For others, however, the new system of policing the amount of clothing, fabric, and shoes civilians could purchase was an enormous adjustment.

The making of a pretty propaganda

Britain's Utility Clothing Scheme was put into action on June 1, 1941. Fabric was at a premium

BY URGING WOMEN TO MAINTAIN SOME FOCUS ON "NORMAL" THINGS LIKE FASHION AND BEAUTY, THE CAMPAIGN WAS DESIGNED TO HELP THEM FEEL GROUNDED AMIDST THE CHAOS OF WAR.

worldwide, and anything available needed to be put toward the war effort. The scheme was carried out by Britain's Board of Trade, under the direction of Prime Minister Winston Churchill – but Churchill was reluctant to restrict civilian dress. Partial to waistcoats and often seen looking dapper in bow ties and bowlers, Churchill understood the social and psychological relationships people had with clothing. He knew that clothes rationing would be detrimental to civilian morale.

Morale was of the utmost importance in Britain from the beginning of World War II until its end because, unlike World War I, this war required the involvement of the entire adult population. World War II, or "The People's War," saw men and women performing both civilian and military duties, and Britain's government recognized that success in what would surely be a long struggle required careful attention to civilian confidence. It wasn't until Britain experienced an extreme clothing shortage, in tandem with a serious economic downturn in 1940, that Churchill would finally declare clothes rationing a necessity. But even before the drastic measure of the Utility Clothing Scheme, Britain had embraced another fashion-centred directive aimed at civilians on the home front.

Beauty as Duty was an official propaganda campaign targeting women, encouraging them to continue to pursue fashion and beauty despite the hardships that they had to endure, and

discouraging the notion that devoting attention to their appearances was trivial or petty. By urging women to maintain some focus on "normal" things like fashion and beauty, the campaign was designed to help them feel grounded amid the chaos of war. Alongside this, the government was addressing the unsettling new reality of women taking on what had traditionally been "men's" work. Morale-centred propaganda campaigns were hardly unusual, but this campaign was aimed specifically at women, a logical result of the unusually high percentage of the female population involved in home front war efforts.

At first, women's involvement in the war was voluntary, but the December 1941 passing of the National Services Act made Britain the first country to conscript women into war-related jobs. While they did not have to bear arms, they worked in factories making munitions, uniforms, and parachutes, or in state-run canteens or child-care centres. All women under the age of 51 were required to register for war work, and by 1943, between 80 and 90 percent were doing their part to support the war effort. Julia herself served in the Women's Royal Naval Service (WRNS) from March 1944 until September 1945. With this level of involvement, and with the majority of able-bodied men away from home, it was not surprising that the ideas of home front morale and the morale of women became almost interchangeable.

Keep your BEAUTY on duty!

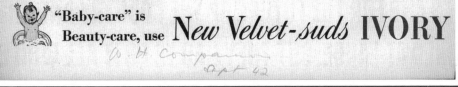

Give your skin Ivory care, Doctors advise!

Defensive care for DRY SKIN!

Keep your skin looking its loveliest even when you're busiest. Give it this *correct care* approved by skin specialists:

1. Use a mild soap. Dry skins tend to be sensitive, to irritate easily. What *gentler* care could your beauty have than that advised by doctors for baby's sensitive skin...New Ivory Soap!

2. Use lukewarm water, never hot. And a *soft* washcloth. Plus Ivory's quick, luxurious lather, it's *so* mild. Then *lukewarm* rinses.

3. Apply lightly a little cold cream. For summer's probably left your skin flaky-dry. And remember this: Ivory contains *no* dye, medication or strong perfume that might be irritating. Get Guest Size Ivory. Most convenient for toilet use.

OILY SKIN? Take the offensive!

You can recapture that cool, lovely look for your complexion. But your skin needs special care, persistent care. Skin specialists approve this cleansing method:

1. Cleanse thoroughly. Work Ivory's thick, lovely lather well into your face and neck, using a *rough* washcloth and lukewarm water.

2. Rinse well. Warm water, then cold. Repeat your Ivory lathering. Go after those oilier areas; your hairline, forehead, nose, chin. Then another rinse.

3. Do this cleansing as often as 3 times daily. See how delightfully smooth and fresh Ivory's mildness leaves your skin. Compare the low price of Guest Size Ivory with that of your present beauty soap.

More doctors advise New Ivory Soap for your skin, and baby's, than all other brands of soap together.

99⁴⁴/₁₀₀ % PURE IT FLOATS

TRADEMARK REG. U.S. PAT. OFF.
PROCTER & GAMBLE

"Baby-care" is Beauty-care, use *New Velvet-suds* **IVORY**

Getting the message to the masses

The Beauty as Duty concept first appeared in popular advertising. In December of 1939, an advertisement for Evan Williams Shampoo was accompanied by the caption "Hair Beauty is a Duty, too!" It was already a woman's job to serve her country and her family; cosmetics ads began to promote maintaining one's personal appearance as another responsibility women had to fulfill. It was an idea that made a lot of marketing sense. Manufacturers wanted to continue selling their products during a time of international crisis, and like everyone else, they shared the desire for the Allies to win the war. It was natural to connect their products to patriotism, and mainstream media's encouragement of consumption helped validate an activity that may have otherwise been considered frivolous or unnecessary.

Lipsticks, soaps, and other cosmetics came with slogans such as "Beauty Is Your Duty" or emphasized the message that it was a woman's "duty to stay beautiful." These ideas were so strongly discursively linked that beauty and resisting the enemy seemed two sides of the same coin. British cosmetics company Yardley ran advertisements in 1942 with the heading "No Surrender," which claimed that ideal women honoured "the subtle bonds between good looks and good morale."

Concerned about civilian confidence on the home front and convinced of the transformative power of fashion, Churchill grabbed hold of the Beauty as Duty idea. He began to turn it into official propaganda, and manufacturers were eager to cooperate. A year before the Utility Clothing Scheme was instituted, the British government assembled a group of editors from various women's magazines to form a committee that would consult on the official message of Beauty as Duty. Their job was to ensure that the new policy was "relayed to women in accessible and appropriate ways." Now, instead of appearing exclusively in advertising, the concept became an editorial mainstay in fashion magazines like *Women's Own* and *Vogue*, as well as in publications like the photojournalistic magazine *Picture Post*.

Putting a little lipstick on a brave face

Between his hesitation to ration clothing and his promotion of Beauty as Duty, Churchill clearly believed aesthetics were somehow crucial to success in the war effort. His

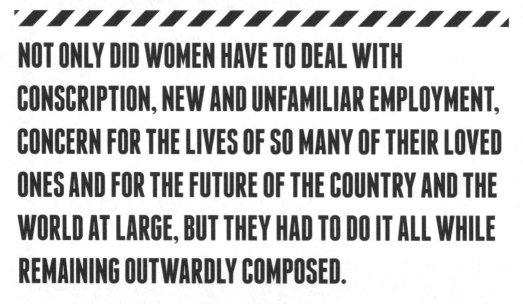

NOT ONLY DID WOMEN HAVE TO DEAL WITH CONSCRIPTION, NEW AND UNFAMILIAR EMPLOYMENT, CONCERN FOR THE LIVES OF SO MANY OF THEIR LOVED ONES AND FOR THE FUTURE OF THE COUNTRY AND THE WORLD AT LARGE, BUT THEY HAD TO DO IT ALL WHILE REMAINING OUTWARDLY COMPOSED.

THE "BRAVE FACE" SHE ASSUMED WAS NOT SYMBOLIC, BUT PHYSICALLY MANIFESTED WITH THE APPLICATION OF LIPSTICK THAT SHE FELT WOULD HELP HER ENDURE WHAT WAS OTHERWISE UNBEARABLE.

opposition to clothes rationing came from his conviction that the government should not interfere with something as personal as "a man and his wardrobe," demonstrating his belief that a person's clothing served a far greater purpose than simply keeping covered and warm. While it was an unusual concern to focus on at such a time, it was also quite astute.

Personal appearance – enhanced through clothing, hygiene, and, in this case, cosmetics – is intensely linked to self-perception. Pat Kirkham, a design historian, author, and professor at the Bard Graduate Center for Studies in the Decorative Arts in New York, has written extensively on this topic. Kirkham describes a woman named Nella Last who kept a diary throughout the war. In one entry, Last writes about using "too bright lipstick" that "on dim days makes the corners turn up when the lips will not keep smiling." The "brave face" she assumed was not symbolic but physically manifested with the application of lipstick that she felt would help her endure what was otherwise unbearable.

Kirkham explains that this emphasis on giving the impression of being "normal," paired with having to take on new and difficult responsibilities, required British women to "make enormous sacrifices while appearing as if they had not done so." Not only did women have to deal with conscription, new and unfamiliar employment, and concern for the lives of so many of their loved ones and for the future of the country and the world at large, but they had to do it all while remaining outwardly composed. To ask someone to appear untroubled during a time of such turmoil and uncertainty is almost absurd, but conversely, it also has the potential to be incredibly buoying.

It isn't easy to do without, but to do without *well* and give the impression that little has changed offers necessary courage to one living in an otherwise terrifying situation. Women had no power over the volatile state of the world, and after conscription was introduced, they also lost control over which jobs they held and where these jobs took them; if they could succeed in appearing strong and unruffled on the outside, perhaps on the inside they might also feel capable of succeeding in the midst of the uncertainty that had become their lives. Fashion was no panacea, but during a time when everyone had worries in excess, it made sense to find comfort, composure, and reassurance wherever possible.

It is difficult to accept the idea that beauty, especially in the middle of a war, should be deemed a necessity – nor was the notion universally accepted at the time. A lot of women in wartime Britain found it difficult to reconcile their inclination toward frugal austerity with the widespread encouragement of beauty. In other countries, notably Germany and Australia, governments urged women to

Hair Beauty—
is a duty, too!

THE ETHICS OF BUYING BLACK MARKET MAKEUP WERE QUESTIONABLE, BUT DOING SO ALLOWED WOMEN TO DEFINE "NEED" IN THEIR OWN TERMS; BY TAKING SOMETHING LUXURIOUS AND TURNING IT INTO SOMETHING NECESSARY, THEY TOOK CONTROL OF ONE SMALL ASPECT OF AN OTHERWISE RATIONED AND REGIMENTED LIFE.

disregard style and present themselves simply and plainly. British women struggled to make peace with their conflicting desires. Indulging in fashion during a time when every last bit of material and energy might be better used supporting the war effort was incongruous.

Although appearance was a concern, clothing was not to be overly extravagant or ostentatious. Women acknowledged that there was a difference between keeping up appearances and being frivolous. The Beauty as Duty campaign redefined concepts of necessity, triviality, and decorum by changing beauty from a matter of individual choice into a public concern. Items such as corsets, civilian hats, makeup, and nail polish were so important to women and such a fixture in women's culture that, despite clothes rationing, the government was willing to set important materials aside to ensure their production.

Frivolity, too, was redefined as women began turning to the black market for stockings and lipstick. The ethics of buying black-market makeup were questionable, but doing so allowed women to define "need" in their own terms; by taking something luxurious and turning it into something necessary,

they took control of one small aspect of an otherwise rationed and regimented life.

Aesthetics, ambivalence, and the luxury of hindsight

Although the positive effects the movement may have had on women's attitudes toward their situations are clear, one cannot overlook that a campaign like this suggests both a condescension to and objectification of women. One of the ideas surrounding Beauty as Duty was that the good spirits of men depended on the good looks of the women in their lives. The same Evan Williams Shampoo ad that claimed "Hair Beauty is a duty, too!" explained that "the men of the services on leave will expect and deserve it."

Another concern this discourse was intended to address was that women's conscription into factory work would lead to their being "masculinized." Before the war, it was unheard of for women to do "men's" work, and their doing so was unnerving to some. Beauty as Duty drew attention to femininity and ensured that it remained a central focus in their lives despite the fact that so many women now spent most of their time in the "male world."

THE POWER OF FASHION IS OFTEN UNDERESTIMATED OR MISUNDERSTOOD, AND A LOVE OF CLOTHING IS TOO FREQUENTLY WRITTEN OFF AS SHALLOW OR SUPERFICIAL. BEAUTY AS DUTY RECOGNIZED THE POTENTIAL FOR FASHION TO FUNCTION AS A WAY TO GENUINELY LIFT SPIRITS AND BUILD CONFIDENCE.

A *Ladies' Home Journal* article published in 1943 remarked that it was evidence of "the free democratic way of life that you have succeeded in keeping your femininity – even though you are doing a man's work!" But if these concerns were a motivation for the Beauty as Duty campaign, they were not its central focus.

The directive, at its core, was aimed at making it all right for women to feel good about themselves, and at encouraging small indulgences and comforts in lives that were otherwise full of sacrifice, in the hopes that boosting their collective self-esteem would help the nation win the war. Kirkham argues that "makeup, corsets and attractive clothes, hairstyles and accessories meant different things to different women; they also had multiple meanings for individual women. Among other things, they brought the comfort of familiarity and continuities, memories of times past, signified femininity and played a part in constructing confident 'fronts' that helped boost individual and collective morale."

Kirkham's words encapsulate many people's ambivalence about this historical moment – why one can find it difficult to be opposed to Beauty as Duty despite the fact that certain aspects of it allude to patriarchal subordination. Yet the campaign is also an acknowledgement of women's changing roles and responsibilities, and an attempt to ease this transition. The power of fashion is often underestimated or misunderstood, and a love of clothing is too frequently written off as shallow or superficial. Beauty as Duty recognized the potential for fashion to function as a way to genuinely lift spirits and build confidence.

Fashion is what stands out most in Julia's recollections of the Regimental Ball. Although growing up she was rarely in the position to afford luxuries herself, the dresses and uniforms at the ball remain bright in her mind. "If not as festive as in peacetime, it was still a grand sight," she remembers. "All of the soldiers in their most formal of outfits ... navy blue and scarlet with plenty of gold braid to brighten things up." A few dances and a fancy cocktail later, it was time for Julia to go. "After midnight the soldiers were allowed to change into less formal uniforms. They would have been quite relieved to be able to wear something more comfortable. My father needed to change too, so we would have gone home, but not to return. The best was now over anyway." ⊠

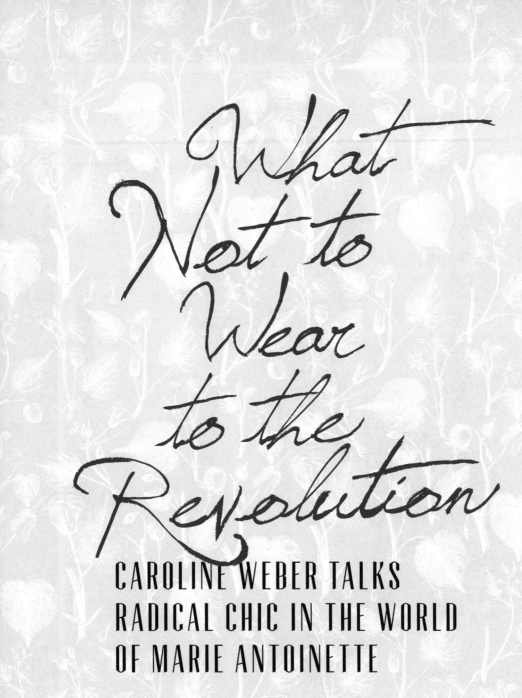

What Not to Wear to the Revolution

CAROLINE WEBER TALKS RADICAL CHIC IN THE WORLD OF MARIE ANTOINETTE

INTERVIEW BY RISA DICKENS

IT'S THE KNIFE BLADE FASHION SITS ON that makes it interesting. Every instant of this super visible and deceptively subtle form of communication teeters between superficial and crucial, silly and symbolic. As Louis the Sun King showed the world – and impressed upon his successors like Marie Antoinette – style, when combined with a good performance, can confer enough power to exert domination. And it can make people angry enough to get you killed.

When Marie Antoinette became a living symbol of the fresh and tenuous alliance between the Hapsburgs and the Bourbons (i.e. Austria and France) she was only 14 years old. When I was 14 I dyed my hair purple with Jell-O. In her world things were more intense. For someone in her position, sartorial revolution actually ripped at the fabric of social reality. She changed the role of queen by loosening her stays, ditching the panniers, and learning to ride forward on a horse, and then she invented a wildly visible hairstyle that seemed to compel imitation: the pouf.

The pouf is such a dramatic example of Marie Antoinette's "revolution in fashion" that the hairdo was the subject of Caroline Weber's talk in Montreal on February 15, 2007. In the basement of the Côte Saint-Luc Library, beneath the thick snow outside, library ladies wore rented 18th-century-ish dresses from Malabar, a costume shop down-town, and had photographs taken with the author in front of tables heaped with gourmet cake. Weber – a Harvard alum, Barnard professor, New York Times book critic, and author of Queen of Fashion: What Marie Antoinette Wore to the Revolution – was gracious and delighted when she took the mic, claiming this spot to be the most fun by far on her ongoing and, according to her husband, endless book tour.

The pouf took the powdered hair that was fashionable in the French court to elaborate new dimensions, telling three-foot stories on women's heads with horsehair, flowers, feathers, vegetables, wood supports, and more. The hairstyle is, it seems, the reason for the apocryphal invention of her most famous phrase. As far as historians like Weber can tell, Marie Antoinette never said anything like the words "let them eat cake." She did, however, use huge amounts of white flour in her hair to create a fashion that was a slap in the face to the starving citizens. Weber's book executes a careful tracing of the swooping movements in style and sentiment that surrounded this alternately loathed and well-loved queen.

You tell of a moment when Marie Antoinette, challenged on her fashion spending, said that if she quit, 200 people would be out of work. Yet she was also so completely unaware – like the silk merchants going broke waiting to find out from her what the new colour would be. Did she see her fashion as having economic implications?
Her lifelong favourite stylist, Rose Bertin, was somebody who, quite amazingly for a young, unmarried, initially illegally working woman, had tailors, seamstresses, lace makers, ribbon makers, and flower makers all in her pay. She was aware of the relations built up around her, certainly. To be a patron of the silk factories was sort of a royal duty for anyone at Versailles.

Even if it was rationalization for all the money she was spending, she was aware there was an economic dimension to it that was actually beneficial to the Parisian luxury industry. Always with her there's the amazing acumen and savvy on the one hand – reinventing her image all the time and coming up with avant-garde styles before anyone else and seeming to grasp what the political resonances would be – and yet she shows on the other hand complete obliviousness or lack of understanding of the negative consequences some of her choices would have. She was unaware that people were hating her for supporting other industries like Belgian muslin, for example.

The contradictions at the time seem all around crazy – especially that no one saw her revolutionary gestures as being part of the larger movement.

This blindness, this selective seeing, is not something we can just ascribe to Marie Antoinette. It's something the populace was guilty of, too. People often ask what surprised me the most, and it was totally that. She basically created the blueprint for female revolutionary dress and nobody gave her any credit! She was anticipating a lot and implicitly or explicitly advocating for it, and yet she's also accused of being the worst possible representative of the royalty. It's hugely contradictory. For me, one of the few places where someone puts their finger on this is in a piece by a feminist revolutionary activist named Olympe de Gouges. She wrote a text in 1791 called the *Declaration of the Rights of Woman* because women had been excluded from the *Declaration of the Rights of Man*, and she dedicated her declaration to the queen.

I was really careful in my book not to say that Marie Antoinette was a feminist and out to liberate women. She was out to liberate herself. But the broader meaning of that was really a broader defining of women's roles. Thinking that a woman could be defined for something other than her success as a mother, travelling alone to the city with her friends, being seen on the street in public – all that was pretty radical and anticipated a lot of later sexual revolutions. It's one of the things I love the most about her story in the end.

I wonder about clothing – costumes, corsets, pants – and the idea that it can allow gestures that will also allow different kinds of thought. I recently read a book about Chinese imperial history and fashion where the author suggests that some women who bound their daughters' feet might have viewed it as a way to convey information about the world. About it being a painful place.

Actually that does work well with Marie Antoinette. Her mother wasn't actively involved in much of her life before or after she left for Versailles, but became incredibly involved around that first fashion makeover. There was a message being conveyed to her in all that trousseau and training: "You will become a perfect French princess by looking this way and you'll have your teeth redone without anesthesia and you'll learn how to walk in these mincing, gliding steps and you'll learn to bear an incredibly painful and restrictive whalebone corset

and to wear these elaborate and difficult-to-navigate pannier dresses." Biographers like to talk about the fact that Marie Antoinette had no political training from Maria Theresa, and that's true – she never sat down and gave her lectures on policy or European politics. But she spent a lot of time educating her about clothes. So that is an interesting idea about cultural transmission.

It's almost like she learned about the Sun King system of rule-by-symbol but then didn't continue with the performance that might have maintained absolutist power, instead creating new styles non-queens could copy. You describe the little girls with white napkins done to look like poufs and the peasant dresses she adopts, and it seems different.
It's appealing to a different kind of public appreciation and respect. And to a different audience. Louis XVI's audience was his courtiers, the aristocracy, the people who had tried to displace him. He was constantly performing within a very restricted circle. Marie Antoinette was performing to a broader public, and the message was not "I'm a god," but "I'm more glamorous than you and you'll think about me and what I'm wearing all the time." It's a completely different kind of authority.

What makes me so sad is how much effort went into ultimately making herself so hated. There was a brief, shining moment when everyone was loving her, and then, as many people point out, they kept copying her even as they began to hate her. They turned against her then. The performance she had chosen was so ill-suited to the circumstances in which she found herself, and it wasn't going to protect her at all. It made her more fatally visible and loathed than she ever could have been just being childless and Austrian at Versailles.

To what extent did she inherit a shitstorm?
Looking back you can see for hundreds of years the moves the French royal government makes and the wedge that's being driven ever deeper between the populace and the royalty, the people on high and the people starving and eating dirt in the provinces. The inevitability seems rooted so far back I don't know that it's fair to say that even Madame de Pompadour and Louis XV could have done something to change it. But they recognized it and said, "Well, not our problem," and they turned it over to these completely inexperienced children with that phrase, *"Après moi, le déluge"* (after me, the flood), which is shocking in its irresponsibility. Marie Antoinette herself, the first time she went to Paris, wrote a letter to her mother saying, "It was so amazing and so touching to me that the people loved us even though they're so burdened with taxes." She understood the economic inequities but didn't make the next step to realize that her own spending was making things worse.

I think that's also the moment when she thought, "The people could love me, even if the courtiers don't."

Do you think there's information you can pass on, like a sartorial communication tip from Marie Antoinette? What not to do? Like Oprah's South Africa episode when she wore the giant diamond earrings....

In an age of blood diamonds! Yes – what not to wear to the revolution. I guess the communication tip is to be really thoughtful and thorough in what your fashion messages are saying. One of the people I often think about, someone who sought privilege and authority by being someone everyone watches, is Madonna. She parades around in unbelievably expensive clothes but preaches kabbalah and asceticism. Adopting the Malawi orphan and then buying him a £50,000 miniature BMW for his nursery is a really strange gesture. One of the things Marie Antoinette becomes such a glaring example of in hindsight is the danger of contradictions and inconsistencies in a PR campaign. I think it was definitely one of the things that laid her low. Even when Marie Antoinette started wearing revolutionary colours and drastically reduced her spending, it wasn't enough to stanch the tide.

Telling the queen's experience of the French Revolution through what was worn – small shifts like colours appearing and matching them up with moments of political and social change – makes the passing of time feel real in a way it rarely does in history books. What other stories can be unpacked from this perspective?

One of the stories that interests me is Queen Elizabeth I. She's someone who had to convey power through appearances. I'd like to know more about how she hit on that stiff, hieratic, statue-like, bejewelled, living icon style. One day she just desexualized herself and dehumanized herself with that white face paint. We know that wasn't hers to begin with – she grew up in wretchedness and it wasn't at all clear that she would become queen. The other person I'm really interested in is Coco Chanel and her relationship to the Nazis in World War II. Before she shut her ateliers down her last collection was super nationalist – it was the "gypsy" collection, but all in blue, white, and red – and she was dating an ultra-right French nationalist, basically a French fascist. These were the people who ended up welcoming the Germans in the name of preserving French purity. It's a period that's generally overlooked by her biographers.

There was an eyewitness when Chanel was dragged out of her hotel room at the Ritz in 1945 by the Committee for the Purification of Public Morals – the people who tarred and feathered women for sleeping with Nazis, a fate she escaped by having money and connections – but the committee nevertheless interrogated her and took her away. She had a gay male ballet dancer hiding from the committee in her closet as this was happening, and he described her as looking like Marie Antoinette walking with her head held high to the guillotine. ✄

Credits

illustration // Emma Rees

KHADI'S GOT A BRAND NEW BAG

THE EVOLVING IMAGE OF AN INDIAN FABRIC

TEXT BY HILLARY BRENHOUSE

LONG BEFORE RETAIL CHAINS and readymades, in the sprawling villages of pre-industrial India, the spinning wheel reigned supreme. *Khadi*, a coarse cotton fabric handwoven using homespun yarn, was then a popular country cloth produced by local peasants and artisans and worn by much of the rural population. That is until the early '20s and the arrival of Mohandas (a.k.a. Mahatma) Gandhi. His vision, philosophy, and nationalist passion transformed khadi into a potent symbol of freedom from British colonialism.

The crude fabric of Gandhi's *swaraj* (self-rule) movement was far from a fashion statement. Tying the country's subjugation to the availability of European mill cloth,

Gandhi implored the Indian nation to burn their foreign-made clothing and devote half an hour per day to spinning. Thus was the humble, indigenous textile reborn as a marker of economic self-sufficiency and political autonomy. Where, though, does khadi stand in an independent and modern India? What room is there in a globalized society for the homemade material now that its nationalist overtones have faded?

Spinning independence

"The householder has to revise his or her ideas of fashion and, at least for the time being, suspend the use of fine garments that are not always worn to cover the body,"

Gandhi writes in *Young India*. "He should train himself to see art and beauty in the spotlessly white khaddar and to appreciate its soft unevenness." Determined to re-clothe the entire country in the ordinary fabric, the nationalist leader imagined that khadi in its simplest form was capable of downplaying divisions in religion, region, occupation, and social status, and effecting communal unity.

Gandhi urged every man, woman, and child to personally take up the *charkha* (spinning wheel) and turn out their own cloth in an effort to establish a sovereign India: "If every person in the country takes a vow today to give some little time of his to spinning, within a very short time we may cease to depend on others for clothing our people and save six crores of rupees for the country." The road to India's freedom, he insisted, began with the rejection of British-made material.

Once the Congress Party lent their support to this ambitious undertaking, adopting khadi as their unofficial uniform, boycotts on the import and sale of foreign cloth were set in place. Public bonfires roared across the motherland, feeding heartily on Lancashire textiles. Patriotic attendees dressed in stark white khadi garments, re-baptized as adherents of the *swadeshi* (indigenous goods) alliance. The spinning wheel, India's new weapon in the fight for self-government, was placed at the centre of the national flag.

Previous exportation of vast quantities of cotton to Europe, however, meant handspun thread was scarce and quite costly. Frantic letters addressed to Gandhi from India's rural poor surged in, expressing a delicate dilemma: they simply could not afford to part with their cheap, imported, machine-spun yarn and mill cloth. Announcing that it would be far better to sport a mere loincloth stitched from khadi than to wear more ample apparel made overseas, Gandhi disrobed. In 1921, the "Father of the Nation" shed his traditional Indian kurta (long, loose shirt) and adopted a short dhoti (similar to a sarong) in its place, identifying himself with the lower classes.

The politics of fashion

For all of his vigour, Gandhi only partially achieved his vision. Critics accused him of attempting to slow the natural progress of the country, and, ultimately, Indian clothing practices remained highly diversified. The population may have espoused khadi as their national fabric, but they continued to underline their differences by dyeing the cloth, experimenting with style and ornamentation, and wearing finer varieties. Khadi silk and khadi wool, while conforming

to the technical definition of khadi, distanced their wearers from the rural poor who were normally dressed in thicker weaves.

Khadi never became the everyday dress of India's inhabitants post-Independence, as Gandhi had dreamt, but his gains cannot be underestimated. The passionate promotion of home industry not only resulted in a full-scale reorganization of the Indian textile trade, but also challenged time-honoured hierarchies that privileged Western garb. Most remarkably, khadi posed a powerful symbolic challenge to British imperialism, exuding political dissent.

Khadi's position in a liberated India has always been tenuous. After all, most of its proponents wore it during the freedom struggle out of a sense of national duty, not on account of love for the fabric or the benefits of handspinning. In the decades following Independence, and with its political implications diluted, the once commanding cloth was left threadbare.

In 1956, in an attempt to remedy the situation, the Khadi and Village Industries Commission (KVIC) was established. Its primary objective was to stem the crushing tide of unemployment in rural areas and migration to cities, and to advance the sale and production of khadi and other small-scale enterprises. In spite of government assistance, however, the KVIC had trouble sustaining the sector and selling handmade goods. The liberalization and globalization of the Indian economy did not help matters, and by the late '80s unsold khadi stock began to pile up in shoddy government shops.

Shri Shailesh Bandyopadhyay, one of the KVIC's 12 members and the affiliate responsible for khadi activities in Eastern India, recalls the regression: "Before, there were about 1.4 million spinners and weavers in the khadi field, but after globalization took off, this number was reduced to almost half. The main reason was that khadi was costlier than synthetic fabrics. Other things being equal, handspun textiles require more labour power than mill textiles." As Indians embraced polyester, Bandyopadhyay laments, hundreds of thousands of dusty homespun metres sat lonesome on warehouse shelves.

Homespun goes high-end
Finally, the KVIC — which operates at a loss — resolved to sharpen its focus and start pandering to the tastes of an entirely new crowd: India's style savvy. Both the National Institute of Fashion Technology and the National Institute of Design were invited to give the heritage fabric a facelift, while a handful of India's fashion moguls

agreed to collaborate with the government on innovative khadi looks. In 1989, the KVIC's first high-profile khadi fashion show hit the runway in Mumbai, showcasing 85 new garments conceived by actress, singer, and activist Devika Bhojwani.

Nearly 7,000 Khadi *Gramodyog Bhavans* (government-run khadi outlets) have undergone upmarket makeovers, and celebrated designers have launched chic, gossamer-fine khadi collections in their own cosmopolitan shops. Labels like "bio-khadi" and "organic, handspun cotton" indicate the textile's recent entry into the elite global arena of eco-friendly capitalism, and publicized exhibitions, like the Wills Lifestyle India Fashion Week, stress the once modest material's new life as a luxury item that can appeal to a young, modish Indian elite.

Eminent Indian designer and revivalist colossus Sangita Kathiwada opened the environmentally conscious high-fashion house Mélange in 1992. Situated in a hundred-year-old cellar, the Bombay boutique offsets natural fabrics with cutting-edge silhouettes, layering, and surface ornamentation, and almost always features khadi in its studio line. Though she extols the local textile as a "great leveller," pointing out that khadi cloth ranges from $3 to $8 per metre, Kathiwada creates pieces

"GANDHI WAS A MODERN MAN AND HE WOULD MAKE A GREAT FASHION DESIGNER." KATHIWADA

that are nothing short of luxuriant. "What we sell at Mélange," she gushes, "is very contemporary, very chic, very modern, and ready for a young woman, or an enterprising woman, or an adventurous woman … The idea is to bring in people who wouldn't normally wear the fabric and prove that it has more than one usage." A testament to khadi's new niche, Mélange's stock suits a clientele composed of Indians and Westerners alike.

Contemporary khadi is marketed as a versatile, valuable textile that is capable of becoming an intercontinental brand. "Yes, we must remember Gandhi," Kathiwada maintains, "but to romanticize khadi in this way is not a great marketing trick. It has a wonderful Gandhian value because of what it does in the villages, but the inherent value of the cloth itself is remarkable because it's unique. Where in the world today can you find a handspun and handwoven cloth? A fabric that is thick to provide insulation in the winter and porous to provide ventilation in the summer? A fabric where every yard looks different and has its own peculiar quality because it's handmade?"

Kathiwada's nationalist orientation is satisfied by the popularization of the traditional textile, and as such she is unconcerned with the moral degradation Gandhi associated with luxury goods. The success of khadi in modern India, she and her contemporaries recognize, depends on the development of a broader taste for handmade goods. "I don't expect a woman of the world to come into this shop and buy khadi because it's India's fabric of freedom. She shouldn't be asked to buy the fabric because it's khadi, but because it's visually appealing and comfortable to wear," she says.

Autonomy, dependence, and the Global Village

Khadi's latest incarnation is not without its critics. Many traditionalists object to the fashion industry associating Gandhi's name with "opulent commercial ventures" that run counter to his anti-consumerist message. Rajiv Vora, a well-known interpreter of Gandhian philosophy and retired member of the Gandhi Peace Foundation, is among them.

In 1992, Vora founded Swaraj Peeth, a non-profit organization that aims to illuminate the nationalist leader's principles. "Khadi is not just a piece of cloth: it is an idea, a philosophy," says Vora. India's autonomy, he feels strongly, involves more than release from British supremacy; true freedom was interpreted by Gandhi as the self-reliance of the Indian nation. "Yes, India has achieved independence from the colonizers. But khadi is not only a symbol of Indian Independence: it is, most

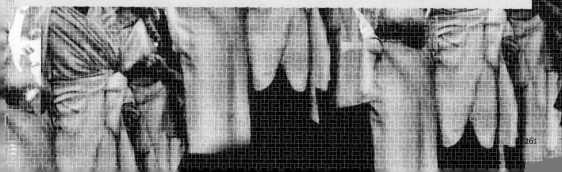

importantly, a symbol of self-sufficiency. And in modern India," Vora contends, "the idea of swaraj has been given the go-by."

As Vora affirms, Gandhi was not simply trying to generate jobs, nor did he intend to create a market based on charity. His premise was that every Indian citizen, regardless of social status, should have access to basic necessities without having to create dependencies on others. Consequently, he hoped that the upper and lower classes would participate in all aspects of cloth production for the benefit of the greater nation. "If he were with us today," Vora says, "Gandhi would only have one question to ask: 'Is India focusing on clothing itself?'"

Rajiv Vora's wife and Swaraj Peeth co-founder Dr. Niru Vora also bemoans khadi's demoralization. "Now we pay three times as much for the same khadi. It's not the people's cloth anymore," she sighs. "It's a rich person's cloth."

Khadi was made to enter the nationalist vocabulary for two purposes, Bandyopadhyay explains. First, Gandhi sought to provide employment to those individuals who, in the '20s, had no other means of income. Second, he was interested in "building a self-sufficient socio-economic order." But, Bandyopadhyay admits, "the current government of India does not believe in this second part. Employment opportunities? Yes. But Gandhi's socio-economic ideology? No. The present government is following the international train, the globalization train. Fashion shows and fashion products are an integral part of the movement of products from one country to another."

It is clear that independent India remains symbolically bound to khadi cloth. Tailoring khadi to meet consumer desires has tempered Gandhi's original ideals, but at the same time it has allowed the textile to assume a new public image. What the history of khadi's revival in the 21st century ultimately reveals is an ongoing tension between capitalist development and a Gandhian-style modernity based on alternative economic and moral principles. Contemporary khadi does not simply evoke the texture of the freedom struggle: it represents a distinctly Indian vision of national progression flanked by the model espoused by the "Father of the Nation" and a globalized worldview.

The production of khadi may not occupy "the idle hours" of the country's inhabitants as Gandhi had hoped, but its use still exemplifies nationalist consumption. Representing the opposition that characterizes an autonomous India, khadi is inextricably woven into the fabric of the country's culture – this much is certain. Whether or not Gandhi would have approved of khadi couture – of this we can never be sure. ✶

A WHIRLWIND TRIP DOWN MAMMARY LANE

THE VERY BASIC EVOLUTION OF THE BUSTLINE FROM 1600 TO 2000

INASMUCH AS CLOTHES GO in and out of style, so do bodies. In one era curvy figures loom large while in another we praise petites. The '20s wanted a Cupid's bow lip; in the '70s, a thin pout prevailed. One might question the wisdom of championing such fixed assets, but regardless of the sense of it, sooner or later some part of our anatomy will fall into, or short of (or possibly even spill over), the prescriptive scale of trend. Nothing illustrates this quite as well as the bustline.

Breasts occupy a uniquely changeable place in fashion history. Perhaps it's because they're rarely wholly exposed; perhaps it's because they have an almost magical tolerance for adjustment. Either way, there's something about the twins that encourages sartorial experimentation. In the 20th century alone,

breast-bearers were asked to boost, flatten, and augment their collective way in and out of corsets, flapper dresses, and bullet bras. And it worked, because boobs can do that. Is it any wonder designers love a rack?

Presented for your consideration is a very basic evolution of the bustline, which proves, once and for all, that fashion has never been anything less than a handful.

NIPPLES, INJURIES, AND IMPRESSIVE TONNAGE FROM 1600 TO 1919

In the 17th century, Queen Elizabeth I made cleavage hot with the masses. By the 18th century, the fashionable décolletage became so low that witnessing an occasional nipple popping out of a dress at Sunday mass was no surprise. By the 19th century, corsets

TEXT BY JAZZ VIRDEE
INTRODUCTION BY
G. STEGELMANN
ILLUSTRATIONS BY
MARYANNA HARDY

became practically mandatory for women of any social ranking or age. The boning inside was made of whalebone or steel.

Cases of cracked ribs, deformed internal organs, and numerous incidents of choking confirmed that the ideal hourglass look, which kept breasts practically at one's throat, came with a heavy price. Warner's began manufacturing looser-fitting "health" corsets in 1894. Nonetheless, women entered the 20th century in pain, still struggling to breathe inside these reinforced undergarments.

During World War I, corsets were taken off the market to conserve steel and redirect it to the war effort. The policy was a huge success, saving 28,000 tonnes of metal, which was equivalent to the amount of steel required to construct two battleships.

Breasts are out, then breasts are in, then breasts are on hold from 1920 to 1946.

The bra, although invented a generation earlier, finally gained popularity in the '20s with flapper girls. Emancipated women were exercising their newly won freedom in political and social life, as well as in fashion. They could be found smoking, drinking, and dancing at jazz clubs. The look was all about youthful exuberance, which translated to bobbed hair, loose clothing, and flat chests – like little girls playing dress-up. Bras were used to flatten breasts to an almost pre-pubescent size, preventing jiggling and allowing long strands of pearls to fall straight over the chest. Breasts were out and legs were in; dancers even applied blush to their knees to help show them off.

A BRIEF HISTORY OF WOMEN'S UNDERWEAR...

2500 BCE Minoan women in modern Crete begin wearing a garment that pushes their breasts out of their clothes

2000 BCE Earliest recorded corsets

450 BCE – 285 CE Greek ladies wear a bodice fastened above the breasts, leaving them popping out and bare underneath

13TH C Women begin wearing bodices that flatten their breasts, emphasizing waistlines instead

14TH C Straight tubular bodices totally flatten out breasts, and many parts of France outlaw belts used to support the bust. An edict of 1370 states: "no woman will support the bust by the disposition of a blouse or by tightened dress"

Breasts started coming back into style in the '30s with Hollywood's emphasis on glamorous feminine styles. It was during the '30s that Maidenform patented different cup sizes for bras that offered a more natural shape. But just a decade later, with the world at war again, resources and materials were redirected, thus limiting the materials available to manufacture bras.

The role of Western women drastically changed as they entered the workforce in support of the war effort. Corsets were too bulky and restrictive to work in, and besides, their production was halted to conserve steel. Women's fashions emphasized utility, often based on military uniforms. It was not uncommon for women to wear suits, though these were still very feminine with

nipped-in waists and subtle detail. Bras were worn, but there wasn't much of a market for innovation. Like so many wardrobe items during this era, the rule was "mend and make do," and women took care of the bras they had to make them last.

BREEDERS, BOMBSHELLS, AND BOOBY-CENTRICITY FROM 1950 TO 1967

The late '40s began a trend that would culminate in the busty '50s. Political discourse focused on repopulation. Women retreated from factory life, and femininity and the home were once more closely interconnected. Women's roles, although home-oriented, took on a new form represented in an almost overt display of female sexuality and

15TH C Breasts are again the focus of fashion; women use bodices to flatten the lower parts of their chest and push the tops up and out

16TH C During the Renaissance period, women stuff their chests with silk and hankies; however, it is much more difficult without the modern bra, as the stuffing ends up all over the place

17TH C What a breakthrough: women's underwear is invented! Drawers are designed as two separate legs attached only at the waist, crotchless for convenience of course

1820S The "corset mécanique" is invented to allow women to get into their corsets with the aid of a pulley system instead of servants

1850S First known bra-like device is registered for U.S. patent; its popularity is short-lived and women continue to prefer corsets

1877 Red flannel combination underwear is invented for women and is, you guessed it, also crotchless!

1889 The first breast support held up from the shoulders, instead of squeezed from the waist, is marketed as a health aid in Paris

1913 Socialite Mary Phelps Jacob and her maid put together the first backless bra for a soiree in New York. It's made out of two handkerchiefs, some ribbon, and cord. Within one year, she has her own patent but tires of the business and sells it to the Warner Brothers Corset Company for $1,500. Within the next 30 years, Warner's makes a profit of $15 million

fertility. The hourglass shape was celebrated with Christian Dior's New Look collection, which required some intense bondage and padding under its glamorous surface. The body was manipulated by corsets and padding, which came back with a vengeance.

This look became the prototype image of the '50s housewife. Though it was popular in North America, it was not universally embraced. Designers themselves, never content to see style in just one way, were often critical of the New Look and what it meant. Coco Chanel famously accused Dior of hating women because he confined them in garments that were not comfortable or practical.

Science also began focusing more on women's sexuality. Alfred Kinsey determined heterosexual intercourse didn't cut it for women, and men needed to do more in bed to satisfy their partners' desires. For the first time in Western civilization, women's sexual identity was being defined as something very separate from that of men, and this attitude was reflected in what women wore. Designer dresses were fitted over lifted, padded, and exposed cleavage. Cone-shaped bullet bras appeared, and by 1949, Maidenform had sold 90 million. Strapless bras also became popular alongside fads for off-the-shoulder shirts and dresses.

In the '50s, big breasts were the ideal. If you didn't have them, you enhanced. Many famous designers of this era worked for Hollywood studios, and film was a crucial medium for marketing women's fashions. Idealized actresses shaped the collective feminine image,

and Hollywood starlets like Marilyn Monroe, Brigitte Bardot, Raquel Welch, and Sophia Loren became objects of fantasy and envy.

Toward the end of the '60s, however, women like Audrey Hepburn and Jackie Kennedy also became style icons. These slender, small-framed women were characterized as brainy and sophisticated next to the more buxom starlets, and they promoted a more practical, less overtly sexual fashion sense.

BURNING BRAS, BURNING CALORIES, AND BACKPEDALLING FROM 1968 TO 2000

By the end of the '60s, the second wave of feminism hit Western nations. In 1968, protesters outside the Miss America beauty pageant crowned a sheep to represent unquestioning adherence to Hollywood's image ideal, and were reported (inaccurately) to have set fire to their bras. Although the notion of bra burning ignited similar protests throughout North America and Europe, bras were seldom actually burned; most of the time they were simply tossed into a big garbage bin. The act symbolized not an attack against fashion, but a declaration of the freedom to choose what (and what not) to wear.

Hippy fashion was characterized by loose clothing, a mishmash of colours, and unconstrained breasts free to fall naturally without bras or corsets. In the spirit of comfort and freedom that prevailed through the '70s, there came a

trend toward a more natural look. Softer, less structured bras became available.

By the '80s, consumer culture returned and fashion and body image were thrust back to the centre of social attention. Skirts got shorter, hair got bigger, and prints got bolder. Shirts and sweaters came with shoulder pads, and breasts remained rounded. The fitness craze popularized the sports bra. Reviving a shape that had been almost forgotten, Parisian designer Jean Paul Gaultier created exaggerated, pointy bras for Madonna's Blonde Ambition tour. They took the '50s circle stitch bullet bra to an extreme and brought it into the realm of outerwear. Big breasts were back, and now if you didn't have any, you could enhance them surgically.

It was in the '90s, as clothes were fitted more tightly against the body with less

structure distorting the figure underneath, that the new curvaceous-yet-thin body ideal came into effect. Manufacturers designed secret padding, creating "bra cookies" to boost breasts depleted by dieting. These puffy inserts were the precursors to things like Wonderbra's push-up and water bras, which attempted to enlarge breasts while keeping their shape and feeling natural.

Fashion's standards no longer demanded restrictive underpinnings like corsets to mold the perfect shape, and old-fashioned padding and waist-cinchers came to be seen as cheating. Control over the female form was achieved by promoting a body-obsessed culture. Arguably, diet restriction and exercise obsession kept women just as restrained as the bondage of the past. ✄

Let's Hear it for the Girls

A GLOSSARY OF BRAS FROM BANDEAU TO SUPERBOOST

TEXT BY CASIE BROWN

RESEARCH BY STEPHANIE FEREIRO

ILLUSTRATION BY ALEXANDRA BARTON

THE BRASSIERE, A TERM coined by *Vogue* in 1907, has changed as dramatically in its lifetime as the fashions it hides beneath. While corsetry had thrust breasts upward from below, the modern bra lifted from above. This innovation kicked the corsets to the curb, providing an adaptable foundation for the silhouettes of each subsequent decade. During World War I, women were urged to abandon the corset to preserve

steel – enough was spared to build an entire battleship. In 1968, feminist protesters of the Miss America Pageant argued the bra was a symbol of oppression, unhooking and hurling their 34Cs into trash-bins. From the Mono-bosom to the bullet, there's no denying that the modern brassiere has, for better or worse, shaped the lives, bodies, and fashions of women. *WORN* offers a well-rounded history of the girls' best friend.

7.

"Falsies," artificial inserts placed or occasionally stitched into the cups of the bra, created the exaggerated bullet shape most fashionable in the late '50s.

This bust shape was revived in the early '90s when Madonna adopted Gaultier's cone-shaped bras as her signature stage-wear.

3. The Kestos-Style Bra
Invented by Kestos director Rosamond Klin in 1926, it gained such popularity that the brand name became synonymous with the word bra: "Women did not buy a brassiere, they bought a Kestos."

Its light compression and support complemented the sleek silhouettes and bias-cuts of the '30s.

Based on a 1913 model by Caresse Crosby, Klin's design featured a handkerchief folded crosswise and darted under the bust. Joined with an overlap in the front and elastic that crossed at the back and buttoned under the bust, these pieces were the beginning of the move toward the shaped cup that followed.

4. The Marks & Spencer Sports Bra
The original sports bra was made from two jockstraps. Hinda Miller and Lisa Lindahl fashioned the garment in 1977 to compress breasts and keep them from bouncing when exercising.

In 1996, Marks & Spencer released their famous version (a Sporty Spice favourite) made from a nylon material called Tactel, which stretched to fit and required no seaming – which is what you want, what you really really want.

With developments in synthetic and stretch textiles, the design moved away from compression, managing to support while remaining breathable.

1. Rudi Gernreich "No Bra" Bra
Originated in 1964 by Gernreich, an avant-garde Californian fashion designer, for the American lingerie company Exquisite Form.

Its transparent tone and streamlined design were the perfect foundation for the adolescent figure deemed fashionable through the '60s. With minimal support, women everywhere achieved the boyish shape personified by models like Twiggy.

A card included with the garment read: "No gimmick, the 'NO BRA' supports yet gives you the natural nude look of a firm, young, bra-less bosom."

Gernreich's designs, despite inspiring imitations, were often considered publicity stunts; his topless bikini featured thin straps that met in a "V" at the sternum, exposing both breasts.

2. Conical Bra
The "torpedo" breasts of Jayne Mansfield and American Bandstanders at large owe everything to this pointed design. Its bullet shape was emphasized with circular stitching, a technique first introduced in 1928.

5. The Ultrabra Superboost

With the relatively flat tagline "Ultrabra, creating the ultimate cleavage," this low-cut bra was thrust into the market by Gossard in 1994. It was the first time a cleavage bra was available in bigger cup sizes, ranging from A to D.

With cups joined by a narrow strip of fabric, the Ultrabra combined diagonal seaming with padding. Breasts were pushed together by the high diagonal angle at which the seam was cut, enhancing cleavage.

The ultimate cleavage proved too much for British airwaves. In 1999, Ultrabra's advertising campaign – featuring the brand's ambassador and model Kate Groombridge – was pulled from television for being too racy.

6. The Bandeau

Though North Americans didn't catch on until the mid-1910s, the bandeau has appeared in different cultures throughout history, originating with the ancient Greeks and Romans who banded their breasts with leather strips.

8.

Quite literally a band of fabric, the bandeau flattened the breasts, creating the boyish figure chic during the Jazz Age. Fabric normally extended at least two inches below the breasts, and fastened with eye hooks or a ribbon tie, in the front or back.

The most common bra of the '20s, versions were available in waist or midriff lengths. Short versions of the bandeau were described by *Women's Wear Daily* as "a novelty" in 1919.

7. The Strapless Bra

Invented in the 1910s, this style didn't become popular until the '50s, when it was introduced as foundational wear for "evening frocks" and blouses. It became a leading style throughout the decade.

Sturdy and sensible, this bra was regarded as an object of glamour, gracing the backs – and fronts – of pin-ups and prom queens alike.

To ensure the ladies stayed afloat, strapless designs took one of two preventative measures: a string of tape extended from the back of the garment to tie in the front or strategic wire boning kept everyone in their cups.

8. The Maidenform

The first licensed "uplift bra" was invented by dress designers Ida Rosenthal and Enid Bissett in 1927. They felt that a naturally shaped brassiere suited their creations better than the flattening undergarments of the '20s.

In the '30s, as uplifted breasts rose in popularity, Maidenform made its way into the drawers of American women, with adjustable elastic shoulder straps to ease the burden or discomfort of extreme lift.

The "I dreamed I… in my Maidenform Bra" advertising series, featuring women wearing the design in public settings, is considered one of the most successful ad campaigns ever, spanning over 20 years. ⊠

FLIGHTS OF FANCY

THE VERY UN-UNIFORM EVOLUTION OF STEWARDESS DRESS

MAR   69

TEXT BY
KATE SCHWEISHELM

RESEARCH SUPPORT BY
STEPHANIE FEREIRO

ILLUSTRATION BY
JENN WOODALL

IN 2006, EX-FLIGHT ATTENDANT Mary Sue Seibold auctioned off her complete collection of Braniff International airline uniforms. Included were 18 ensembles comprising 90 individual items amassed between 1963 and 1983, a period notorious for its bold and, at times, off-the-wall style. Bidding started at an incredible $100,000 (USD), reflecting the collection's rarity and its connection to a bygone era when the fashions of the sky mirrored those on the runway.

Now defunct, Braniff was once the fore-runner in modish fashion for "stewardesses" (as they were then called), and for good reason. In 1965, the company hired couturier Emilio Pucci to re-design their uniforms. Pucci's bold, playful designs were a significant departure from the way airlines had clothed female employees up to that point, kickstarting competition among Braniff's rivals to update their own in-flight looks. American Airlines introduced knit, short-sleeved mini-dresses with matching fishnets; TWA briefly flirted with the idea of paper dresses; and Southern Airways tried out belted tunics over "wet-look" vinyl pants. As one journalist marvelled in 1969, "The stewardess uniforms have now become so chic that it is sometimes hard to tell the cabin crew from the paying passengers."

It would be hard to imagine anyone fawning over contemporary uniforms, which are largely composed of basic pant suits in subdued colour palettes. But while they may not reflect the latest trends, they do point to a cultural shift in attitudes toward women and their role in the workplace. In her book *Femininity in Flight*, Kathleen Barry observes that, historically, "female wage-earners in many clerical and service fields have been expected not only to perform gender on the job, but to perform gender as the job." This was never truer than for those women working 40,000 feet above the earth, acknowledged less for their safety training than for their sunny dispositions. The demands of femininity were fundamentally intertwined with their job requirements and reflected in the clothes they wore.

The new shape of air travel
In the beginning of passenger flight service, young men were employed as "cabin boys," but the industry was forever altered in 1930 by the crafty thinking of a woman named Ellen Church. Early air travel was a bumpy ride and air sickness was common. Church,

a trained pilot, wanted to work in aviation but knew she would never be hired as a commercial pilot. Instead, she proposed a new position, one for which she was also trained: on-board nurse. Initially, Boeing rejected her idea, but soon changed their minds – not for her flight training but for the publicity. People considered air travel risky; having a female on board would demonstrate its safety. After all, if a young woman wasn't afraid, how dangerous could it be?

Chosen less for their medical knowledge than their gender, the company hired several young nurses. Yet those early stewardesses' uniforms were austerely practical. Made up of high-lapelled, double-breasted blazers and boxy, loosely tailored skirts, they reflected both their status as trained professionals and the military influence on aviation. Fashion had not yet trumped function.

Learning curves
Other airlines quickly picked up the idea of hiring female nurses as in-flight attendants, but, because they were anxious to dispel any idea of danger, cabin attendants' medical backgrounds were increasingly downplayed. Eventually the requirement of a nursing diploma was dropped entirely. Though attendants still saw their primary duty as ensuring the safety of passengers, the airlines' marketing stressed the courteous service and delightful companionship their lovely attendants provided. By the '50s, the label "hostess" defined the public's perception of their work – to facilitate, as Barry phrases it, a "luxurious, leisurely party among the clouds."

Pleased with the ongoing success of their campaign, airlines demanded stewardess hires comply with rigid (and rather arbitrary) requirements: to be white, female, young, slim, attractive, and unmarried, and to possess a certain "poise" and agreeable demeanour. Quasi-military uniforms were

MAR   69

softened into neatly tailored three-piece
skirt suits accessorized with ladylike
hats and gloves. The aesthetic message,
writes Barry, was that "stewardesses were
glamorous but reassuringly domesticated
young ladies." (In fact, some media
referred to the job as a "bride school,"
churning out lovely, well-mannered
hostesses who would make ideal wives.)

Hidden, of course, was the intense effort
required to maintain desirable bodies and
perky personalities while performing the
hard work of customer service and safety.
Airlines issued bulky manuals covering all
aspects of appearance from hair colour to
accessories. Christine Lautsch, who started
flying with Pacific Western in 1976, remembers, "things were sort of dictated to us, like
the colour of pantyhose we were allowed
to wear, the colour of shoes, the style, the
heel-height, the look." Lautsch recalls
that when her mother was a stewardess
in the '50s, "they had to wear girdles, and
garters to hold up their stockings. They
were required to wear heels at work at all
times, and they never had pants – only
skirts and dresses." Some airlines sent new
stewardesses to "charm farms": retreats
where they were trained in decorum and
given "beauty makeovers." Barry even

SOME MEDIA REFERRED TO THE JOB AS A "BRIDE SCHOOL," CHURNING OUT LOVELY, WELL-MANNERED HOSTESSES WHO WOULD MAKE IDEAL WIVES.

3

cites cases of airlines having stewardesses' teeth filed to create perfectly even smiles.

Lilla Wright, part of the first group of flight attendants for Air Jamaica in 1968, remembers their stringent rules: "We had to be made up and we had to have the whole schmear – foundation, blush, lipstick, eye shadow, eyeliner, mascara, the whole works. And of course you had to be well-manicured. I remember going to bed at night with my hands on top of my coverlet trying not to smudge my nails because if they were smudged, oh dear!" Michael Gillevet began his flight attendant training in the late '70s and recollects, "one young

lady in the class was advised that her hair style was unacceptable, and after being told this three times, she was asked politely to leave the class and not come back."

On some airlines, it was common for supervisors to verify whether stewardesses were wearing bras or to perform unannounced weight checks – anyone who "failed" was grounded immediately. Often, though, these expectations went unspoken. "Let's put it this way," says Wright, "if your uniform was tailor-made for you and you were a certain weight when it was fitted.... We weren't told that we were not allowed to gain weight, it was kind of understood." Upholding these implicit standards of femininity required work on and off the clock, yet it was never recognized or compensated.

Hemlines and bottom lines

The '60s spelled major changes for the airline industry, inspired by cultural changes surrounding the sexual revolution and the introduction of jetliners able to transport much larger numbers of passengers. All things being equal in technology and pricing, airlines looking to expand their market share turned to their stewardesses to entice

with optional bubble helmet for inclement weather, through a bright raspberry skirt suit for welcoming passengers and 'Puccino' shift for serving dinner, to a clingy mock turtleneck and knee-length 'harem' pants for serving after-dinner drinks." It was hardly a burlesque show, but ads for Braniff's "air strip" made it seem as if hostesses performed an actual striptease mid-flight, capitalizing on titillating notions of the modern, "sexually liberated" single woman. The campaign was, in part, responsible for doubling the airline's revenue in a year.

> "WE WEREN'T TOLD THAT WE WERE NOT ALLOWED TO GAIN WEIGHT, IT WAS KIND OF UNDERSTOOD."

potential clients – especially businessmen travelling on expense accounts. As one journalist noted in 1967, "Since most aircraft look more or less alike to the average traveler, and fly more or less alike, and give more or less the same service, competition has driven the lines to find a new ploy – dress, or undress – for their hostesses." The "undress" was a direct reference to Braniff.

Braniff introduced its "air strip" in 1965. Emilio Pucci designed a uniform composed of four different outfits that the women would remove piece by piece during the flight. Barry's book documents the routine: "The fashion show progressed from a coat

Other American airlines adopted equally risqué ploys. Southwest (the "love" airline) dressed its workers in tiny shorts and white knee-high lace-up go-go boots. Lautsch describes Pacific Western's "stampeder uniform," an outfit on Calgary flights consisting of "a very short miniskirt, a blouse, a little vest with a fringe, a cowboy hat, and cowboy boots." She says, "you couldn't have worn it without having someone see up your skirt if you bent down. It was a really racy uniform." The new styles actually impeded women from doing their jobs; when asked how to work in a miniskirt, Wright replies with a laugh: "Very carefully! You sort of bend at the knees, and

if you had to put something in the overhead bin, you make sure there's no men peering around and then you quickly shove it in."

If they didn't actually invent it, the airlines certainly perpetuated the notion of the "swinging stewardess," the available and adventurous female flight attendant stereotype of the '60s and '70s. Their promotional philosophy was best summed up by Mary Wells, the brain behind the marketing overhaul of Braniff who, in 1967, famously said, "When a tired businessman gets on an airplane, we think he ought to be allowed to look at a pretty girl."

Airlines took advantage of the sexual liberalization of the time, suggesting that the "service" and gratification one could expect to receive from a hostess was of a decidedly sexual nature, making her an object of erotic fantasy for passengers. Ad campaigns were laced with libidinal innuendo. In 1971, National introduced its controversial slogan, "Fly Me." This phrase appeared in ads featuring individual stewardesses introducing themselves, saying, "Hi, I'm Cheryl – Fly Me." Braniff asked, "Does your wife know you're flying with us?" Continental offered the slogan, "We Really Move Our Tails For You."

Some hostesses also provided in-flight entertainment, performing in fashion shows on Air Jamaica or Braniff liners. "After the

277

5 & 6. From the '30s to the '50s, stewardess uniforms were designed with a sharp military influence. Dependable and highly trained, stewardesses were primarily nurses and emergency personnel.

7. In the '60s, uniforms like these from Pacific Southwestern came with a whole new job description. Advertisers and airlines promoted stewardesses as in-flight hostesses, waitresses, and increasingly racy fashion plates.

8. With the dawn of the politically correct '90s, flight attendant uniforms reflect a more egalitarian and respectful attitude. Form follows function – not fashion.

meal service was over," Wright explains, "we'd go to one of the washrooms and change.... The person who was in charge would be on the mic describing the fashions, and we'd walk the length of the plane, back and forth, and change into something else." Wright enjoyed modelling, but only "up to a point" – that point being lascivious passengers who used narrow aisles as an excuse to "accidentally" brush their hands against the hostesses as they passed by.

Wright's recollections encapsulate the power imbalance stewardesses faced at work. Although they consistently believed their primary role was ensuring passenger safety, airline advertising encouraged customers to view them as sexual objects. As Lautsch observes, "Our union used to stress to the company that we were there for safety, and the companies viewed that we were there for service." This discrepancy inevitably led to bitter disagreements.

The beginning of the end

Many stewardesses liked their new outfits, finding them easier to manoeuver in and much hipper; they didn't like the airlines' domination of their physical appearances and the increasingly lewd attitudes of male passengers.

Subtle forms of resistance became more common throughout the '70s. Paula Kane, author of *Sex Objects in the Sky: A Personal Account of the Stewardess Rebellion*, describes wearing a uniform two sizes too big and "forgetting" to wear her name tag to be more anonymous. Five stewardesses protested by showing up for work in comfortable, flat, crepe-soled shoes rather than regulation heels. When their supervisor said nothing, the women adopted the new footwear permanently. Groups like Stewardesses for Women's Rights (SFWR) formed to

as a profession requiring skills that came no more naturally to one gender than the other. Uniforms shifted accordingly toward simpler, more gender-neutral styles. After a 36-year run with CP Air, flight attendant Diane Cox could see the effect: "By the end of my career, the hats and gloves were gone. With the business suit, they went into a more professional image." Lautsch credits union involvement, "because they put out surveys to the flight attendants and asked what they wanted. Maybe that's the difference now – there's actually

WHILE SOME OF THE GLAMOUR MAY HAVE FALLEN BY THE WAYSIDE, THAT "BORING" NEW WARDROBE BROUGHT A NEW LEVEL OF RESPECT.

object to their work being viewed as simply a "natural" outgrowth of women's supposedly innate caregiving dispositions rather than a profession requiring particular training and a skill set. (The SFWR was founded by one woman who had been fired for going over her maximum weight and another who had quit after her skirt was ripped off mid-flight by a drunken passenger.) A rebellion bubbled up against what sociologist Arlie Russell Hochschild calls the "costumes, the script, and the general choreography" of the stewardess.

Following these protests and stewardesses' unionization, the job began to be seen

feedback from the people wearing the uniforms. Before, we didn't have any say." So, while some of the glamour may have fallen by the wayside, that "boring" new wardrobe brought a new level of respect.

It's perhaps telling that, up until the auction, Seibold stored her old uniforms in her hope chest, an item whose intended purpose was never realized because her job barred her from marrying. In that sense, then, there are some parts of this history that are worth letting go. Still, I can't be the only one who wishes the bubble helmet would make a comeback... an un-gendered version, that is. ⊠

FASHION IS
IDENTITY

07

FASHION AFFECTS HOW PEOPLE SEE YOU. Dressing an infant in pink dictates a response very different from that to an infant in blue and something as simple as a hairstyle can channel history. The styles we assume affect how we see ourselves. We know better than anyone if the reflection in our mirror is true to the person inside.

Fashion is a cultural and social signifier, extending one's ability to fit in or stand out. Our clothes can unite us with a community and create a feeling of belonging. At a glance, or from a distance, our outfits offer clues about belief and affiliation. They show what we value and how we live. Our subtlest details – the flower on a lapel – can help us find allies in a sea of strangers. Fashion offers a way to challenge others' assumptions. We can use clothing to establish new truths more beautiful and complex than categories of he or she or us or them.

We are all born with bodies that come with expectations – sometimes cultural, sometimes gendered. But whoever *you* are, whoever *you* want to be, whatever part of yourself needs to be explored or revealed, clothing can convey an expression of desire and being. Fashion is identity. ⊠

Out of the Closet

The evolution of identity in gay men's fashion from green carnations to hot cops

text by Max Mosher ✿ illustrations by Sara Guindon

THE BLACK-AND-WHITE PHOTO could have been taken in 1945 — a victory celebration snapshot at the end of World War II. That is, until one notices the two hunky sailors locking lips amid the confetti. Of course, the image captures an era in which a gay man was more likely to have a rock pitched at him than an ad, but that's what gave the image its clever irony. By the time Diesel ran the racy picture in fashion magazines in 1999, homosexuals were already well on their way to becoming a coveted marketable demographic.

But from prejudice to purchase power, gays have had one constant companion: clothes. The marriage (or civil union, if you will) of gay men and clothing long predates advertisers' flirtation with queer culture. "For gay men," says Shaun Cole, principal lecturer at London College of Fashion and author of *Don We Now Our Gay Apparel*, "clothing has always acted as a signifier of identity." And from the Edwardian dandy to the Armani-clad bodybuilder (discussing adoption with his common-law partner over brunch), there have been as many ways of dressing gay as colours in the rainbow.

Whereas homosexuals had once relied on surreptitious, coded accessories like red ties and pinkie rings, by the '70s, entire outfits were shouting, "We're here, we're queer, get used to it!" Through progressively more bold and unapologetic fashion, gay men were trying on identities that allowed them to explore their sexualities, create communities, and announce their orientation to an increasingly savvy public. For gay men, what was in their closet helped them come out of it.

Clap if you believe in fairies

In Victorian England, the trials that would publicly "out" playwright Oscar Wilde (and see him imprisoned on charges of gross indecency) firmly linked homosexuality with effeminacy, witticisms, and radical fashion. Along with his velvet suits and shoulder-length

For gay men, what was in their closet helped them come out of it.

hair, Wilde popularized the green carnation buttonhole, adopting a queer symbol used by London's rent boys. That meme, connecting gay men to effeminate fashion, held strong for the next four decades. During the "pansy craze" of the '20s and '30s, fey, tuxedoed gentlemen made risqué quips in screwball comedies, and New Yorkers headed to Harlem to gawk at the elaborate costumes at annual Drag Balls.

Pansy, nellie, swish, queen: the fairy went by many names, but one thing universally acknowledged was that he wasn't a "real man." Sexual theories of the time suggested that homosexuals were women in men's bodies, unnaturally devoid of masculinity. But the easily recognizable identity proved useful for lonely men desperate to find each other. Gay men flocked to the stereotype like fairies to a flame.

Fear of arrest and harassment dissuaded men from being overtly effeminate in day-to-day situations. Instead, fairies developed a series of coded accessories to announce their sexuality, adapting them as styles changed. At the turn of the century, it was red ties, pinkie rings, and white kid gloves. By the '50s, pink shirts, sneakers, and mohair sweaters were the "swishy" staples. In England, pale blue socks signified homosexuality; in France, green cravats. Because secrecy was essential, even the subtlest cues counted – a pointed suede shoe was a quiet wink at the initiated in the same way an offhand reference to Judy Garland could determine whether a stranger was a fellow "friend of Dorothy." The codes worked so well that early researchers, baffled at gay men's ability to find each other, theorized some sort of homosexual "sixth sense." But not everyone wanted to be a fairy. "For many men, effeminacy was a way into a gay lifestyle," writes Cole. "Many embraced an overtly effeminate style before later rejecting it." Masculine gays felt alienated from an identity that didn't represent them; early queer activists worried that the fairy stereotype gave the community a bad name.

As communities grew and the need for secrecy decreased, many queers dismissed the red tie and everything it stood for. Fairies became the butt of jokes, jeered at on the street and even denied entry to gay bars. But they were not turned away at the Stonewall Inn, a mafia-run bar in New York destined to enter history.

Revolution's a drag

"If we want to be employed by the federal government, we have to look employable to the federal government," said Frank Kameny of the Mattachine Society, an early gay rights organization. Mattachine members followed strict, conservative dress codes (suits for men, dresses for women) and, for two decades, fought for incremental changes with little success. But all that changed on the night of June 28, 1969.

Inspired by either the civil rights movement, anti-war protesters, or the recent death of Judy Garland (depending on who's telling the story), patrons at the Stonewall Inn retaliated against raiding police. They incited a riot that lasted two days and gave birth to the gay liberation movement. Accommodationist goals were gone in an instant and shame was replaced with newfound pride. Buoyed by years of pent-up frustration, queer activists were ready for a revolution, and their wardrobes provided a good starting point. Influenced less by drag queen performances than by transgender sex workers, proponents of what came to be known as "radical drag" blurred the line between masculinity and femininity by adopting extreme elements of both: tutus and army shorts, gold lamé gowns and work boots, bearded faces caked with makeup. Occasionally, the look was characterized by the lack of clothing, as radical drag queens joined the first Pride marches wearing bikini bottoms and nothing else.

Taken off the stage and put on the street, what was once a camp performance became a political act, questioning what, if anything, gender meant. "Drag took on the increasingly unfriendly appearance of the 'gender-fuck,'" writes Daniel Harris in *The Rise and Fall of Gay Culture*, "the bearded nun in a sequined habit, clown-white face and fishnet stockings, shrieking obscenities like a snarling pit bull straining at her leash." (The parodic nuns were part of activist group The Sisters of Perpetual Indulgence, whose original habits were borrowed from an actual convent with the explanation that they were staging *The Sound of Music*.) Though it was an early precursor to punk, radical drag was never a widespread movement: few thought dresses made of tin pie plates and Christmas tinsel were practical for everyday life. But radical drag queens had shown that gays didn't mind being called freaks anymore (and that being freaky was

The Clone Look went mainstream in the '80s, adopted by heterosexuals who apparently missed the irony of straight men dressing like gay men dressing like straight men.

rather cool). By the mid-'70s, a new style was already nipping at its platform heels.

Previous gay fashions had mixed the feminine with the masculine – the fairy did so subtly, the radical drag queen flamboyantly. This new identity would stick determinedly to one extreme and, remarkably, by mining traditional masculine culture, gay men would find a way to announce their sexuality to the world.

Attack of the clones

In *Cities on a Hill*, her study of San Francisco's gay neighbourhoods during the '70s, journalist Frances FitzGerald was surprised to recognize the same styles over and over again. "The Castroids," she wrote of the denizens of Castro Street, "were dressing with the care of Edwardian dandies, only the look was cowboy or bush pilot: tight blue jeans, plaid shirts, leather vests or bomber jackets, and boots. The new look was 'gender-eccentricity.'"

Men who had grown up thinking "gay" meant "feminine" were suddenly indulging in the icons of manhood: the construction worker, the mechanic, the lumberjack, the cowboy. Athletic clones (as they came to be known) wore tennis shirts, grey hoodies, and shorts paired with knee-high socks. Whatever the look, close-cropped hair and handlebar mustaches were the perfect final touches.

Though the style aped straight culture, it should not be confused with trying to "pass." Straight onlookers saw a man in jeans and a plaid shirt, but fellow gays noted the trendy style of a pair of Levi's and meticulously chosen flannel. FitzGerald quotes one gay man: "You can't go to the laundromat at 10 a.m. without the right pair of jeans on."

Quickly dubbed "the clone look" because of its uniformity, this style became the defining gay aesthetic of the disco era. According to Cole, "gay men realized that it was fine to be overtly masculine … that sex and sexual freedom were something that they could freely embrace." In the '70s, gays were much more visible and less concerned about being recognized as gay. Clones had taken the look of the working-class male and sexualized it, emphasizing muscles through tight t-shirts, and shapely buttocks through deliberately shrunken jeans. As Cole observes, "Some men even left the top or bottom button of their Levi's undone, in part to signify sexual availability, and in part to suggest that their genitals were so large they had popped a button through sheer size."

The clone look was, in fact, a deconstruction of the traditional male, a kind of "butch drag." By dressing like "real men," clones had discovered that masculinity was a performance with costumes no less contrived than the fairy's tailored suits or the radical drag queen's gowns. The clone told the world that even men who looked like men might sleep with men.

Some homosexuals had been uncomfortable with the style of the effeminate fairy, associating it with a time when they had been oppressed and ashamed. When the closet doors burst open and gays declared their sexuality to the world, the vibrant colours of the fairies' accessories became the colours of the rainbow flag. The clone look, the first style to say it was okay to be both gay and masculine, may have encouraged thousands of men to come out.

A touch of leather
Some men wanted to get even farther away from the fairy – so far they needed an engine. By the '70s, leathermen were a common sight in queer communities, recognizable by their head-to-toe biker ensembles: black jacket, cap, vest, studded wristband, metal-plated boots, pants, and chaps. Some even carried around motorcycle helmets (despite many not owning bikes) to avoid undue attention from police. For those worried about wearing their leather look on the street, bars catering to leathermen had dress codes posted at the entrance, but offered changerooms in the back.

"If you think about the highly effeminate stereotypes that existed at that time," says Peter Hennen, an associate professor of sociology at Ohio State University and author of Faeries, Bears and Leathermen, "you can see why men in this position might be powerfully attracted to the hyper-masculine image of the leather biker." Hennen claims that gay men were responding to the same alienated feeling that biker clubs did in the anxious post-war years. "Men in general were looking for a way to rescue the wildness, the impetuousness, and the danger of a kind of frontier masculinity that was increasingly seen as being tamed by the niceties of contemporary culture and quiet suburban living." The sex appeal of Marlon Brando in The Wild One didn't hurt either.

While S/M sexual practices were a component of leather culture, Harris argues that they were secondary to the desire to connect with other masculine gay men, who couldn't care less about Hollywood musicals or interior design. Despite the social and legal victories the movement had achieved, gay men in the '70s still felt politically vulnerable and helpless against gay bashing on the street. With the tough-as-nails biker look, gays were replacing victimhood with virility. The Tool Box, the first leather bar in San Francisco, hung castoff running shoes from the ceiling with a sign that read: "Down with Sneakers!" The previous era's symbols were now being discarded like old shoes.

Leathermen had first indicated their sexual proclivities by the placement of keys on their belts (a motif lifted from biker culture), but this was replaced by the "hanky code." A handkerchief, according to its colour, pattern, and placement, signified a man's fetish and whether he would take an active or passive role. (According to legend,

By the '70s, Leathermen were a common sight in queer communities, recognizable by their head-to-toe biker ensembles.

the tradition dated back to California's Gold Rush days, when men tied handkerchiefs around their necks to take the woman's role at a dance.) A multiplication of fetishes reflected an explosion of sexual activity. Gay men saw hooking up as an essential part of their hard-won freedom. "Clothing in the '50s and '60s had operated either as a secret code for those passing, or as a very visible marker of a feminine identity," Cole says. "The '70s offered a range of new styled identities – clones, gender-fuck, counter culture, punk even – that allowed a very visible engagement with sexuality."

Coded accessories had gone from the red tie whispering, "I'm a gay man," to the red hanky that declared, "this is precisely what kind of gay man I am!"

Closet space
In time, all these gay identities would overlap, awkwardly mingling with each other at marches and bars. A 1977 cartoon from The Advocate showed a classic fairy presenting his purse to a skeptical clone: "Well, it is leather, isn't it?" The clone look went mainstream in the '80s, adopted by heterosexuals who apparently missed the irony of straight men

dressing like gay men dressing like straight men. This, of course, killed the look for many gays. But as nipple rings gave way to wedding rings, fashion remained a relevant and inextricable part of queer identity and culture.

Just as the Stonewall Riots didn't invent the desire (or struggle) for gay rights, gay fashion existed long before the first clone trimmed his mustache. During hostile and homophobic eras, fairies displayed their sexuality as openly as they could. Their red ties and blue socks were subtle signs pointing to an alternative way of living, helping pave the way for the outrageous and openly queer fashions that followed.

Fashion reflects the story of the gay rights era as it evolved from secret symbols to raucous revolution, and from fear and oppression to fierceness and pride. With the freedom to be gay came the freedom to be different kinds of gay, and the multiplying of queer identities has only increased since the '70s. Though some once thought that homosexuality was homogeneous, encouraging gays to "come out" proved the opposite: gay men are as diverse as any group, and have as many ways of being gay as they had hangers in their closets. ⌧

COLOUR (ME) YOUR COLOUR, BABY

THE GENDER-FICATION OF PINK & BLUE

text by Kate Schweishelm · photography by JeongMee Yoon

I WAS BORN A BIG, FAT BABY. In the delivery room, my copious rolls and folds somehow confused even the doctor who first pronounced me a boy before correcting himself seconds later, bewildering my overwhelmed mother who thought maybe I was both. She would soon get used to this mistake; with my beefy, tanker truck physique and wispy, barely there hair, I was never the portrait of a delicate, dainty girl-child. In fact, as an infant, strangers assumed I was a boy so often that my exasperated mother started making a conscious effort to accessorize my outfits with pink bows, pink booties, and pink lace.

And why pink? Because pink is for girls, and blue is for boys. The gender significance of each colour needs no explanation – it's a custom that has been passed down in Western culture for generations, a tradition so longstanding we can only guess at its origins. Or so we think.

A manly shade of pink

Just over half a century ago, there was no consensus on the "right" colour for little boys and girls. In general, any pastel shade was considered appropriate for babies' clothing and nurseries. Even when pink and blue emerged as the dominant baby colours, there was no widespread agreement on which colour belonged with which gender. In Louisa May Alcott's 1868 bestseller, *Little Women*, twin babies are distinguished in the same way we're now accustomed to – a pink ribbon for the girl and a blue ribbon for the boy; however, the practice is described by one character as "French fashion," implying that it wasn't necessarily the norm in North America.

In fact, modern parents might be shocked to hear that for the first third of the 20th century, it was often argued that blue was the natural colour for girls, and pink the proper hue for boys. In 1918, one baby magazine explained: "The reason is that pink being a more decided and stronger colour is more suitable for the boy; while blue, which is more delicate and dainty, is prettier for the girl." The ease with which the magazine is able to rationalize these opposite colour choices indicates just how arbitrary colour associations were – and are.

The utter lack of consensus on gendered colours was proven in a 1927 article in *Time*. The magazine surveyed a handful of the biggest department stores in the United States, asking which colour was appropriate for each gender. The results were evenly split – half designated pink for boys and blue for girls, and the other half claimed the opposite. One Cleveland chain even suggested pink was the correct colour for both sexes. The article concluded that there seemed to be "no great unanimity of U.S. opinion on Pink v. Blue."

Dr. Jo Paoletti, clothing historian and author of *Pink and Blue: Telling the Boys from the Girls in America*, speculates that the confusion stemmed from the diversity in North American immigration during this period: people were arriving from disparate parts of Europe, bringing with them a variety of local customs. Ultimately, though, the greater significance of the pink and blue debate lies in what the notion of gendered colour conventions says about our evolving attitudes toward the nature of childhood.

From nature to nurture to knickers

In the 19th century, visually signifying the difference between boys and girls was not the norm. Children under the age of five, regardless of gender, wore the same thing – essentially, a variation of the styles worn by adult women. All infants wore bonnets and long, white dresses, similar to christening robes, trimmed with lace or embroidery. When they began to walk, toddlers graduated to shorter dresses and suits with skirts in various pastel colours. The differences between "boy clothes" and "girl clothes" were subtle – perhaps the style of buttoning or trim. The importance was placed not on distinguishing genders, but on marking children as a group separate from adults.

At that time, childhood was viewed in highly sentimental, romanticized terms. Children were seen as unspoiled cherubs, not yet corrupted by sin. Parents wished to shield their progeny from the wicked world of adulthood for as long as they could, and this meant prolonging

IN THE 19TH CENTURY, THE IMPORTANCE WAS PLACED NOT ON DISTINGUISHING GENDERS, BUT ON MARKING CHILDREN AS A GROUP SEPARATE FROM ADULTS.

the time children spent in gender-neutral clothing. As Paoletti explains, "Sexual awareness … would come soon enough; there was no need to hurry it by dressing babies like little men and little women."

Parents of this era were confident that masculinity and femininity were innate characteristics that would surface as children matured, regardless of how they were treated (or dressed) as babies. It wasn't until the turn of the 20th century, and the emergence of modern psychology, that this viewpoint shifted. By the 1890s, popular magazines were telling parents that gender roles were learned, and that they had a responsibility to begin teaching their offspring as early as possible. A swing from a belief in the power of nature to the power of nurture was now evident.

Whereas parents of the 19th century thought of gender identity as a natural development, parents of the early 20th century came to believe that it was a result of their own parenting practices. Coddle your boy and he may grow up to be too feminine; let your girl spend time roughhousing and she may become too masculine. Paoletti points out that it is perhaps no

BY THE 1890s, POPULAR MAGAZINES WERE
TELLING PARENTS THAT GENDER ROLES
WERE LEARNED, AND THAT THEY HAD
A RESPONSIBILITY TO BEGIN TEACHING
THEIR OFFSPRING AS EARLY AS POSSIBLE.

RATHER THAN SLOWLY GROWING INTO A GENDER THROUGH SEVERAL RITES OF PASSAGE, GENDER IS NOW THE FIRST THING THAT DEFINES US AT BIRTH AND IS AN IDENTITY MARKER THAT IS CONTINUOUSLY REINFORCED THROUGHOUT CHILDHOOD.

coincidence that it was also around this time that homosexuality began to be seen as a preventable psychic disorder, influenced in part by one's upbringing. Combine this view with the first wave of feminism and the fact that adult women were adopting more androgynous clothing, and it suddenly seemed highly important to ensure that children understood their gender roles from early on. The change was especially noticeable in boys' clothing, since traditional children's dress more strongly resembled feminine styles than masculine ones. Boys began wearing their hair short, tossing the dresses, and transitioning to trousers or knickers earlier than ever before.

The photographs that make up JeongMee Yoon's *The Pink and Blue Project* vividly illustrate just how rigid these definitions have become. Yoon takes male and female children from her native South Korea and photographs them surrounded by their possessions. The results – boys dwarfed by an ocean of blue, girls marooned in a sea of pink – demonstrate how relentlessly gendered the colour schemes of these innocent playthings are. But to what end?

Studies have shown that colour-coded clothing has little to no effect on infants and toddlers, who can't yet grasp the concept of gender. What clothing does significantly affect is how people

HOW AND WHY DO WE ALTER OUR BEHAVIOUR AND THE TOYS WE OFFER IF WE KNOW A CHILD IS A BOY VERSUS A GIRL?

Our babies, ourselves

As the 20th century advanced, the rules for separating boys from girls became progressively more restrictive, to the point that putting a male newborn in a pink dress now seems blatantly absurd to the majority of new parents. What is most interesting about all this, Paoletti observes, is that "even as gender roles have supposedly become less distinct, boys and girls are dressed more differently than ever before in American history." And at an earlier age, too – we sexualize even infants, regarding them as nascent men and women long before sexual maturity is reached. Rather than something we slowly grow into through several rites of passage, gender is now the first thing that defines us at birth and is an identity marker that is continuously reinforced throughout childhood.

react to a baby – essentially, it functions as a visual cue for adults interacting with the child. But if that's the purpose all this colour-coding serves, it brings up a big question – what difference does it make? How and why do we alter our behaviour and the toys we offer if we know a child is a boy versus a girl?

In a culture that fancies itself highly egalitarian, it is curious that we're so preoccupied with interacting with a baby in a "gender-appropriate" way, especially when we recognize that this "time-honoured" tradition is actually a very recent phenomenon. Because, really, the androgynous infant me didn't suffer from occasionally being treated like a burly little guy, nor from at times being seen as a sweet little gal; as long as you had a hand on the refrigerator door, hulk-baby was more than okay with being whatever you wanted him/her to be. ✉

Modest Introduction

TEXT BY EMILY RAINE • ART BY CELESTE RAMOS

IN RECENT YEARS, words like burqa and hijab have worked their way into the western lexicon, but there is still a lot of confusion over their meanings, stalling many discussions before they begin. In an effort to more clearly identify these terms (technically, if not ideologically) WORN uncovers a few definitions.

In Islam, hijab refers to covering part or all of oneself for modesty. It is part of purdah, the separation of the sexes, and both men and women have codes for appropriate cover that vary widely by region. The rules for veiling are closely aligned with kinship – one covers up to circulate in public, or any time there will be interaction with those who are not family (non-mahram). The imperative to dress modestly, or khimar, is outlined in the Qur'an, but many of the specific veiling practices are local and long predate the advent of Islam.

In the West, hijab is generally applied to women alone, and often denotes the headscarf or mantle used to conceal hair.

Abaya: A long, loose black cloak worn over other clothes to conceal one's figure from throat to foot. Abayat are mostly worn in the Khaleej (or Persian Gulf) region of the Middle East, although they are growing in popularity among Pakistani conservatives as well. While most are a plain chiffon-like material, some are adorned with embroidery, decorative trim, or even intricate patterns rendered in Swarovski crystals. A variation is the jilbab, a floor-length coat accompanied by a mantle.

Burqa: A single garment that covers both face and form, slipped on over other clothes before going out. In Afghanistan and northern Pakistan, burqa are also known as chadri. These long, flowing covers have

Abaya

Dupatta

Burqa

Bushiyya

Khimar

Chador

Niqab

haik

Al-Amira

a mesh grille over the face and slits for hands and come in a range of mostly pastel hues. The term burqa is often misused, incorrectly describing *niqab* or abayat.

Dupatta: Multi-purpose scarves worn by Hindu and Muslim women of all classes throughout much of South Asia. Available in a wide range of fabrics and styles, some are part of coordinated outfits, and many are heavily decorated with metallic embroidery, sequins, mirror and beadwork, insets, and tassels. While dupatta are generally draped over the head and allowed to fall past the shoulders, they can also be worn as thin shawls. Dupatta predate Islam by a long shot – some estimate by as much as 5,000 years – and though considered a key part of modest dress, they are also fashionable accessories.

Bushiyya: Most commonly worn in the Persian Gulf region, this is a loose black cloth without eyeholes draped over the whole face and made of a fabric sheer enough to see through. A bushiyya is secured over the forehead and under a headscarf. It's worn loose so that it can easily be flipped up to expose the face beneath, although many women wear this piece with a tighter niqab underneath for maximum coverage.

Niqab: A veil that covers the bottom half of a woman's face but leaves her eyes exposed, typical of the Arabic Persian Gulf region. Most are loose-fitting squares of black fabric tied on under a headscarf, sometimes with another band of cloth covering the forehead to form a slit that exposes the eyes. A variation is the half-niqab, which is worn over the bridge of the nose and fixed tightly under the chin (like a ninja mask). In the United Arab Emirates, a few older women still wear traditional stone niqab: dull grey casts with carved-out sockets to

protect the eyes. The stone contains minerals that moisturize and cleanse the wearer's skin as she sweats underneath it, serving at once as sunshield, windbreak, and facial.

Chador: A long black semicircle of fabric, with no sleeves or slits for hands, that covers both head and body, and is held fast by one hand under the chin. This form is unique to Iran, and has been worn there since long before the birth of Islam. The chador was initially a class, rather than religious, prerogative: wealthy Iranian women wore them to distinguish themselves from those who worked.

Khimar: A headscarf used to cover part or all of a woman's hair, sometimes exposing her face or throat depending on the mantle's cut and how it is tied. Lengths and designs vary by region. These are generally black and are known as *shayla* or *buknuk* (a longer version) in the Middle East, *türban* in Turkey, and *tudung* in Malaysia and Indonesia. In the west, we usually refer to this as hijab.

Haik: An all-white full-body cover worn by North African Muslims, usually made of cotton, wool, or silk. A haik is wrapped over the head and around the body, and held together with one or both hands on the inside. The women who wear them cover their faces either by wrapping the haik tightly enough so that only one eye is exposed through a triangular gap, or by adopting a facial veil as well.

Al-Amira: A two-piece headscarf composed of a tight wrap of stretchy fabric that binds the head to prevent any stray hairs from escaping and a longer, looser tube of material that is wrapped to hang overtop. The two pieces can be made of the same or complementary fabrics. ✄

HAIR APPARENT

photography by Alyssa K. Faoro

Credits

hair // Sydney Woods
modelling // Paul Comeau, Chris De Castro, Ryan Marr,
Ryan Nangreaves, & Chris Cheeseman
styling // G. Stegelmann
styling assistance // Chelsea McBroom

◇◇◇◇◇◇◇

"I want minimum information given with
maximum politeness."

JACKIE KENNEDY

◇◇◇◇◇◇◇

"I tried to drown my sorrows,
but the bastards learned how to swim...."

FRIDA KAHLO

"Elegance is not the prerogative of those who have just escaped from adolescence, but of those who have already taken possession of their future."

COCO CHANEL

"I have the heart of a man...
and I am not afraid of anything."

QUEEN ELIZABETH I

◇◇◇◇◇◇◇

"For me, sitting still is harder
than any kind of work."

ANNIE OAKLEY

THE F WORD

Finding a Place for Fashion in Feminism

TEXT BY EMILY RAINE

FASHION HAS ALWAYS BEEN TREACHEROUS terrain for feminists. They must carefully negotiate critiques of the toll fashion sometimes takes on women's bodies, wallets, and self-esteem, while still recognizing its capacity for pleasure, power, and entrepreneurship. Though feminists have proven quite skilled at attacking fashion's many shortcomings, I have consistently been saddened and disenchanted by their failure to notice its many benefits.

Feminism has a long history of disdain for clothing that is expressive, decorative, or extravagant – in short, everything about fashion that is fun. Generations ago, Simone de Beauvoir described her female predecessors' painful whalebone-and-steel corsets and spine-jarring heels as a means of depriving women of their physical power; even before that, in the late 1800s, George Sand (a woman) advocated cross-dressing as liberated. Since then, feminists have critiqued the fashion and beauty industries for manipulating desires and condemned women who dress up for objectifying themselves.

The rank and file of the '60s women's liberation movement sported a "natural," unisex look: t-shirts, no bra, sandals, and jeans. This generation of feminism was steeped in revolutionary Marxist rhetoric that saw fashion as the epitome of capitalism. Any visible attempt at self-decoration implicated the wearer in contributing to her own oppression by dressing up for the sexist gaze. The movement was so popular that the "natural" feminist look itself became trendy, making the no-fashion look the very height of fashion. The theme, it appears, is that a woman can dress like a feminist by giving up everything frilly, brightly coloured, and tight; above all, a woman is dressed like a feminist when she is dressed like a man.

As a feminist, a scholar, and a girl who likes clothes, I often find myself caught in the crossfire. I have watched my friends give up their vintage finds, big earrings, or dresses splattered with fruit prints when they get "real" jobs or have kids. Call it the *Legally Blonde* effect. But, like many women, every time I catch myself doubting whether I look intelligent in knee-high boots or if grown-ups are allowed to wear hot pink, I wonder: if I'm a feminist, then why can't I dress like a girl?

A distraction for delicate creatures

Although playing with clothing is one of the great daily joys of many women, those who are sympathetic to feminism often feel guilty for it. Sociologist Iris Marion Young has said that fashion theory constructs a rigid idea of "the woman well dressed for the male gaze, then endows with guilt the pleasure we might derive for ourselves in these clothes." The fashion-conscious feminist is made to feel doubly shamed for having twice betrayed the feminist cause:

first for falling into the old patriarchal trap of mugging for the objectifying sexual gaze, then again for enjoying it.

This position doesn't leave much room for the satisfaction of playing with the spectacular identities that clothing can signify as an activity in and of itself. It assumes that a woman's interest in her attire is purely frivolous, seeking only to outdo her peers or impress sexual quarry. It ignores the relationships that clothing nourishes between women, the pride and power that can be gleaned from

the presumption that everything women do or take an interest in is completely asinine. Though fashion today is considered largely a woman's preoccupation, it has not always been so. Until the 18th century, wealthy women and men wore elaborate costumes to broadcast their wealth. Fashion was a class, not a gender, prerogative. When rich men took to the office after the Industrial Revolution, however, they gave up the satin, jewels, and furs of yore in favour of a modified hunting costume, easily recognizable in

FEMINISM HAS A LONG HISTORY OF DISDAIN FOR CLOTHING THAT IS EXPRESSIVE, DECORATIVE, OR EXTRAVAGANT — IN SHORT, *everything about fashion that is fun.*

a solid outfit, and the game of using garments as costumes to craft public personas. Above all, it takes for granted that women who invest energy in their appearances are incapable of realizing they are being manipulated; they are lambs who willingly nestle themselves in the fashion industry's rapacious jaw rather than rational, empowered individuals who choose to communicate using apparel.

By following this line of logic, feminism rehearses an older, very sexist condemnation of fashion as silly and impractical, based on

today's three-piece suit. Bourgeois women continued to exploit fashion's riches, flaunting expensive clothes in order to demonstrate their husbands' abilities to pay for them.

Since then, men's apparel has changed little, and even their accessories are muted and bland. Psychoanalyst J.C. Flügel calls men's rejection of fashion "The Great Masculine Renunciation," arguing that it represses an innate human drive for exhibitionism and self-display. He finds that masculine narcissism has since been forced to find

other outlets, such as professional or athletic ostentation, and he proposes that the leering gaze and the fetishization of women's images may also be consequences. Flügel's theory suggests that fashion fulfills a basic need to communicate something of ourselves to one another in the vast anonymity of city life.

Recognizing some of these factors – or perhaps eager to wear lamé to conferences – feminists began to explore ideas of fashion that legitimize the enjoyment of clothing without abandoning a critique of the fashion industry.

Feminine Renunciation" and submission to *Vogue*. She sees wearing vintage as a positive feminist practice because it plays up the commonalities among women of different eras, highlighting, for example, similarities between '40s fashions and '80s feminist theory. "Because it establishes a dialogue between the present-day wearers of that clothing and its original wearers, vintage also provides a means of salvaging the images that have traditionally sustained feminine subjectivity, images that have been consigned to the wastebasket not

BUT LIKE MANY WOMEN, EVERY TIME I CATCH MYSELF DOUBTING WHETHER I LOOK INTELLIGENT IN KNEE-HIGH BOOTS OR IF GROWN-UPS ARE ALLOWED TO WEAR HOT PINK, I WONDER:

If I'm a feminist, then why can't I dress like a girl?

It seemed that the solution lay in finding a system of dress that operates outside of mainstream media – the magazines that dictate colour coordination, the correct body type for the season, and the (inevitably high-end) brands we should buy – yet still allows women to play with clothing to create looks and personas. To many, vintage clothing provides such a system.

Second wave second-hand
Kaja Silverman argues that second-hand rags offer an outlet that avoids both a "Great

only by fashion but by 'orthodox' feminism."

Vintage also subverts fashion's built-in obsolescence, returning the value to past seasons' discards. This is a vital issue, considering that textile and garment manufacturing requires (mostly) female workers in the Global South to labour under appalling sweatshop conditions, creating seasonally disposable wares for (mostly) female consumers in the North. The relative cheapness of second-hand goods also allows less-privileged consumers to buy more and

better clothing, enabling poor women to take greater risks and freedoms. Think of it this way: if you can only afford one pair of pants, you'll make damned well sure to get a pair that you can wear to work and that matches everything. With two pairs, you might be able to buy the slinky red ones, too. Buying used goods makes room in even the tightest budget for a bit of frivolity, provided you have the time to seek it out.

Eighties feminism also praised vintage for providing women with both entrepreneurial and social opportunities. The vast majority of vintage retailers are female-owned small businesses patronized and staffed mostly by women. They facilitate a semi-closed cycle of consumption, disposal, retrieval, and re-consumption peopled almost entirely by women. Used clothing stores, where fledgling design houses share store space with hand-picked vintage items, are commonly used to launch or subsidize small, independent designers – again, mostly younger women. Vintage vendors are part of a broader collector economy of "rag picking." Seasoned buyers comb used-goods depots for particularly nice second-hand pieces to collect or resell. Determining which goods are worth saving involves a trained atten-tion to details and a solid dose of taste.

Casual rag picking is a rite of passage for many, enabling young girls to learn about fashion history and experiment with different looks on the cheap. Buying vintage individualizes taste, as the goods available

are set apart from mainstream fashion media trends. Scouring second-hand racks is also highly social – the fact is, females of the human species prefer to hunt in packs. Second-hand shopping allows us to share knowledge about brands, textiles, or design and tailoring details; to cultivate knowledge of old fashions; and to boast about past finds.

Vintage shopping is much like record, stamp, or coin collecting among men – each is a collector culture operating its own hierarchy of value that only connoisseurs can appreciate, each accords status in demonstrations of this skill, and each is dominated by one gender, almost entirely to the exclusion of the other. With vintage, experience fosters a level of connoisseurship to distinguish the

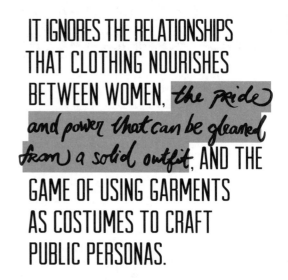

IT IGNORES THE RELATIONSHIPS THAT CLOTHING NOURISHES BETWEEN WOMEN, *the pride and power that can be gleaned from a solid outfit*, AND THE GAME OF USING GARMENTS AS COSTUMES TO CRAFT PUBLIC PERSONAS.

Fashion is a positive feminine practice WHEREVER AND WHENEVER WOMEN USE CLOTHING MEANINGFULLY AND CREATIVELY.

difference between, say, a '50s crepe shift by an obscure designer and a dime-a-dozen '70s polyester op art dress. It trains us to treat vintage pieces as art objects, each with its own peculiar character and history.

Scholar Angela McRobbie claims that in making such distinctions seasoned pickers "can attain the status of a connoisseur, an achievement that mitigates against established associations of fashion consumption with irrational and hysterical traits." When we share our acquaintance with vintage goods, both the garments and the collectors who know to nab them are validated. Vintage is rare in its cultivation of such feminine specialized knowledge because it is a collector field that is not perceived to be dominated by men. McRobbie also points out that women tend to feel more comfortable developing skills in realms stereotyped to be outside of male cultural expertise, and fashion is one area where women are seen to reign supreme.

Perhaps the greatest thing about vintage is that each piece is unique and exclusive, worn in a personalized way. Feminism, too, makes compelling arguments in favour of second-hand clothing. The common message is the conviction that fashion is a positive feminine practice wherever and whenever women use clothing meaningfully and creatively. It reminds us that fashion is ultimately about using garments to express oneself and that what is powerful and fashionable in a well-put-together outfit is the woman who shines through in it.

Since the '80s, the tide of vintage cheerleading has abated as feminist fashion critics turned their attention elsewhere. However, this period of fashion theory is dear to me for having opened up a space where women who identify with feminist issues can feel okay about their desire to dress up, without fear of being criticized by their peers for "selling out." It authenticated especially the weirdest, most idiosyncratic fashions as art objects that are testaments to the women of their times. Every piece is somehow brilliant because it is girly, a signifier of something that women are extremely good at. The feminists' attention to rag picking makes the jangling bangles and flapper fringes and the endless mountains of crap that accumulate in my smelly wardrobe a source of pride, and each hard-won find becomes a trophy for hours of scouring. Because of this, I can finally consider myself a feminist fashionista. ⊠

UNBINDING BINARIES

Using clothing to unlock the door of gender identity

TEXT BY ALYSSA GARRISON // PHOTOGRAPHY BY WYNNE NEILLY

LANDON WHITTAKER ROLLS OUT OF BED having hit the snooze button at least twice. He showers, combs back his short brown hair, and brushes his teeth. Next, Landon pulls on a binder, a mesh undershirt used to create a male chest contour and, although he owns a number of packers, opts not to put one down his pants. "I don't want to look fully male," he explains. "I like not having anything obvious in my pants. It's contradicting because I don't need a packer but I need a binder, but that's what makes me comfortable." Lastly, Landon turns to his sparse closet and chooses the clothing that will most likely help him pass as a man.

Today, the queer community is more visible than ever before, but many of the practices within it are still misunderstood. For many trans, genderqueer, and butch people, the misunderstandings start early in life and create a lasting resentment toward getting dressed. For Sonya Cams, a 31-year-old queer person, the rules of dress were decided before she was born. "My mom already had a walk-in closet for me full of dresses. She used to have to pin me down kicking and screaming to get them on me before kindergarten." For Sonya's mother, preconceived notions of gender came before what made her daughter comfortable, but it was a losing battle. "Half of the dresses ended up going to Goodwill, the tags still on them." Sonya's tense relationship with clothing and her mother lasted until she was finally able to use her own money to buy the clothes she liked – from the boys' section. "I loved my Adidas tracksuits with matching knee-high socks and sneakers. And I always wore the same hat, trucker style with a mesh back. For a long time I even slept with that hat on because I hated to brush my hair so much."

Though she eventually found the clothes that made her comfortable, Sonya had internalized her mother's expectations: "I was conditioned so much as a small child to be the feminine girl she wanted me to be. Even now, when I go home to my family, I soften it up." For Wynne Neilly, a queer person who grew up in the suburbs of Oakville, Ontario, dressing in boys' clothing could only mean one thing: "My mom has always thought because I wore men's clothing, I wanted to

"I don't think that masculinity is exclusively attached to maleness."

WYNNE NEILLY

be a man. In the weeks after I came out to her, she found a pair of men's underwear in the laundry hamper and lost it. She couldn't wrap her head around me wearing men's underwear if I was a woman. She still can't."

Sex, sexuality, and gender are completely different pieces of a person's identity. Sex is based on the reproductive organs one was born with, and cannot be changed without surgery, whereas gender is fluid and can act as a chosen aspect of one's identity. Sexuality is separate from both, indicating to whom one is attracted as opposed to how someone identifies. Gender, however, is a social construction, and a spectrum with many hues.

In the case of the above – female-to-male trans people and masculine-identified people – this can mean those born into a female body but identifying as male, those who reject gender categorization, and those who identify as women but dress in a way considered to be culturally masculine. Others may appear traditionally male and take testosterone, but choose to keep their female reproductive organs and identify

as female among friends. Still others may choose to be completely androgynous, opting to be referred to as "they" to avoid gender labelling and expectations. J, a University of Toronto Women and Gender Studies major, identifies as trans-queer, just started hormone treatments, and prefers others use gender-neutral pronouns. Although very masculine when first coming out as a trans person, J now feels comfortable indulging in "femme-ininity," mixing men's and women's clothes to explore a femme identity on the trans-masculine scale. "I've recently heard the term 'trans fag with dyke roots.' It's great." But the complexity of identifying outside the gender binaries creates a new set of problems when it comes to shopping.

Stores divide their goods between men and women, from socks and jewelry to jeans and t-shirts. These clothes fall into "fit" guidelines that subscribe to normative gender ideals and send some very pointed messages: women are dainty and slim-waisted, with larger chests and smaller feet, and embellishments are key. Men have massive shoulders, long legs,

> ## "I don't think of myself as masculine, I just think of myself as me. If anyone were to look at me they would think I was masculine, but that's based on an idea of masculinity created by society."
>
> LANDON WHITTAKER

and narrow hips. Even if women's clothing is made in a menswear style, details like the small back pockets on pants or the side a dress shirt buttons on are giveaways that can prevent passing. This garment binary makes it nearly impossible for some people to find clothing. "Places for the masses need to recognize the reality of the human figure, because people aren't all Barbie and Ken; they're diverse," says Wynne. Wynne and Landon, friends for the past five years, often joke about fighting off the smaller gay boys to grab the few sizes that fit their slender frames. For Landon, the hunt for men's clothing has become easier as his upper body broadens from testosterone injections.

Travis Clark, a 19-year-old trans guy, also found his relationship with clothing changed as his body became more male: "Before I started hormones, I always wanted to make sure people knew I had this masculine feel about me. I had anxiety being around people in public because I didn't exude enough of a masculine voice or a masculine face. Once I started hormones I got a lot more comfortable in my body and how I represent myself, and I've gotten a lot more fluid in my clothing choices. You would never catch me in a tank top six months ago. I was uncomfortable in my body and anxious people would see my binder. Now I've embraced my trans identity and am totally comfortable with the masculinity I exude. But I'm also not super concerned.... I just don't think about it anymore."

As each person occupies their unique place on the gender scale, they also have varying needs when dressing their specific shape. J has to deal with finding clothing in the right size without drawing attention to a large chest: "The biggest size in men's clothing often isn't big enough, because of the shape of my body. Even if I want to wear men's clothes I can't fit them." And the one problem on which there is consensus is shoes: although men's shoes are produced in a size seven, it's rarely available and almost always too wide for a smaller foot. This leaves male-identified dressers with the option of finding masculine women's shoes, which are often narrow and finished with subtle, feminine details.

"Gender is just something someone made up a long time ago, to me it doesn't really mean anything."

SONYA CAMS

Fitting problems continue in dressing rooms, where shoppers are forced to pick a side. Gender divisions in the changerooms of clothing stores create the same conflict as gendered washrooms. Kyle Lasky chose to completely avoid men's changerooms until taking testosterone and passing as a man. Others, like Wynne, have been turned away at the door. "I'm trying on men's clothing because I want them to fit me in a masculine way, so how is that any different from a man?" With all these issues of fit and availability (not to mention the potential for conflict), it might make one ask, why bother? But as in so many other areas of self-identification, clothing is a big deal.

Although clothing may have its limitations, it provides the freedom to express oneself and create a new body without altering the surface of the skin. "Clothing is so important. Initially when you see someone, how they're dressed is one of the first things you notice about them. Especially since clothing is often used as a gender identifier," says Travis. Wynne adds, "I wouldn't be able to

live with myself if I didn't have the option to choose what I wear. The clothing that I choose to wear gives me confidence and helps me feel strong in my own skin."

Strength is a common ground for people who identify with masculinity, but Wynne feels masculinity has little to do with being male: "I think it's interesting because if you were to ask somebody who was born male and identified as feminine or was trans female, they would probably say the same thing about feeling feminine; it makes them feel strong." Although each person has a different take on what masculinity means, they repeat again and again that it's not about the aesthetic, but the energy they find when they are truly comfortable with themselves. "When you think of a group of people you can't just place one image on them. We are all very individual people. Not every trans guy is going to want to have this insanely masculine look. Just because we're trans doesn't mean we all have to look alike," says Travis.

Everyone, regardless of gender, sex, or body type, wants to wear something in which

"I think masculinity all has to come from within, really; it depends if you have a masculine energy, a masculine feeling."

TRAVIS CLARK

they feel comfortable, and be free to make that choice, even when it challenges the norms society has built. Fabric and thread don't conform to a gender, so why do we impose gendered labels, and force people into categories that don't fit? The fashion world purports to celebrate self-expression and individuality, yet the by-products and ideas of fashion really only exist for two kinds of people. The truth is, even people who fit into the normative categories are often left out – and their opinions ignored and choices limited.

For those outside the lines, it can be daunting. But if clothing can give us the power to reinvent ourselves and to show the world the person we want to be, if fashion is aspirational, then it shouldn't be hard to understand why people would want to push the boundaries and find the fit that others take for granted. As Wynne says, "How everyone chooses to represent themselves is equally amazing. It's awesome when people can be brave enough to step outside of preconceived gender boxes, and the world just needs to back off and let them dress the way they want." ⊠

Finding the Words: A list of commonly used terms

BINDING: To flatten one's breast tissue either with a store-bought binder or tensor bandages.

BUTCH: Notably masculine in appearance and/or behaviour, but not necessarily identifying as male.

FTM OR F2M: Slang for female-to-male transgender people.

GENDERQUEER: An identity that involves no gender labelling whatsoever.

PACKING: Using a store-bought packer – molded to resemble a flaccid penis and scrotum – or sock to create a bulge visible through pants.

PASSING: In this context, a trans man being publicly recognized as male.

STEALTH: A person who chooses not to be identified as transgender by those around them.

TRANSGENDER: An all-encompassing term used to define individuals whose gender expression and/or gender identity differs from conventional or cultural expectation based on their sex.

TRANSVESTITE: A person who cross-dresses, meaning they dress in clothing traditionally related to the opposite sex.

TRANSSEXUAL: An individual whose gender identity does not match the sex that was identified with/assigned to them at birth.

T: Slang for testosterone, or hormone therapy. Can be administered through creams or patches, orally, or most commonly, through direct injection.

FASHION IS

IDEAS

08

FASHION IS MORE THAN CLOTHING or trend, history or object — it represents ideas. It inspires ideas. Why do we choose the things we wear? What drives our consumption? What are the terms under which we assign clothing value and how does that value shift over time? Because fashion is a living, evolving thing, and reflective of its age, examining the ideas behind it can help us identify less externalized cultural ideals we too easily take for granted.

In this chapter, the ideas behind fashion are paramount. Collectors examine why establishing a clothing museum is complicated by both choosing its contents and asserting its credibility, a fashion scholar looks at the changing perception of "vintage" in definition and significance, and the production of a traditional fabric wanes in the shadow of outsourcing and the global market. In these photo shoots, stylists draw inspiration from everyday sources like literature, food, and pop culture. And while some of the ideas have serious implications and some are just for fun, they all use clothing as the starting point for larger conversations.

Invariably, how we think about our selves, our economy, and our culture — every aspect of our lives — informs how we wear our clothes. WORN believes careful consideration of our response to fashion might lead us to ask how we could use clothes to influence culture. As Alexandra Palmer says, you can use fashion to "change who you are, or who you think you are, or who others think you are." It may be grammatically awkward, but fashion is definitely ideas. ⬨

biblio filles

creative direction by Serah-Marie McMahon
photography by Alyssa K. Faoro

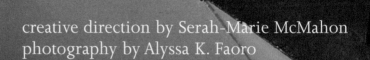

Reading list

Reading list

Reading list

opposite page
The Secret Garden //
Frances Hodgson Burnett
Dune // Frank Herbert

this page
*I'm with the Band: Confessions
of a Groupie //* Pamela Des Barres
& Dave Navarro

Credits

styling // Casie Brown, Rose Flutur &
Eliza Trent-Rennick
assistant styling // Alyssa Garrison
hair styling // Jamie Furie & Renee Clement
assistant photography // Melissa Alcena
makeup // Tammy Wong & Karen Lindblad
modelling // Jo Jin, Wynne Neilly, Ave
Smith, Laura Duncan, Nura Yunus,
Sara Williams, Amanda Caswell, Jessica
Chen, Laura Kloepfer, Alexandra Barton,
& Melissa Alcena

CURATOR, CONNOISSEUR, CONSUMER
A MIDLIFE CRISIS AT THE PARIS ETHICAL FASHION SHOW
TEXT BY SHANNON BELL PRICE

I WAS BORN AT THE BEGINNING of the end of the world. At least this is how my beatnik, baby boomer parents and I came to see it. 1968 seemed the postmodern end of liberal idealism. It was the year Nixon was elected, Martin Luther King Jr. was assassinated, and international anti-war protests and student unrest peaked. Then again, it was also the year Andy Warhol survived an assassination attempt and Jane Fonda played a sexy space cadet in *Barbarella*. It was the year Theodore Roszak coined the term "counterculture" in his book *The Making of a Counter Culture: Reflections on the Technocratic Society and Its Youthful Opposition.*

Forty years later, I still see the world through this oppositional lens of despair over the past mixed with hope for the future. Ideological soul-searching doesn't easily reconcile itself with a career in fashion, but here I am, and I am not alone. I don't work in the fashion industry per se. I am a fashion curator, connoisseur, and, of course, consumer.

I grew up in Berkeley, California, where we have recycled, composted, and saved water for as long as I can remember. Organic food and natural cosmetics have long been the norm. From an early age I shopped at thrift stores and sewed my own clothes. In my teens and twenties, this DIY aesthetic came to define my personal style. But when I moved to New York City a decade ago, I found the lure of avant-garde designer clothing, the relative expense of vintage, and having less time and space to sew changed my shopping habits, how I dressed, and even my perception of self. My then-new position at an uptown museum eventually inspired a full-blown fashion identity crisis.

As a result, I began to look for more meaning in my work as a fashion historian and curator. While I am still drawn to the formal and artistic merits of high fashion, I realize I need to reconcile these interests with my environmental and social concerns. I can also see that this eco-chic moment is part of an evolving fashion history, and its success or failure hinges on whether or not it really can be both eco and chic. If environmentally concerned designers cannot manage to produce beautiful clothes that people want to wear, there's no hope of creating a sustainable fashion industry. Ultimately, I found I wanted a crash course in the issues, and that's how I ended up in Paris in October of 2007 at the fourth annual Ethical Fashion Show (EFS4).

THEORY

While the idea of combining environmental concerns with fashion has been around at least since the decade I was born, by 2007 it had only seriously been on the fashion industry's radar for less than 10 years. But in 2006, London Fashion Week launched Estethica, an ethical and environmentally friendly exhibition sponsored by the British Fashion Council, and that same year Paris' Prêt-à-Porter trade fair featured a So Ethic section with 70 socially and environmentally conscious designers.

In 2007, Sweden, Singapore, and Australia had fair trade and organic-centric fashion shows, and in North America there were ethical fashion shows in Los Angeles, Portland, Seattle, and Vancouver. Yet whatever the competition, Paris' EFS is the oldest and largest ethical trade show dedicated solely to *la mode éthique*. Founder and organizer Isabelle Quéhé strives to make Paris the ethical fashion capital of the world and to prove ethical fashion can be cutting edge.

Organized by a non-profit, Universal Love, EFS attracts a wide variety of sponsors and partners to its cause, including the French Ministry of Economy, Finance and Employment; the United Nations Environment Program; and PPR (the umbrella company for design houses like Gucci, YSL, and Balenciaga). The corporate and governmental support ethical fashion receives in Paris was impressive, and I wondered why our own fashion capital, New York, had not organized around these important issues.

France is a smaller, older country with a long history of supporting its apparel arts, so it may be cultural (and easier to organize on that scale), but the United States is one of the largest nonorganic cotton producers and consumers in the world. While there are certainly serious private efforts being made (Loomstate, Rogan, and Barneys' 2007 Green Christmas), it's far more enthusiastically organized overseas in terms of both government support and nonprofit involvement. We need to get our national act together.

AND PRACTICE

EFS4 was held at the Tapis Rouge (built in 1784, it was the first department store in Paris). Three floors of over one hundred vendors – the first EFS only had about two dozen – kept visitors busy day and night. There were all-day discussion panels and fashion shows highlighting the best of the participating ethical designers. Vendors ran the style gamut from couture to kidswear, and each was classified according to their environmental emphases, like organic textiles, traditional skills, or fair trade practices.

More than 40 countries were represented at EFS4, from Afghanistan to Britain to the Ivory Coast. Many designers worked in international collaborations between European and developing nations, combining traditional skills with organic cotton, or social projects with recycling. Gafreh, a women's collective based in Burkina Faso, hires local weavers to transform recycled plastic bags into cloth. But although these projects were interesting, some looked a bit hippyish to me (must we still do tie-dye skirts?) and were, for the most part, far too bohemian for an upscale fashion market.

It was nice to see there was plenty of design that wasn't.

DESIGN

French designer Caloli practises fair trade and highlights the traditional skills of the Chinese Miao women through the beauty of their thousand-fold pleated skirts. In my museum work, I have done much research on and acquisition of Miao dress and their exquisite sculptural silver jewelry because I thought it would be an inspiration to Western designers. It was incredible to finally see the extreme ruffled silhouette of their traditional dress effectively translated into contemporary fashion.

Celine Faizant, who trained with Chanel and Lacroix, produces a sort of demi-couture out of organic textiles and dyes such as her *manteau à tournure*, a chic merino and Jura black wool coat. Also, Sakina M'Sa, a collective of French women who have been unable to find work in high fashion due to social and cultural restrictions, makes luxurious silk dresses in solid colours, detailed with twists, pleats, rolls, tucks, and draping that create a refined ultramodern style.

Satoshi Date is a Japanese designer who has worked with such illustrious contemporaries as Alexander McQueen and Gareth Pugh. Date is a multidisciplinary artist, but it was his

PLANNED OBSOLESCENCE, THROUGH EVER-CHANGING FASHIONS MADE CHEAPLY AND REPLACED OFTEN, HAS BEEN IMPORTANT FOR THE WORLD ECONOMY – BUT IT'S TIME WE FOUND A NEW WAY.

fashion work that was a hands-down highlight of EFS4. Date denounces homogenization, consumerism, and disposable decoration, and does his part by hand-felting and dyeing the organic wool he uses to make his one-of-a-kind, decidedly avant-garde, semi-futuristic line. The combination of the wool's uneven texture and the fugitive pastel colouring creates an uneasy but thoroughly satisfying *wabi-sabi*. Date also uses all of the offcuts from his work to create unique pieces of wool jewelry, and his signature runway shoe is a pump with a paper spat that creates a silhouette both charming and jarring.

DEBATE

About 5,000 buyers, trendspotters, market researchers, and fashion professionals (some aspiring) attended EFS4. This demographic was a stark contrast to the academic conferences I usually attend, where people talk about fashion rather than participate in the cycle of consumption. However, there were a handful of people like me with academic leanings, and the daily panel discussions were exactly what I wanted to delve into, more than just the aesthetic effect of ethical fashion.

Panels featured broad discussion of the economic, social, and environmental issues at stake. They stressed the need to advocate and support organic cotton (nonorganic cotton comes with a side of harmful pesticides, chemical runoff, and dyes). There was consensus that although the gap between ethical and mainstream fashion is wide, awareness is increasing. Consumer pressure can compel large corporations to act responsibly. The panels also touched on partnerships with developing countries with respect to gender (it's usually women's work in these countries) and colonization (it's the first world "collaborating" with the third). Talk of supporting traditional skills is beneficial, but I noticed a tendency to assume that native craftsmen will enjoy the work we ask them to do. Ethical fashion do-gooders must be careful not to idealize (and primitivize) their collaborators.

One notable panel outlined the life cycle of an apparel object (extraction, production, fabrication, distribution, consumption, care, disposal) and highlighted how these processes contribute to global warming and resource waste. Fashion is responsible for a lot of the waste our consumer society produces, and it was fashion that introduced the seasonality that other product industries would follow. Planned obsolescence, through ever-changing fashions made cheaply and replaced often, has been important for the world economy – but it's time we found a new way.

> # LUXURY COULD BE DEFINED AS AN ETHICAL CHOICE, RATHER THAN BY PRICE OR BRANDING.

MORE WITH LESS

The final conversations of EFS4 dealt with consumption and changing the way we use and define fashion. There was talk of evolution among fashion consumers who may begin to see a product in relation to its real environmental and social costs. Luxury could be defined as an ethical choice, rather than by price or branding. We must look at consumer trends and the fast, novelty-driven fashion cycle that creates so much waste, and we must slow it down, ignore seasonality (sadly, this has become easier to do, as climate change has already altered the way people shop), and look for quality over quantity. Fashion does not have to be about constant change, but it can be, and actually always has been, about quality, longevity, beauty, and personal expression.

LESS AND MORE

My European muse was a French fashion professional who wore the same Balenciaga outfit for five days straight while we were working on a project. She looked absolutely stunning every day, and it proved to me that it's better to spend more on a few high-quality outfits than to choose lousy quality for the sake of quantity. I have used this as my model and dedicated myself to a year of less shopping. While I cannot afford Balenciaga, privileging quality over quantity has helped me to make peace with what's already in my closet, wear my clothes with style and often, and feel freer to do things other than shop and worry about what to wear.

Though in Europe understanding of the ethical fashion industry has been growing, in the United States, the home of Walmart, disposable clothing, and the absurd idea that we shouldn't be seen in the same thing twice, this is not yet the case. EFS4 proved to me what I hoped it would: there are enough talented ethical designers to begin a fashion revolution – now we just have to buy into it. In Paris, I found a balance and a merging of aesthetics and ethics that I believe fashion must achieve to survive in the 21st century. ✖

Cut to the Chase

Credits

modelling // Nonto
photography & art direction // Jasa Baka
for Parlour Treats

PULLING A MUSEUM OUT OF A HATBOX

FASHION COLLECTORS JONATHAN WALFORD AND KENN NORMAN TRANSFORM A PRIVATE ◈ STASH INTO A PUBLIC INSTITUTION ◈

INTERVIEW BY KATE SCHWEISHELM
PHOTOGRAPHY BY ALYSSA K. FAORO
ART DIRECTION BY G. STEGELMANN

KENN NORMAN WAS READING A BOOK on Fortuny when Jonathan Walford first approached him 25 years ago. The book signalled a shared and lasting interest in fashion history, and the two have been a couple ever since. Jonathan, who was the founding curator at the Bata Shoe Museum, is an admitted shopaholic with a history of emptying his wallet to further his personal collection of vintage clothing. Kenn, a bibliophile who was once fired from a job at Ports International for piercing his ear on his lunch break, has a background in crunching numbers in the corporate and arts administration worlds. Out of these combined talents, a museum was born. After five years of planning, the Fashion History Museum received its charitable status in early 2009, and the pair is now searching for the best site to host its impressive collection of artifacts.

When did you first take an interest in fashion?

JW: The first time I consciously remember looking at clothes and thinking they were cool was while watching *The Six Wives of Henry VIII* on TV. I was 11 years old and I cried because it was on after my bedtime and I wanted to see it. The clothes were absolutely fascinating to me.

Do you remember the first thing you collected for collecting's sake?

JW: It was a black net dress from the 1890s. It was English and so theatrical. I paid $60 for it, which was every penny I had from my paycheque. I had it until a few years ago, when I finally sold it on eBay.

What was the vintage market like when you started collecting as a teenager in the '70s?

JW: There was no real market – it was just old clothes. I used to pick great stuff at Value Village – I got a Courrèges at one. I could shoot myself over the things I didn't buy – I'm now buying stuff that I wouldn't have even looked at 20 years ago. I used to get Ceil Chapmans and then re-sell them for $15. I didn't care! I thought Ceil Chapman was boring! You don't find stuff like that anymore – in the '90s everything changed, and the prices suddenly started doubling and tripling. I think a lot of it is overvalued now. When it comes down to it, it's still old clothes. Fabric gets tired, seams get weak. Old polyester with body smell – it's going to have that smell forever.

What's your strangest story of how you acquired something?

JW: Around 1980 I worked at a museum in North Vancouver. On my drive to work one morning I noticed a pile of hatboxes outside a house, which I thought was weird. After work I went back and the hatboxes had been picked up by garbage already, but I noticed that the house was abandoned and the back door was open, so I went in. For some reason, the people who bought the house had decided to throw out all the hats, but the clothes were still hanging in the closet. So I went to the corner store, bought a box of garbage bags, went back to the house, and loaded up. I filled every square inch of the car.

Was your family supportive of your interest in fashion?

JW: My father was a buyer for the fancy schmancy Room at the Bay. He bought wedding dresses, hats, and eventually cocktail dresses. He'd go to Davidow in New York and the guy would ask what size his wife was and a suit would arrive later for my mother. She had Davidow, Ceil Chapman, Lilli Ann – all those names. Nowadays we call them kickbacks, but in those days they were called "gifts." [Laughs.] There were a lot of clothes around, but the funny thing is I have nothing but my mother's wedding dress and a couple of other things.

What about your family, Kenn?

KN: My father used to work in the industry too, back in the '50s and '60s, and one of my sisters was a runway model who did a lot of in-house work. I actually applied to be with the Academy of Fashion Design when it was still brand new. At that point, students were still doing one year in Toronto and one in Chicago, so I would have been interning under Oscar de la Renta – but I just couldn't afford to go in the end.

Pierre Bergé has said, "A collection is like a dinner party. It is made up of the people you invite, but also the people you don't. There are also, of course, those who couldn't make it." Who wasn't invited to your collection?

KN: Don't say her name! [Laughs.]

JW: Well, I have a problem with Chanel.

She was a hard-nosed businesswoman — nothing wrong with that — but she screwed people to get where she did. For a while I said I didn't want to collect her stuff, but that was also when I couldn't afford it! But really it's the modern company I have a problem with — it's very litigious. They've decided that they're pulling back the word "Chanel" as a trademark, whereas the one thing Coco Chanel was not was very litigious. In the '60s, she would show her stuff to other designers ahead of time to make sure it was copied, to underscore the importance of her work and to make people want the real stuff. Now you can't even say something is "Chanel-like." [Chanel has strictly stated the name may only be used in direct references to the company and its products — supposedly to prevent any dilution of the brand's status.]
KN: At the same time, she did have a lot of importance. We do have Chanel in the collection.
JW: Lagerfeld did a brilliant job of reviving her in the '80s. They never talk about Chanel in the '70s — they were still making clothes; they were just really bad clothes.

Is there anyone you wish could come to the dinner party? What's your holy grail?
JW: We don't have a Fortuny.
KN: We had one exceptionally briefly, which was worn by Lauren Bacall. Unfortunately it was too damaged, so we returned it.
JW: What I'm willing to pay always seems to be $1,000 less than what they're actually selling for.
KN: We're always the underbidders. It's like the bridesmaid rather than the bride.
JW: The bridesmaid of Fortuny.

Baudrillard says that it is inevitably oneself that one collects. Do you think your collection says anything about you?
JW: It does in that I have a hard time collecting what's not my taste. Put it this way: if I were a

◈ · ◈

"I COULD SHOOT MYSELF OVER THE THINGS I DIDN'T BUY — I'M NOW BUYING STUFF THAT I WOULDN'T HAVE EVEN LOOKED AT 20 YEARS AGO."

◈ · ◈

woman in the '50s, I'd be living in suits and cocktail dresses. I don't like loud colours; I have problems buying clashing colours. I appreciate Lacroix, but you can only wear that once and then everyone knows — "oh, there's the Lacroix again." I like novelty, but it has to be cheap, like a paper dress. That I get — it's fun, you wear it once, you throw it away.

How did the idea for a museum begin?
KN: The seed for it was Jonathan's collection.
JW: The fact that we have this huge collection taking over the house and I don't know how to stop buying!
KN: Over the years, I've seen the need out there and the connection people have to clothing. We just came back from New York and every exhibit we went to that involved fashion was packed. Anybody who is interested in the field wants to see whatever is out there, and they want to see it all the time. So that's why we decided it was a really good idea to have a permanent museum dedicated to fashion. It's a decorative art that isn't taken seriously. The more that we can promote the success of our organization, the more others — like smaller collectors or even

collections within museums – can gain credibility. It's not about competitiveness; it's for the betterment of all of us.

How big is the collection currently?

KN: Ten thousand pieces. Plus, there are magazines and books – the library archive is already over two thousand items, and that's not even including documents and photographs. One of my dreams is to create the best fashion-related library archives possible in the world, in multiple languages. I've always been a collector of books.

Is there a difference between acquiring and collecting?

JW: A lot of museums make the mistake of thinking more is better. It's not about getting the most – it's about getting the best. The best means not necessarily the top quality; it means the best examples. A good curator will collect, which means defining, discerning what you want. If something comes in that's better than what you've already got, you get rid of the other one. A lot of museums don't do that; they just grab more and more to the point where they have stuff that will never see the light of day. One of Marie Antoinette's dresses was recently on display at the Royal Ontario Museum for the first time in 40 years – and that's an important dress! I try to remember that with my own collection: it has to be worthy, and it has to have a value; if not, it has to be resold to someone who can wear it or a museum that can use it.

Do you ever regret getting rid of things?

JW: Sometimes I get too hasty. Here's a classic case: I had this silly little painted oilcloth box from the '20s that I thought was a child's hatbox. I got it at a garage sale for $2. I had it for years and thought it wasn't terribly useful, so I sold it on eBay. It turns out that it was actually for bathing suits. After the beach, you took off your wet bathing suit and put it in this waterproof oilcloth bag to carry it home. I was a bad curator – I should have understood the object before I got rid of it. Sometimes I also get too picky. I used to get rid of a dress if the belt was missing – I considered that profoundly damaged.

How did you come up with the name, the Fashion History Museum?

KN: The word history is important – my personal motto is "once we understand our history, we know who we are in the present, and we're inspired for the future." I think that's the connecting piece for Jonathan and me: we both love social history. Social history is the museum's main focus, in a way – what makes people tick.
JW: And how the clothing fits in.
KN: You have to understand where fashion has come from to know where it is right now.
JW: I think one thing that's missing is a place where you can take a class to see a chronology of the history of fashion and where you can actually see designer works, so you can say, "this is typical Lanvin, typical Dior, typical Chanel – and here's what makes it typical."

You could have become a fashion scholar without actually buying the pieces – so why did you?

JW: They're my tools. I read them like books – when you feel them, handle them, know them, then you begin to understand the quality, the taste, the style of the period, the type of woman, the type of occasion, everything. You need to understand it all, and you really only understand by holding them.
KN: The full story is there.
JW: I've always thought of it as more than just a pretty dress – it's what's behind the pretty dress that matters. ⬦

J Eat Style

Photography by Lisa Kannakko

Credits

photography assistance // Thomas Lee
modelling // Van Dao Bich Le,
Avery Moore, Ama Girard-King,
Sara Falconer, & Stephanie Fereiro
art direction // Stephanie Herold
styling // Dana De Kupyer
makeup // Bella B.
hair // Jamie Furie
editorial supervision // G. Stegelmann
& Serah-Marie McMahon

FOSSILIZED & RAREFIED

AN INTERVIEW WITH FASHION SCHOLAR ALEXANDRA PALMER ABOUT DEFINING VINTAGE IN MODERN TIMES

interview by Bella Butscher

IN THE WORLD OF FASHION, "vintage" is a ubiquitous term, used to describe anything from a '30s feedsack dress to shoes picked up at the mall last year. Consumers, collectors, and connoisseurs apply the term according to their own – often discrete or overlapping – definitions, making it difficult to navigate the differences between terms like vintage, antique, and plain old second-hand.

Alexandra Palmer is an author, curator, professor, and fashion scholar. She has spent her career studying fashion and history, and her extensive study and hands-on experience have allowed her to develop a well-measured perspective on all things wearable. As she offers her unique insight into marketing, referential style, and the accelerated cycle of fashion, one thing becomes clear: when it comes to clothes, the word "vintage" might say more about us than about what we're wearing.

As vintage clothing progresses from being the domain of those who consider themselves in the know to being made more widely accessible (like buying second-hand and vintage clothes in Urban Outfitters or Holt Renfrew), do you anticipate a diminishing of the cachet that's currently associated with vintage?
The whole idea around vintage is that it's limited stock and it's a claiming of history. For the consumer, it's something that, ideally, is irreplaceable. That's what's interesting about it. And that's why it's so fashionable now, because we've sort of out-licensed ourselves and out-mass-produced ourselves. You can go into a Gap anywhere in the world. A large part of the interest in vintage is to gain exclusivity and to have something that's unique. Otherwise, that is hard to do, or a lot more expensive if

you're going to an artist or a craftsperson. Unless you can do it yourself, which is a skill that's getting less and less common.

What sort of a role do you see vintage clothing playing for people involved in retro scenes, like rockabilly kids with their seamed stockings and their cuffed jeans, and punks with their safety-pinned jean jackets and bondage pants?
Those are clear signifiers of what is now often called "tribalism," or conformity to a group – an adherence to social and cultural norms within a group or subculture. Clothing is used as a clear signifier to others, either in or out of the group. It's the most overt sign – kind of the litmus test. Also, you have to put clothing on your body. You can also take it off. You can change. By wearing clothes, they are transforming. You can change who you are, or who you think you are, or who others think you are, by what you wear. That's why they're so intriguing.

Do you see that kind of meticulous copying of a past style as unimaginative?
No, I don't. It's a way of belonging to a social-cultural group, and we all do it in different ways. We all do it through clothing, we all do it through religion, we all do it through non-religion, we do it through food, through design. Clothing is just such a clear signifier as you move through the world. I must say that the idea of modernity is interested in these sort of fossilized forms of clothing. It's called "subculture," but in other contexts you would describe it as "fossilized clothing." Servants' clothes, or the Playboy bunny, or certain types of uniforms like that of a New York City doorman, are fossilized clothing. I happen to think that rockabilly and punk are also types of fossilized clothing, but we call them "subcultures" because that's cooler. I was in my late teens and 20s in the

> ❝ **The whole idea about vintage is that it's limited stock and it's a claiming of history. It's something that, for the consumer, is ideally irreplaceable. That's what's interesting about it. And that's why it's so fashionable now.** ❞

'70s, so punk doesn't seem radical to me at all. Personally, I don't understand why a modern person would be into punk – to me it's not at all modern. But of course, punk today isn't the same as punk in the '70s. It's completely different; it's shifted. So those things shift, as everything does – as regional dress does, as any kind of dress does. There are nuances, and you read those codes. Anyone who has worn a uniform knows that; you all dress the same, and yet you're all really different in the way you wear your uniform, even when the markers are very marginal.

At what point does vintage clothing become artifact?
It depends on the collection, it depends on the museum, and it depends on the numbers of the piece. Obviously, mass-manufactured is more common than haute couture, or something that was an artist's piece, or was not made in large numbers. Everything cannot be saved. Things are saved through time; some things disappear due to the nature of the material. A lot of things don't survive because the material is too delicate

or disintegrates, like the early plastics and rubbers. All these kinds of materials are very corrosive – it's in their nature; they self-destruct. There's a whole history of things that, due to the material, do not survive, and there's nothing much we can do about it. Anyone who's had "wet look" Courrèges stuff knows what happens – it falls apart. Spandex in the '80s… there's a whole history where it will remain to be seen what ends up in museums. A lot of it is destined not to look so good. And in fact, a lot of the earlier pre-synthetic stuff lasts better than the synthetic rayons.

Do you think that it's possible for fashion designers to make clothing that is completely devoid of references to the past?
No. I think that a lot of the history of dress is the history of manufacturing, cutting, and textiles – so, very practical craft issues – and I don't think you can get away from that. Basically, it's still a human being you're designing for. The form that one is dressing – no matter how abstract you make the piece of clothing – is still the same: two arms, two legs, a head. It's actually a really boring armature to be stuck with. If you were a sculptor you could create your own armature. Essentially, the craft of sewing is a history in and of itself, and innovative designers like Galliano, like Margiela, like the Japanese [Rei Kawakubo, Yohji Yamamoto], are intensely involved in the craft.

What does the word "vintage" mean to you?
It's sort of a meaningless word, and it's become more meaningless because stuff from little more than a decade ago is now considered "vintage" in some circles. Now it seems the word just means something is old, and there is no real timeline. So it's not a word I would use to describe a museum artifact; it's definitely common parlance. Second-hand or – I'm apprehensive about using the word now – vintage clothing is sold in thrift stores and in extremely exclusive and expensive boutiques. Can you reconcile the difference between spending $1,200 at Holt Renfrew for a '60s dress versus the same dress at a Salvation Army for less than $10? You can't reconcile it. They're two completely different markets.

If you walk into a high-end store, the goods are preselected. They've gone to the trouble of going to a million Salvation Armies for you, or whatever, and that's what you're paying for. Also, obviously what you want are the goods; you're not interested in the rummaging, and getting your hands really dirty, and the smells, and the other nasty people who might be there. And you have to look at a heck of a lot of stuff too, to find anything that's acceptable to you. Perhaps you have a different ethos that raises the unacceptable to the acceptable and is more arty and avant-garde. At the other end of the spectrum, you're probably not that arty or avant-garde if you're going to an extremely high-end vintage store where everything has been tamed and selected and cleaned and sanitized. Wealthy shoppers don't often want to spend the time provisioning in flea markets, so they go into the high-end boutiques where they're likely to get what they want, and they're willing to pay for it. Ultimately, they may as well be buying the latest Louis Vuitton handbag.

And how do you react upon seeing racks of mass-produced clothing that is just 10 years old being labelled "vintage" by second-hand store owners?
Well, I mean, it's not for me to say, but I just find it fascinating that people consider that worthy of the label. Usually, historically, the

❝ It means whatever you want it to, and it'll be completely different if you're talking to a 20-year-old about vintage, or if you're talking to a 60-year-old about vintage. The two will have an entirely different concept about vintage. The word is, in some ways, completely meaningless. ❞

most recent past is considered undesirable, and that's what has pushed fashion forward and made something new. But we seem to have accelerated ourselves so that anything from the very recent past seems to be able to attract some cachet among certain people, and that is actually different. That is modern. I can't say that I completely understand it, but it is a phenomenon that is different.

Picking up on your interpretation of vintage, I remember walking through a shopping mall last summer and seeing fluorescent pink t-shirts with rhinestone letters spelling out the word "vintage," and it seemed to me that that term was almost like a designer label in and of itself.
I think you're right. But I guess it separates the men from the boys, too. Everything has the "vintage" appellation now. I saw "vintage cut" jeans from Old Navy and I looked at them and thought, "What does that mean?" I don't get it – what are they actually trying to say? Either I'm out of it or they're just trying to sell jeans with a desirable and fashionable word with these evocations that are completely confused and arbitrary. It means whatever you want

it to, and it'll be completely different if you're talking to a 20-year-old about vintage or if you're talking to a 60-year-old about vintage. Each will have an entirely different concept about vintage. The word is, in some ways, completely meaningless.

So, a Britney Spears t-shirt that's three years old is already ironic to some.
Yeah, it's exhausting. But with mass media it takes very little time for things to permeate through large numbers of people. If there is no internet, or even if there is no photography, the time lapse is a lot longer. It takes people a lot longer to see maybe a tourist coming to their area wearing something different. It's a different kind of correspondence. And now, through visual images and all the stuff that's extremely rapid, we hardly have time to assimilate it before it becomes passé. And we have a very low attention span as well, so it's much more complex. To find something that's different and new is a lot harder because we have access to too much information that we can't even process. That's where I think vintage becomes intriguing, because it is something that is more rarefied. ⊠

POLITICAL COVERAGE

KEFFIYEH AND CULTURAL
OUTSOURCING

THE LAST KEFFIYEH FACTORY in Palestine belongs to an elderly man named Yasser Hirbawi. In Hebron, where his workshop is located, there were 120 factories before 2000; in 2009, only 10 remain. His is the last that exclusively produces keffiyeh, and even he only runs a fraction of his machines for a few hours a week, hard pressed to sell the 70-80 pieces woven daily.

Benoit Faiveley's short documentary, *Made in Palestine*, profiles the dislocation of keffiyeh production from Palestine. It reads as a microcosm of the vaster economic collapse of a region despoiled by decades of warfare, political deadlock, and sanctions choking off trade and foreign relief. Hirbawi makes for a sympathetic protagonist, hand-some and stooping in a black and white keffiyeh. He speaks softly over the clicking thrum of his few active industrial weavers, blackened with old grease. Protesting that he cannot compete with cheap imports from China, he says: "The keffiyehs shouldn't be imported from the outside. I'm ready to fulfill the need of the market. I would bring more machines if needed…. They should stop the import gate, especially for this specific thing, this Palestinian symbol."

The story of keffiyeh, or *hattah*, is entangled with its status as a symbol of Palestinian identity and resistance. It accumulates ever more layers of meaning as it moves farther away from its place of provenance – of anti-imperialism, pan-Arabism, Palestinian solidarity, anti-Zionism, attachment to the romantic figure of the revolutionary fighter or hatred of the terrorist, and, finally, to fashion. Its material production is similarly implicated in an onion of meaning; globalization and market demand from sympathetic foreigners, fashion mavens, and curious tourists unintentionally endanger the very bonds that link the fabric to a specific place, a place rather like Hirbawi's small workshop in Hebron.

An iconic commodity: the evolution of modern keffiyeh

When Hirbawi started his factory in 1961, the fabric was not yet entrenched as a symbol of Palestine; it was merely a normal part of everyday local dress. If anything, keffiyeh conjured Arabic peasant labourers or, in the West, signified exotic Arabia. The cloth was first tentatively positioned as a symbol of resistance through the Arab Revolt during and after World War I, particularly in the Western fixation with the British envoy and Arabic advocate T. E. Lawrence (later committed to celluloid – in keffiyeh – as Lawrence of Arabia). Keffiyeh became inextricably aligned with Palestinian resistance through the figure of the late Palestine Liberation Organization chairman and Fatah leader Yasser Arafat, who was seldom seen without one. Arafat wore his either secured with an *agal* or draped over his right shoulder to form a triangular shape mimicking the contours of Palestine.

The keffiyeh began to resonate as a symbol in the West during the First Intifada (1987–1993), an uprising of Palestinians living in Gaza, the West Bank, and East Jerusalem. Images coming out of Palestine at the time were brutal, frequently featuring young men with keffiyeh wrapped to hide their faces lobbing stones and Molotov cocktails at heavily armoured Israeli tanks. In the winter of 1987 to 1988, American hipster girls began sporting keffiyeh bundled and twisted around their necks as scarves. The trend sprouted in activist circles, where they were worn to display solidarity with the Palestinians, and slowly filtered out into the broader fashion underground. The keffiyeh that generation wore were still Palestinian-made – many, in all likelihood, produced by Mr. Hirbawi himself.

Shortly thereafter, the keffiyeh faded out of fashion's spotlight. But at the outset of the Second Intifada in 2000, it again began to enjoy a certain countercultural currency. Journalist Sonja Sharp pinpoints this as the moment of the Palestinian-made keffiyeh's decline: "By the time the Second Intifada happened in 2000, hardcore activists and the super cool already had them. Then the keffiyeh trend reached its tipping point, and hipsters' insatiable lust for the scarf lured

WHEN WE CONSUME COMMODITIES, THE CONDITIONS OF THEIR PRODUCTION ARE LARGELY OBSCURED, REPLACED WITH SWIRLING CONNOTATIONS ABOUT THE KINDS OF PEOPLE WE BECOME BY CHOOSING THEM.

Chinese manufacturers into the gig. Fast forward a decade, and Chinese keffiyeh are the norm. Ironically, global support for the Palestinian-statehood-as-fashion-accessory has put yet another nail in the coffin of the Occupied Territories' beleaguered economy."

Her mildly hipster-baiting tone aside, Sharp has a good point. It was the Western desire for keffiyeh that made it worthwhile for Chinese textile manufacturers to produce the pieces,

WHAT IS A KEFFIYEH?

The practice of wearing keffiyeh is older, almost, than time, and is an ancient Bedouin strategy of protection from the harsh elements of the desert. The keffiyeh (transliterated phonetically, so spelling variations abound) is a piece of white material woven from cotton with a bit of wool, usually bearing a net-like checkered pattern in a red or black colourway.

The fabric is woven loosely for porosity, so it protects skin from the

sun but is permeable enough to let any cooling breezes pass through. They have traditionally been strictly menswear, although some styles of women's hijab serve a similar function. Keffiyeh can be pulled over eyes and mouth to guard against the sudden and violent sandstorms that rip through the desert, but are mostly worn either draped around the shoulders or secured on the head with a black circlet of rope known as an agal.

The lined pattern woven into keffiyeh is ancient, a Mesopotamian representation of fishing nets or ears of grain, traditionally rendered in either red (mostly in Lebanon and Jordan, where decorative cotton strings and tassels are also frequently appended) or black (in Syria and Palestine). Its cousins include the Turkish *shemagh* and the spotless white *ghutrah* popular in the Persian Gulf region, although many Arabic men wear different regional variations as a matter of taste.

although not quite in the traditional way and never of the same quality. While this innovation might have had no effect on Hirbawi and his compatriots, who were not allowed to export their wares across borders, economy-of-scale manufacturing and the powerful stick and carrot of competition and profit margins did.

The offshore keffiyeh were not merely sold to sympathetic foreigners in the West – they also inundated the local economy, filling market stalls throughout the Middle East with their cheaper, shoddier wares. The imported pieces sell for about a quarter of the price of Hirbawi's, so even vendors sympathetic to the politics of Palestinian-made symbols cannot risk losing tourist dollars by proffering only the higher-end pieces. The market, it seemed, simply would not bear a $12 price tag.

Inflammatory fashion: not-quite-keffiyeh comes to the mall

In 2007, Nicolas Ghesquière draped the wraiths stalking his Balenciaga runway with the cloth as part of his "multi-ethnic" Fall/Winter line. Shortly thereafter, the scarves were available at Topshop, Urban Outfitters, Le Château, and every mall accessory store in between. These mass-produced pieces came in a plethora of colours, including numerous fluorescents, houndstooth, and skull prints to mark the tastes of the moment.

One multinational chain took heat for their offering, particularly for the

LINKED TO PACIFISM, TERRORISM, FREEDOM, SOLIDARITY, POLITICAL CONSCIENTIOUSNESS, AND APATHY ALL AT ONCE, IT IS DIFFICULT TO IMAGINE A GARMENT THAT MORE SAVAGELY RAISES THE HACKLES OF PUBLIC OPINION.

contentious marketing of the pieces as "anti-war scarves" to capitalize on growing popular opposition to the Bush regime and its martial interventions abroad. The company was subsequently accused of shilling symbols of "Islamic militancy" and shamed into removing keffiyeh from their shelves. Before this, they had sold well at several times the price of Hirbawi's better-quality organic weaves – which, of course, pales in comparison to the Balenciaga pieces retailing for a hefty £3,000 (about $5,200). Thus, it appears that what the market will bear depends greatly upon who's selling.

Keffiyeh were ubiquitous for most of 2007 to 2008, and have been celebrity-spotted on figures ranging from Ricky Martin to Kanye West to Trent Reznor to Lauren Bush to a Jonas brother. There may well be one languishing in your closet right now. Rachael Ray unintentionally produced a political uproar (albeit a mild one) after wearing a similarly patterned scarf in a Dunkin' Donuts commercial. Bloggers complained that her apparel was anti-Semitic, causing the company to pull the ads – and it wasn't even a proper keffiyeh. Clearly, as far as symbols go, this one's loaded.

When we consume commodities, the conditions of their production are largely obscured, replaced with swirling connotations about values and lifestyle, about the kinds of people we become by choosing them. In the case of keffiyeh, *Made in Palestine* pulls back the curtain somewhat by revealing where the textile is not produced – in the ravaged economy of Hebron.

Keffiyeh is at once meaningless – as Kibum Kim wrote in the *New York Times*, "[It] appears to be the dubious successor to last year's Che Guevara tee-shirts, a symbol denuded of any potent political associations by pop culture" – and clouded by a palimpsest of overlapping and conflicting attributions.

THE THINGS WE WEAR HAVE LIVES, BOTH AS MATERIAL OBJECTS WITH HISTORIES, AND AS IMAGES LOADED WITH SIGNIFICANCE.

It seems, at times, that it means so much as to say nothing. Linked to pacifism, terrorism, freedom, solidarity, political conscientiousness, and apathy all at once, it is difficult to imagine a garment that more savagely raises the hackles of public opinion, as the Rachael Ray "scandal" clearly demonstrates. Even fur pales in comparison.

But, if there's a trend that can trigger Trent Reznor and Ricky Martin sharing an accessory, who knows what this fabric can do? These no doubt well-intentioned appropriations of keffiyeh serve to remind us that the things we wear have lives, both as material objects with histories and as images loaded with significance, and that sometimes it's worth digging into our closets to think through where all this fabric came from. 🝔

FASHION IS

FUN

09

EVERYONE HAS THOSE MOMENTS. Maybe you're on your way to a party or a wedding, or maybe you're going to work, and you stand in front of your closet feeling lost. Though you have managed to get dressed on every other day of your life, you no longer understand your clothes, which seem bent on making you foolish and dowdy. The thing you need to remember in those moments is that, first and foremost, fashion is fun.

For all we discuss clothing as a signifier, a message, and an artifact, fashion doesn't have to mean everything all the time. Once it has served its purpose in keeping us warm or dry, what appeals to us in a garment is purely subjective. Style doesn't sustain us physically – there is no recommended daily requirement of sequins or pyramid guide to tell us we're not getting enough toile de Jouy. We can approach the act of dressing with impractical joy and creativity, deciding for ourselves the weight it carries in our construction of self. Fashion is a lot of things, but one thing it's not is a test; you can't do it wrong.

While *WORN* strives to discuss the complexity of fashion, we are also a bunch of people who came together because we get excited about getting dressed. We want to talk about fashion as history, but we also want to find out what the hell is with Elvis Presley's jumpsuits. We want to examine the possibility that Jim Jarmusch exists exclusively in black and white and tell you the story of Salvador Dalí chucking a bathtub through a department store window. And we'll insist it was absolutely necessary to put a zebra in a photo shoot because if you have access to a zebra, what other choice do you have? ⧓

PRETTY
THEFT

PHOTOGRAPHY BY HENRY SAMSON

STYLING // G. STEGELMANN
MODELLING // WEI GUO
MAKEUP // BELLA B.
PAINTING // GEORGE BOUCHER

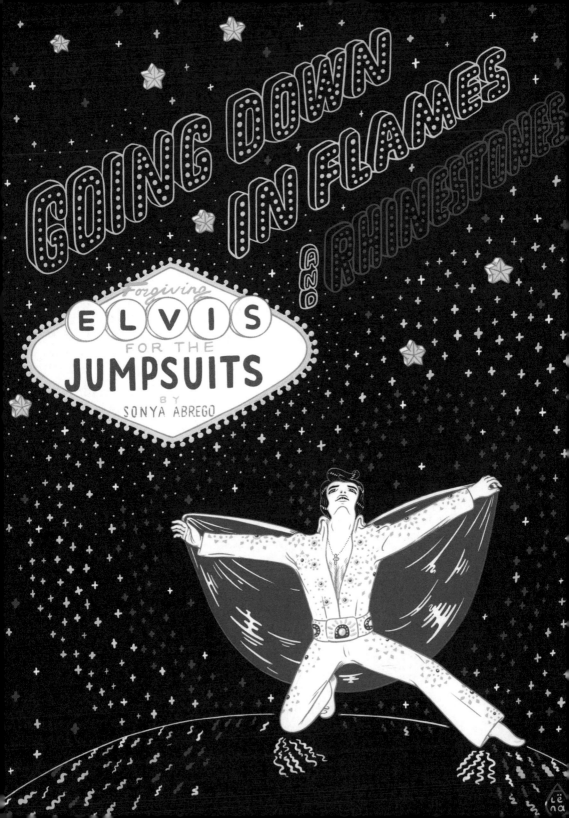

"WHEN PEOPLE TALK ABOUT ELVIS and make fun of him as, like, this goofy guy in the funny jumpsuits, I get upset." This is what I told the bartender who hired me for my first weekly deejay gig in my hometown of Edmonton. In Elvis we found common ground, and I was booked. It was one of the first times, but definitely not the last, that the King has come up in conversation.

Fast-forward five years to today, and I'm in New York City writing my master's thesis on the clothing Elvis wore, focusing on 1954 to 1958, my favourite Elvis years in terms of both music and style. In a setting where "19th-century women's fashion consumption in constructions of female identity" would carry more academic clout, "Elvis" never fails to get a reaction. It has also become my social litmus test – if you're not down with Elvis, you're not down with me.

I was introduced to Elvis in the same way as I was to many other pop idols of past generations: by working my way backward through imitation, kitsch, and parody. He certainly wasn't around the house when I was growing up. My folks were a few years too young to have seen Elvis as a threatening misfit from the South, as a rebel. The rebellions of my parents were rooted in the '60s, and by then Elvis was already singing and dancing for Hollywood.

I don't remember being told who Elvis was – I can't isolate a first image or song. He was just there, as background noise, as "the '50s," as Americana, as a hairstyle. He was a symbol without referent. I do remember loving Andy Warhol's Elvis and seeing him in other pop artists' work. I read critical articles about the appropriation of Elvis' image as a symbol before I really got into his music or biography. Check off the appropriate trope: '50s American masculinity, bad taste, Hollywood, camp, etc.

It may have worked to my benefit, because I hear Elvis' early recordings for the amazing pieces they are. His music was never contaminated with the sordid tales of his descent into drug-induced puffiness and

THE OSTENTATIOUS EXCESS BETRAYS A TOTAL DISCONNECTION FROM THE OUTSIDE WORLD.

✛ ✛✛ ✛✛ ✛✛ ✛✛ ✛✛ ✛

multiple after-death sightings. Being young 20 years after Elvis died, I couldn't have expected to encounter anything about him free from interpretation, and now I can include my own.

MEETING THE KING

In January 2008, I finally made it south to the great state of Tennessee. This was my pilgrimage to the holy land, and I was elated. In Tennessee, I could eat fried foods and listen to old music sans judgement. But most importantly, I was going to see Sun Records, I was going to see Stax, and dammit, I was going to Graceland! At the end of each busy day of my trip, my brain bristled with the overstimulation: everything from rhinestone Nudie Suits (the famously flamboyant outfits designed by Nudie Cohn for everyone from Roy Rogers and Hank Williams to Cher), to Cadillacs mounted with chrome pistols and steer horns, to trinkets in gift shops. Then came the seventh of January, which will live on in my memory as "Graceland Day."

Graceland stands as a representation of Elvis' taste in the late '60s and early '70s. Almost every room is haunted by a headless mannequin dressed in his old clothes – mostly dark, narrow '60s suits with high collars and accessorized with gold jewelry. If they lack Elvis' liveliness, they help make up for it by driving home a point often touched upon in the literature: the isolation and loneliness that came along with his being confined to Graceland.

Although this is probably not the message the management of Elvis Presley Enterprises is trying to deliver to fans, I felt it weigh on me. The ostentatious excess betrays a total disconnection from the outside world. If one were to judge from the artifacts that make up Graceland – without knowing a thing about who Elvis Presley was – one could easily conclude it was assembled by a teenager who was materialistic to the core, a thrill-seeker obsessed with novelty, luxury, and whatever might be the opposite of sophistication.

The jumpsuits were out in full force at Graceland. I had nothing against the jumpsuit era, but it had never been my thing. I was all about Rockabilly Elvis: the sexy, controversial Elvis who inverted musical and sartorial conventions. Yet, to focus exclusively on the earlier part of his career is to deny a substantial chunk of his contribution as a performer. The thing about Elvis was always his universal appeal. His long-time manager, Colonel Tom Parker, a carnie Svengali, knew he had found in Elvis a child of popular culture and an uncanny composite of everything American. This boy could reach the masses.

This idea is reiterated through Elvis' multiple incarnations as a commodity. At the Graceland gift shops you can buy novelties and postcards featuring the Elvis of your choice, like a series of comic book action heroes. There is '50 Elvis in Lansky Brothers pink and black, Army Elvis in fatigues, Karate Elvis in a red and white gi, '68 Comeback Special Elvis in black leather, Elvis as each and every one of his movie characters, and finally, Jumpsuit Elvis of *Aloha from Hawaii* and fabulous Las Vegas. Elvis existed in multiples before Warhol had anything to do with it, and every iteration had meaning.

I found more jumpsuits in cases on the former racquetball court, its walls covered to the high ceiling with gold records. I can understand why people see the whole jumpsuit thing as easy to make fun of – it's just too much. But the detail of the sequins and embroidery is impressive. Even if you don't appreciate them aesthetically, you can't help admiring the workmanship.

These notorious suits were the work of Bill Belew, a costumer who studied design at Parsons

HE HAD FOUND IN ELVIS A CHILD OF POPULAR CULTURE AND AN UNCANNY COMPOSITE OF EVERYTHING AMERICAN. THIS BOY COULD REACH THE MASSES.

✛ ✛ ✛ ✛ ✛ ✛ ✛ ✛ ✛ ✛ ✛ ✛

in New York and worked with theatre and TV stars. Beginning with the famous black leather outfit of the '68 Comeback Special, Belew worked with Elvis until his death. He designed Elvis' baroque stage costumes and some of his more elaborate daywear (although Elvis continued to patronize Lansky's, a Memphis menswear store that sold him and other '50s icons their show-stopping styles). I found out later that the seventh of January 2008, my Graceland Day, was also the day Mr. Belew passed away.

In addition to those on the racquetball court, a separate exhibition entitled *Sincerely Elvis* is exclusively devoted to jumpsuits. Along with Belew's original sketches for the costumes, there are over 30 outfitted mannequins fully lit and glittering behind glass.

The first thing I noticed was the size of them – the waists measure a slim 30 to 32 inches. But aren't these jumpsuits supposed to represent Fat Elvis? Isn't that part of why they were funny? Chubby man + tight clothes = hilarious? If that's the way the story goes, and the myth of Elvis has outgrown the man, does it even matter that he wasn't big at all, not until the very last year of his life? Why should we respect accuracy or separate fantasy from reality? Elvis didn't. That was part of the fun.

THE EVOLUTION OF A JUMPSUIT

The suits are narrow and designed for motion. He was obsessed with karate training and wanted stage clothes that resembled the white karate gi. Admittedly, when you're looking at a white jumpsuit emblazoned with rhinestones and accessorized with a matching wrestler-sized belt and cape, the simplicity of a martial arts costume may not spring to mind, but it becomes more apparent after closer inspection.

Belew took into account that lighting on the Vegas stage was subpar; wearing white was a way to be seen clearly. The original two-piece gi-style outfit morphed into a one-piece jumpsuit for practical reasons. Elvis would kick and jump on stage, which often tore his tight pants and untucked his shirt, so a one-piece suit made it easier to move. And there were other familiar things, too.

The flared pants, pointed high collars, wide belts, ascot-like scarves, leather fringe, flared legs – these were all characteristic of '70s menswear. This was the age of *Superfly*, *Saturday Night Fever*, and glam rock. The imagery on each outfit is literal: a phoenix, a tiger, an Aztec calendar, a dragon. Some designs are borrowed from historical western wear or Native American garments. Fringe, macramé, studs, and sequins are ubiquitous, and their application grows more and more unrestrained as the years pass.

+ + + + + + + + + + + + + + + +

THE ORIGINAL TWO-PIECE GI-STYLE OUTFIT MORPHED INTO A ONE-PIECE JUMPSUIT FOR PRACTICAL REASONS. ELVIS WOULD KICK AND JUMP ON STAGE, WHICH OFTEN TORE HIS TIGHT PANTS AND UNTUCKED HIS SHIRT, SO A ONE-PIECE SUIT MADE IT EASIER TO MOVE.

THE EARLIEST JUMPSUITS ARE ACTUALLY QUITE PLAIN, WHILE THOSE OF THE LAST YEARS LOOK AS THOUGH THEY WOULD NEED TWO PEOPLE TO HOLD THEM UP.

+ + + + + + + + + + + + + + + +

The earliest jumpsuits are actually quite plain, while those of the last years look as though they would need two people to hold them up.

Belew recounts how the two were trying to think up a particularly novel design for his 1973 *Aloha from Hawaii* special. Ever patriotic, Elvis wanted something very American. Instead of being draped in stars and stripes, they settled on an eagle with wings outstretched to cover the back of a floor-length cape. But the original was, apparently, so long and heavy Elvis could not move. His friend Joe Esposito claims Elvis fell onto the floor, laughing under its weight.

Elvis indulged his taste for flash and spared no expense. In Bill Belew he found the perfect partner in crime. Elvis was never one for moderation, and he and Belew took '70s men's fashion to the limit. Although components of the suit are easily linked to contemporaneous styles, Elvis made them his own. The exhibition name *Sincerely Elvis* starts to become synonymous with "signature style." Even though the jumpsuit was only one incarnation of Elvis' aesthetic, this is the one Graceland promotes.

THE CONSEQUENCE OF EXCESS

For all their excess and shocking visual impact, there is something disconcerting about the jumpsuits – especially seeing them standing en masse so still, stuffed, and alien. On one hand, this moment in his career is pictured as his triumph: the full realization of Elvis as singer, performer, and spectacle. His music may not have been strictly rock and roll anymore, but he took all the irreverence and joy that was rock and roll farther than anyone had ever thought it would go, including Elvis himself.

On the other hand, it demonstrates what happens to this ideal once it becomes a commercial product – orchestrated, choreographed, and dressed at the height of opulence. Elvis' daring, African American–influenced styles of the '50s were an inspiration – people wanted to be like him and look like him. When others had their fingers on the pulse of a burgeoning youth culture, Elvis cut open an artery.

The '70s look was more extreme, yet the edge had been dulled. Music had changed and culture had changed, largely because of Elvis' influence.

no one is challenged and no one is threatened." It makes me sad, despite all the glitter.

Elvis and his image have always been awash in contradictions. The jumpsuits may be silly, but you don't need to take something seriously to be captivated by it. Anything connected to his physical being, not least his clothes, has taken on a spiritual significance to rival the medieval cult of relics. The myth surrounding his rise to fame and tragic decline is the quintessential American story. People love to celebrate a poor boy's making good in the world as much as they relish watching him crash and burn once he's wealthy and famous.

Elvis is too much to live up to, but the impersonators who try tend to conform to the

FOR ALL THEIR EXCESS AND SHOCKING VISUAL IMPACT THERE IS SOMETHING DISCONCERTING ABOUT THE JUMPSUITS – ESPECIALLY SEEING THEM STANDING EN MASSE SO STILL, STUFFED, AND ALIEN.

But when everything is permitted and there's nothing to rebel against, then every indulgence can be satisfied, and there is nowhere to go but down. Now the only ones willing to take on the jumpsuit are impersonators and those looking for a laugh. These garments represent someone who was, for better or worse, out of touch with reality.

Greil Marcus says it best when he sums up an Elvis concert from the mid-'70s: "There is great satisfaction in his performance, and great emptiness.... Elvis has dissolved into a presentation of his myth and so has his music. The emotion of the best music is open, liberating in its commitment and intangibility; Elvis' presentation is fixed. The glorious oppression of that presentation parallels the all-but-complete assimilation of a revolutionary musical style into the mainstream of American culture, where

jumpsuit look. Maybe it's a better disguise: it's more costume than person and thus easier to assume. Despite the jumpsuit phase being the most popular for impersonators, when the United States Postal Service ran a contest in 1993 to select which image would be used for the Elvis Presley commemorative stamp – an Elvis from 1957 or a later jumpsuit-clad version – the youthful example won overwhelmingly.

Belew's designs for Elvis are iconic, but what most people want preserved is more ephemeral: an explosive young rebel who changed the world before collapsing under the weight of a rhinestone cape. ✄

Credits

illustration // Elena Viltovskaia

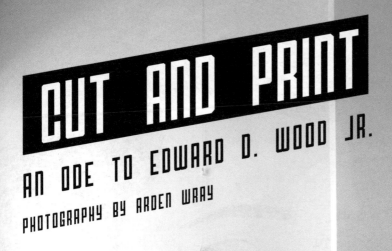

CUT AND PRINT

AN ODE TO EDWARD D. WOOD JR.

PHOTOGRAPHY BY ARDEN WRAY

Credits

art direction // Serah-Marie McMahon
styling // Peghah Maleknejad & Casie Brown
makeup // Bella Butscher
hair // Renee Clement
modelling // G. Stegelmann, Ted Kulczycky, & Nando Martins

Director Jim Jarmusch, by most accounts, virtually invented contemporary independent American film (*Stranger Than Paradise*, *Dead Man*, *Broken Flowers*) and ranks among the finest living directors. This has no relevance to the musings at hand.

FIVE REASONS WHY JIM JARMUSCH IS THE COOLEST PERSON ON EARTH

(OTHER THAN THE FACT THAT HE MAKES GREAT MOVIES)

TEXT BY TED KULCZYCKY

1. "I NEVER TRUST ANYBODY WITHOUT HOLES IN THEIR CLOTHES."

He's well off but still proudly wears thrift shop. The sharp lines and dapper trims on most of his outfits scream "style," but despite this attention to his appearance, he never seems especially handsome or pretty. His clothes look old, but they don't convey the preciousness of vintage. Even with the odd hole, they don't have that ratty feel you sometimes get with thrift. His stuff looks sharp but still – for lack of a better

word – worn. One further note on fashion: he's a film director. He likes baseball. He's almost never seen in a baseball cap. Thank you.

2. THE HAIR.

The straight-up shock of salt and pepper has progressed, through the years, to a straight-up shock of salt. During the halcyon days of punk, while everyone on the Lower East Side was using chemicals, food colouring, and bodily fluids to make a "striking new 'do," Jim Jarmusch's hormones styled his hair naturally.

3. HE'S A MEMBER OF THE SONS OF LEE MARVIN.

There is, apparently, a secret society (with meetings and handshakes and everything) that also includes Tom Waits, Neil Young, Nick Cave, and several other celebrities. Membership requires the individual to bear "more than

a passing resemblance" to the hard-living, horse-faced, and gravel-voiced star of *The Wild One* and *The Dirty Dozen*. With his stretched features, thick eyebrows, and premature white, Jarmusch was one of the founding members.

4. HE SMOKES.

Smoking is bad. It kills. It stains your teeth. It harms your unborn baby. People who smoke are bad. *Bad*. But it's cool! And very few of us look as cool as Jarmusch while smoking. What could possibly frame that hair as well as a cloud of smoke?

In *Blue in the Face*, Jarmusch has a cameo as a man about to quit smoking. He philosophizes about the filthy habit for 15 minutes before taking his last puff: "Why do the Nazis always hold their cigarettes in a funny way in movies? Does it signify their evilness?" Among Jarmusch's own films, *Dead Man* comments

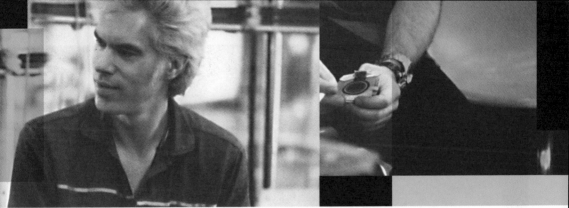

on the differences between Native American spirituality and Western capitalism via a running gag about tobacco; *Coffee and Cigarettes* is a two-hour meditation on what my uncle commonly refers to as a "whore's breakfast."

Jarmusch has been quoted as saying, "I hope I'm not a notorious smoker."

Sorry, Jim.

5. HE'S ACTUALLY BLACK AND WHITE.

I recently noted to a friend, in casual conversation, that I'd never seen a colour photo of Jim Jarmusch. My friend was polite enough not to correct me, but I soon realized the absurdity of my statement. I'd seen the movies *Blue in the Face*, *Tigrero*, and *Sling Blade*. All three are in colour and all three feature Jarmusch. Hell, I've seen him in person a couple of times. So why can't I get a colour image of him in my mind?

Sure, there are other people it's impossible to visualize in colour – Charlie Chaplin, Ralph Kramden, Hitler. But this seems to be a consequence of familiarity. Most of the images we've seen of these people are over 40 years old and in black and white. But I saw two documentaries with a colour Jarmusch in them a month ago. I checked my magazine collection for interviews and articles, and Jarmusch is usually photographed in black and white, even for full-colour magazines. I still don't think that's it. I think the fact that he seems made up of shades of grey is what leads photographers to shoot him devoid of pigmentation.

I've racked my brain trying for an explanation, and it could be 1) An odd geometrical visual phenomenon caused by his hair and the length of his face. 2) A strange psychological condition related to the way people perceive colour in dreams. 3) *He's actually black and white.* ⊠

Amidst
the
Clutter

PHOTOGRAPHY
BY ALEJANDRO
ESCAMILLA

Credits

styling // Andi Gilker
modelling // Andrienne Irving

A Century on Display

A brief overview of window dressing in the 20th century
and an introduction to three men who put fashion under glass

TEXT BY MAX MOSHER
ILLUSTRATION BY CAITLIN SHEARER

"WINDOW DRESSING IS AT FIRST GLANCE so gorgeously useless that it resists all comparison with other derided professions." So says Simon Doonan, arguably the most famous window dresser in the world. He likens his chosen profession to the hairdressers of 18th-century Versailles. But the man whose displays at Barneys department store brought him international renown is being facetious. He knows that however frivolous, whimsical, or controversial a window display might seem, its real purpose is clear.

Stores have had displays almost as long as they've had windows, but it wasn't until the rise of the department store in the early 20th century that window dressing became serious business. Retailers in growing cities faced increasingly stiff competition for customers' dollars. Rival department stores used their windows to vie for the attention (and patronage) of passers-by, turning their displays into vibrant three-dimensional advertisements. And it was up to the people who decorated those windows to devise the strategy of battle.

Window dressers (also known as visual merchandisers) created what has come to be known as "brand." Martin M. Pegler, of the journal *Retail Design International*, claims that window displays "are the store's first opportunity to distinguish itself, to say 'Here I am!' and 'This is what I sell and who I would like to sell to!'" Ultimately, it is the dresser who needs to understand what that means. In the early 1900s, visionary window dressers would dazzle customers with "new" technology – dreamlike displays of bright lights, colours, and moving parts. Later on, when technology alone failed to impress, stores would seek more esoteric minds, combining advertising with installation art. By the end of the century, an increasingly cynical consumer required tactics that were more street-savvy than salesman. In any case, only creative minds need apply.

In the profession's early days, however, women need not. Although recognized as both effective sales associates and decorators, women were often barred from being window dressers due to the late hours and the unsavoury reputation of stores' technicians. But where there's a window, there's a way; enterprising women like Cora Scovil (credited with creating the first mannequins with movable joints) simply started their own freelance merchandising companies.

Though elaborate window displays survived the Great Depression, in the post-war decades they were nearly defeated by the middle-class flight to the suburbs, the advent of slab-like malls, and the rise of television advertising. In the '80s, the art of window dressing re-emerged as a means of giving a store a hip corporate identity. Risk-takers used the traditional medium as a platform to address an almost insatiable appetite for irony. But as handmade props are replaced by flat-screen monitors, and shopping moves online, it's not difficult to imagine a future in which a mannequin looks as antiquated as a crumbling Roman statue.

Yet rather than ask what this means for retail, we might better ask what this means for us. Because one thing is absolutely clear: our windows – and our window dressers – reflect us in more ways than one.

L. FRANK BAUM

Store windows of the 19th century were cluttered affairs as shopkeepers piled up goods, emphasizing quantity over quality. But advances in plate glass manufacturing made windows wider and left owners with a lot more space to fill.

In 1900, L. Frank Baum published two books: *The Wizard of Oz* and *The Art of Decorating Dry Goods Windows and Interiors*. (The latter is less well known, having never been turned into an Oscar-winning film.) Billing itself as a "complete manual of window trimming," *The Art* was a summary of *The Show Window*, Baum's own publication and the first window dressing trade journal. As an optimistic entrepreneur of his expansionist time, Baum had worked as a travelling actor, playwright, set designer, and journalist, but he discovered a passion for display when designing the windows for his own shop, Baum's Bazaar, in Aberdeen, South Dakota. (Sadly, his store was stocked with items deemed impractical for a frontier town and soon closed.)

Much like his soon-to-be-famous wizard, Baum understood the power of smoke and mirrors. His signature "illusion windows" featured the latest technologies, such as electrical revolving stars, incandescent globes, and fluttering mechanical butterflies. Window-shoppers became an audience, gasping at a disembodied – but talkative – head protruding from a pedestal, and the "vanishing lady" who disappeared only to return in a different hat.

To construct his fantasies, Baum turned to ordinary household goods; for a hardware store window, he built a human figure with a wash boiler as a torso, stovepipe limbs, and a funnel hat. This particular design would later be reborn as Oz's Tin Woodman.

Despite his romanticism, Baum understood that the real purpose of any display was to move the goods. "If the show window is arranged with sufficient artfulness," he wrote, "customers will want what they see whether they need it or not." And so, he ushered in the age of modern advertising, although not without ambivalent feelings. Baum was wary of outlandish sales pitches that reminded him of snake oil sellers and carnival barkers. His skepticism provided the cautionary twist to his tales of wizards and witches; even as his windows beguiled adults, he encouraged his child readers to keep their wits and be aware of "the man behind the curtain."

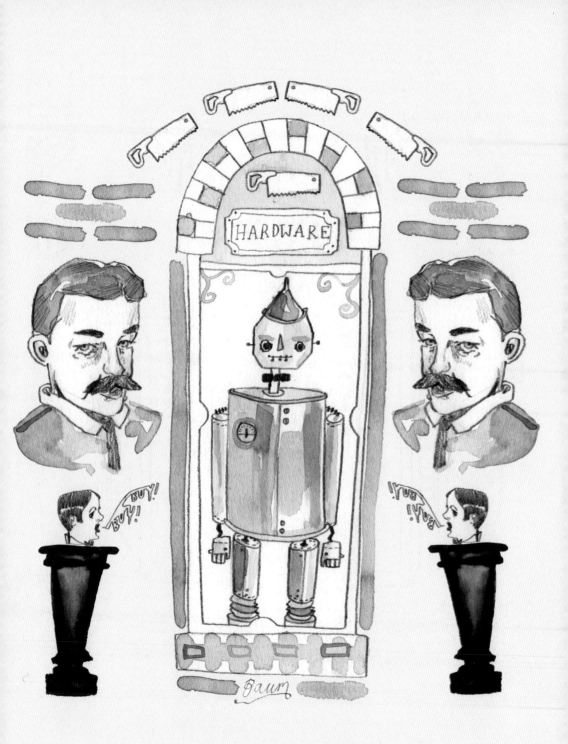

SALVADOR DALÍ

The first 30 years of the 20th century proved to be the golden age of the department store – and the golden age of window display – but in 1929, the Great Depression hit the retail industry hard. Stores needed new and interesting ways to lure back penny-pinching customers. Hiring celebrated artists to install avant-garde displays seemed like just the thing to catch pedestrians' eyes.

Saks Fifth Avenue in New York hired celebrated Hungarian artist Marcel Vertès, an illustrator who would go on to create advertisements for Elsa Schiaparelli and design Academy Award-winning costumes. In reference to Freudian analysis, he installed a reclining mannequin with a "dream dress" materializing above her head to great success. So when department store Bonwit Teller commissioned a window from Salvador Dalí in 1939, they hoped to cause at least a minor stir. Little did they realize that Dalí was as dedicated to scandal as he was to mustache wax.

The Spanish surrealist filled his window with a bathtub containing three disembodied arms, a taxidermied buffalo head, stuffed pigeons, and naked mannequins with blood streaming from their eyes. It took all night to install, after which Dalí retired to his hotel. It didn't take long for perturbed Park Avenue patrons to complain, and Bonwit Teller's managers replaced the nude mannequins with clothed ones. All seemed well until Dalí returned that afternoon. What happened next was best covered by *Time* magazine: "Into the store to the company lawyer rocketed Salvador Dalí, sizzling in Spanish and French. Next thing Bonwit's knew, the Surrealissimo was in the window with the bathtub. 'Ooomph' went the tub as he jerked it from the moorings. 'Crash' went Bonwit Teller's beautiful plate-glass window as the small struggling artist and his tub went through it and hit 'bang' on the sidewalk." Dalí was detained in the ladies handbag storeroom. Later in court, a magistrate handed him a mild sentence, noting, "These are some of the privileges that an artist with temperament seems to enjoy." Years later, Simon Doonan, himself a provocative window dresser, pointed out that the whole fracas had benefited all involved: the store got publicity, Dalí's eccentric reputation was enhanced, and Bonwit Teller's window dressers "probably got the best laugh of their entire careers."

SIMON DOONAN

In 1977, punk revolutionized fashion. In comparison to the rebellion around him, British freelance window dresser Simon Doonan began to find his own displays bland and "aesthetically turgid." He decided to risk his career with a display as outrageous as mohawks and nose piercings. Commissioned to create a window for a posh shop on London's Savile Row, he covered men's suits with toy rats, each wearing a diamond bracelet as a collar. A gawking crowd soon gathered to witness what would become Doonan's signature style.

Though consumers had become cynical about advertisers' promises, Doonan's shocking window displays forced people to pay attention. Referring to a series of wildlife attacks, in one store Doonan positioned a stuffed coyote dragging away a mannequin baby. In another, a mannequin emerged from a coffin like a vampire. The "Sistine Chapel" of his tacky oeuvre was his series of celebrity-themed Christmas windows of the early '90s, featuring grotesque papier mâché caricatures of public figures: Queen Elizabeth burying a deceased pet corgi and Madonna prancing about

nude. Doonan had no fear of being accused of bad taste; indeed, he revelled in it.

His bad-boy reputation got Doonan hired at Barneys in New York. They saw him as a visionary who would help rebrand their store as it went global, and even his most outrageous concepts were indulged. Behind Barneys windows, he smashed TV sets, tore up mattresses, and hung toilet paper from the ceiling (later returning it to the store's supply closet to be used).

Along with his singular sense of irony, Doonan's work is a nod to his predecessors, combining the fantasy of Baum with the shock of Dalí. No fan of windows featuring video screens, Doonan believes you "are much more likely to win the hearts of your customers with some pathetic low-tech animation, such as a malfunctioning papier mâché butterfly on a string." But whereas once upon a time Baum's magical butterflies inspired awe, Doonan's catch our eye precisely because they are hokey and out of date. His style reflects an era in which shoppers have become so immune to slick, big-budget advertising that nothing short of a mannequin boxing match will win our attention. ⊠

FIELD

GUIDED

styling & art direction by Avyn Omel
photography by Alyssa K. Faoro

Credits

styling assistance // Deua Medeiros
modelling // Sam Xu, Chelsea Omel,
& Nicole Pearson
hair & makeup // Jamie Furie
title illustration // Janice Wong

photo // Arden Wray

CONTRIBUTORS

Sonya Abrego
Bree Apperley
Alexandra Barton
Shannon Bell Price
Natasha Bigioni
Hillary Brenhouse
Casie Brown
Bella Butscher
Shea Chang
Renee Clement
Darren Curtis
Vanda Daftari
Risa Dickens
Nate Dorr
Alejandro Escamilla
Robert Everett-Green
Alyssa K. Faoro
Benoit Faiveley
Stephanie Fereiro
Maegan Fidelino
Rose Flutur
Sara Forsyth
Jamie Furie
Alyssa Garrison
Pascale Georgiev

Andi Gilker
Pamela Grimaud
Sara Guindon
Peter Ha
Maryanna Hardy
Carl W. Heindl
Stephanie Herold
Esme Hogeveen
Marlena Kaesler
Lisa Kannakko
Margot Keith
Laura Kloepfer
Adriana Komura
Paulina Kulacz
Ted Kulczycky
Stacy Lundeen
Peghah Maleknejad
Emilie Marzinotto
Chelsea McBroom
Chris Mejaski
Haley Mlotek
Christopher Morris
Max Mosher
Wynne Neilly
Catie Nienaber

Avyn Omel
Hillary Predko
Danijela Pruginic
Emily Raine
Celeste Ramos
Tyler Rauman
Emma Rees
Henry Sansom
Sarah Scaturro
Karolin Schnoor
Kate Schweishelm
Caitlin Shearer
Hailey Siracky
Tessa Smith
G. Stegelmann
Emily Taylor
Monika Traikov
Eliza Trent-Rennick
Lise Treutler
Jazz Virdee
Samantha Walton
Janice Wong
Jenn Woodall
Arden Wray
JeongMee Yoon

THANK YOU

To every writer, designer, photographer, and illustrator who put all their creative tears into this fantastic beast.

To Drawn & Quarterly, for taking a chance on an unknown kid. You are awesome, Chris Oliveros, Peggy Burns, Tom Devlin, Tracy Hurren, and Julia Pohl-Miranda.

To Jane Pratt for providing such a lovely foreword, and for giving teenage me hope to cling to in a small Canadian town. *Sassy* and *Jane* may not have saved my life, but they certainly saved my sanity.

To Sonya Abrego, Risa Dickens, Emily Raine, Sara Forsyth, Janice Wong, Michelle Sayer, Danielle Sayer, Anna Fitzpatrick, and Liz Byer, whose fingerprints are all over this book.

To Juul Haalmeyer, Courage My Love, Mrs. Huizenga, Roger at Flashback, and Lynn at Exile, for loaning us so many of the smart dresses and sweet shoes that populate our photoshoots.

To stellar copy editors Martina Bellisario, Karen Fraser, and Stephanie Fereiro, for crossing all our t's and dotting all our i's.

To Daniel Reis for making us look so good in video form.

To the girls of Victoire, Clayton Evans, Nathalie Atkinson, Stacey May Fowles, the Quinn family, the Ontario Arts Council, Anita Clarke, Tavi Gevinson, and Claudia McMahon, for being early and constant champions and supporters.

To the Type Books staff for tolerating me while I put this whole thing together, including Derek McCormack, whom I promised I would mention in the book if he covered my shift on Saturday.

To Morgen Young, Dan Wagstaff, and Bruce Martin, for answering so many crazy questions about this business we call publishing.

To Ted, for hauling all those boxes up the stairs every new issue, and an unimaginably huge number of other things. There is no way *WORN* could even exist without you. I love you always.

And truly, most of all — thank you to every Wornette everywhere. Whether you spent years editing issues, afternoons making cat ears, or a moment telling a friend about this glorious product of independent fashion publishing, you are a Wornette and this book is for you. ⬦